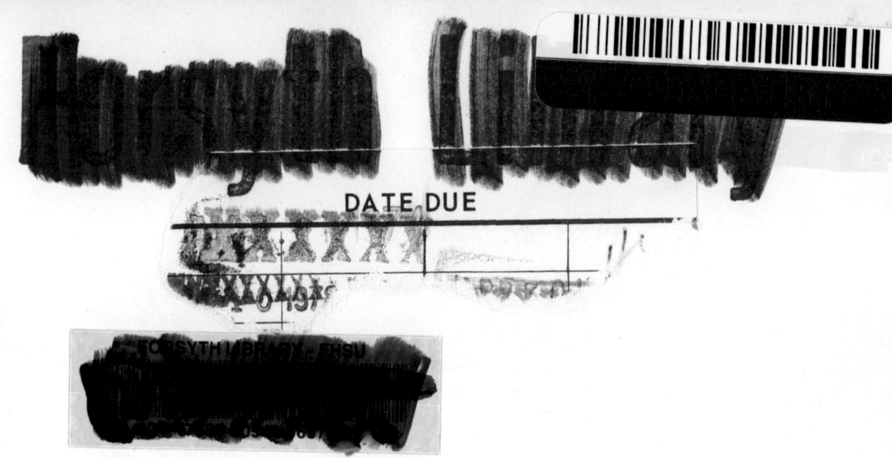

A History of Epic Poetry

A History of Epic Poetry

(POST-VIRGILIAN)

BY

JOHN CLARK, M.A.

Second Classical Master in the High School of Dundee

Author of "Manual of Linguistics"

Il ne suffit pas, pour connaître l'épopée
d'avoir lu Virgile et Homère.

VOLTAIRE, *Essai sur la Poésie Épique.*

HASKELL HOUSE

Publishers of Scholarly Books

NEW YORK

1964

published by

HASKELL HOUSE

Publishers of Scholarly Books

30 East 10th Street • New York, N. Y. 10003

Library of Congress Catalog Card Number: 65-15876

PRINTED IN UNITED STATES OF AMERICA

PREFACE

THE following pages are meant to exhibit the different national renderings of a variety of poetry that perhaps more than any other has given status to the literature possessing a great specimen of it, and supremacy to the poet of that specimen.

I have restricted my formal examination of poems to those of the post-Virgilian period. So much excellent criticism has been made on Homer and Virgil that it seemed presumption on my part, as well as a needless increase of the bulk of the book, to adventure a full statement of the epical position of these two princely poets. It is clear, however, that no history of epic poetry could be called satisfactory that did not contain some reference to these poets—that did not, indeed, to a definite if limited extent, take into account and appraise their work. I have therefore in the Introduction devoted some pages to a consideration of certain aspects of the epical quality of their respective poems. Other pre-Virgilian epics than those of Homer claim, and have received, a certain amount of attention.

A study like mine, to reach true conclusions, needs observation not only of the great masters of epic, but also of humbler poets whose good intentions have not been reinforced by potent inspiration. It needs an examination not only of mature specimens of varying quality, but of those earlier specimens that are often immature only as regards poetic dressing and amplification, and that have a movement and vigour not always associated with maturity. I have tried by the consideration of some three dozen poems representing different qualities and different stages of the epopee to supply what is needed.

I should say that the history of the literature of a particular poetry ought, by a comparison of poems and by reflection on the facts of the evolution of the species, to be able to set down something of value regarding its nature and possibilities. This I have essayed to do according to the measure of my ability.

Although I have treated the subject under national names, my reader must not expect from me a full history of national epics. Such a work would have required several volumes for its satisfactory completion, and would, I think, by the size and independence of the separate accretions have defeated my aim, which was, to write a short history of a poetical variety as such.

All my quotations are translated. I think the author of a book like this, which professes to be the history of a poetry in which all are interested, has no right to inflict on the general reader the presumably slow understanding of numerous quotations from poems written in different tongues.

The history of literature has been written in various ways. It has been written in panorama, it has been written in periods, it has been written from national standpoints, it has been written with reference to the work of individuals. I think there is much to be said for writing it under the head of literary variety.

I wish in this place to thank Mr A. Taylor, M.A., of Dundee High School, for assistance in reading the proof-sheets.

J. C.

CONTENTS

INTRODUCTORY

THE DEVELOPMENT AND NATURE OF EPIC POETRY

CHAPTER I

THE LATER ROMAN EPIC

CHAPTER II

THE ENGLISH EPIC

CHAPTER III

THE FRENCH EPIC

CHAPTER IV

THE GERMAN EPIC

CHAPTER V

THE ITALIAN EPIC

CHAPTER VI

THE SPANISH AND PORTUGUESE EPICS

LIST OF POEMS

DATE	POEM
B.C. 1100	Kalevala
,, 850	Iliad Odyssey
,, 300	Ramayana
,, 235	Argonautica (Apollonius)
,, 200	Mahabharata
,, 19	Æneid
A.D. 65	Pharsalia
,, 72	Argonautica (Valerius Flaccus)
,, 85	Punica
,, 95	Thebaid
,, 300	Fingal
,, 600	Beowulf
,, 1000	Shahnameh
,, 1080	Song of Roland
,, 1150	Poema del Cid
,, 1200	Nibelungenlied
,, 1314-1317	Divine Comedy
,, 1375	Bruce
,, 1461	Wallace
,, 1516	Orlando Furioso
,, 1572	Lusiads
,, 1575	Jerusalem Delivered
,, 1589	Araucana
,, 1590-1596	Faery Queen
,, 1667	Paradise Lost
,, 1671	Paradise Regained
,, 1726	Henriade

DATE	POEM
A.D. 1742	Henriqueida
,, 1748-1773 . . .	Messiah
,, 1814	Roderick
,, 1859-1885 . . .	Idylls of the King
,, 1867	Jason

Certain of the dates are quite doubtful, certain are only approximately correct.

INTRODUCTORY

THE DEVELOPMENT AND NATURE OF EPIC POETRY

Earliest heroic. Widest definition of epic

I SHOULD like to begin this introduction with a passably correct account of the development of epic. I wish to work along the literary line that has led to the heroic species proper of literature, so that it may be possible to have a retrospect that will be at once clarifying and fact-binding. The account will be, in a way, hypothetical, but still, I believe, of some validity, presenting a bridge from the known into the unknown, or rather, in regard to my procedure, part of an arch and a pier that rests on cloud thrown forward to meet part of an arch and its pier that rests on fact. This bridge will, I hope, form some sort of pathway, in spite of the queerness of the pontifical art. I shall, of course, have to isolate a mode of literature that did not for a long time exist in severance, but that certainly was always present in noticeable development, or in embryo, even in those parti-coloured efforts at expression that we may, by a stretch of imagination, call literary strivings. I am here giving the term 'epic' its most comprehensive meaning, and, if I define an epic as *a tale of dignity about individuals*, I think that very far back we shall find foreshadowings and adumbrations more or less amorphous, potential of our variety of literature, and of much else.

We can imagine savages taking one another by the

hand, and in wild chant, accompanied by movement, expressing their feelings. These utterances of entreaty or thanks to the beings who frightened or gladdened them were the beginnings of literature. They were acts of worship, and such dignity as was in the world then must have been in them. There could have been no story in these chants, for it was not definite personality that was addressed. Personification, doubtless, was operating, but rather indistinctly, I should say, and personification does not necessarily give personality with its predicate of rational activity. The beings worshipped, malevolent or benevolent, or both, were vaguely imagined, with fiats for attributes, and caprice for forethought.

The beginnings of literature

Early man was not an individual. He was a unit in a group. He acted and thought with his fellows. He lived for his tribe, and believed in its permanence, and in its past. Dead tribesmen were this past, and these were revered, especially those great ones who had served the tribe well. As time went on these tribal worthies were brought into line with one another. Between them there would very often have existed the relationship of father and son, and paternity, and dignity with it, would be thrown always backward, until some conspicuous ancient would have transferred to him all the reverence that was owed to the past as past, and as the cause of the present. His position as ancestor, representative, and protector of the tribe, was one that conferred dignity. He became the tribal god. At tribal ceremonials he was worshipped, and invoked, and the story of his birth and deeds was chanted. His glory would be that of the ideal tribesman, and although this would not mean possession of the individuality of a heroic personage, yet his apotheosis would by-and-by work into the story of his life notions of independence and authority. We may call this story a

The tribal god and individuality

narrative-chant, addressed to, and celebrating, personality.

Chants to a divine power were only worship, choral hymns; the story of the tribal god was a part of worship that must have put off incoherence and put on sequence, must have had, in fact, the semblance of a narrative. My point is, that no hymn to a god would, as such, give a story, which, in days when imagination was weak and only existed in the shape of emotion, could not have been uttered save about the experienced and the known, and that only the feats of the tribal god recited in the act of worship—and worship was then the one thing that charmed the imagination of men into recital—supplied materials with enough human interest and human scope to be called a narrative. Further, that the humanity of the story, being that of the society of the period, would have been very deficient in the self-sufficingness that ought to belong to what is called pre-heroic energy, had not the godhead of the tribal hero imparted a quantum of this quality to it. With our narrative-song we are still a good way from heroic quality of narrative, and from the kingship among men that is the property of the hero, but we have got a promising beginning. We may call this epoch, a long one, and gradually entered on, that of Rudimentary Literature, and, under that aspect of literature now being considered, that of Primitive Epic. It was an epoch in which every man was, so to speak, his own poet.

Beginnings of narrative. Primitive Epic

When the deifying faculty increased the number of gods, who, at first, had been the creations of terror and interest, and anthropomorphism was endowing deity with human attributes, many subjects for narrative-song of big import and of human bearings were provided. The multiplication of tribal heroes went on with time, and these, as protectors of the tribe, being associated with gods, were trans-

Early actors and early actions

figured as actors in matters that concerned their special activity. Gods with human attributes on the one hand, and tribal heroes with divine affinities on the other, speedily, by the mouths of their worshippers, spread notions of detached and self-determined activity, while the record of their co-operation for some given object imparted body to the chanted narrative, and was an anticipation of an epic feature. The sphere of action was, as yet, too confined to have much in it of the nature of heroic action, limited as it was to energy, sometimes man-like, along the lines of the divine and the semi-divine.

Outstanding individuals

I have emphasised the dignity and purposefulness that the superhuman functions of heroes gave to their deeds celebrated in official lays, but the conditions of life were rapidly becoming such, that heroes who had not been admitted to the heroic pantheon, and even live heroes, were beings of outstanding excellence.

Let us suppose a leader in war to have been slain. His tribesmen meet to sing his death-song. They describe his feats of war, his glorious leadership, and his noble death. Be it granted that these are the self-sacrifices of a number of the tribe, yet the stuff is not unlike that of a heroic lay. Again, a warlike brave has won for his tribe a victory in war. At the next feast of the tribal god a song is added to the tribal song celebrating him and his feats, and comparing him to the tribal god. This is something like a pæan to individual excellence. The similar surnames of heroes and gods, as benefactors of the community, would cause confusion, transference, and commingling of services. Stories told of heroes would be tinged with matter derived from stories of the gods. Therefrom would arise an exaggeration in matter, a proudness of style, and a mixture of legend and myth that we find in some specimens of early heroic.

I think I may say that at the end of this epoch the narrative-song had become something more than an act of worship or semi-religious commemoration, that it had, in fact, assumed proportions, and a tone that entitled it to be called the predecessor of ordered rhythmical narrative. It is to be thought that adorations and litanies addressed to the gods, and sacred recitals of their deeds were in the preparation of a religious brotherhood, and it is likely that lays which could not be known off-hand, being more than formal invocation and entreaty, but which needed attention to details in the secular activity of the heroes, were arranged by forerunners of the professional bards of a later age. The tribesman is no longer his own poet, but a listener to the poetical renderings of others. The epoch, with its rhythmical recitative and its high-toned narrative, may be justifiably named the epoch of Potential Epic.

Heightened narrative. Potential Epic

The wider life of men and an incipient distribution of tasks were subtly originating feelings of isolation and self-interest. The leaven of individualism was in operation. Combination for purposes of conquest and defence necessitated leadership, and special positions, and subordination. Tribal narrowness and levelling began to disappear. Leaders awoke to the consciousness of personal power, and fondness of this, and circumstances made permanent the assumption of superiority. Great war-lords acquired not only place, but property and a following, and, tribal ties being broken, men became personally devoted to a leader as leader. These great ones took the place of the tribe in the minds of the many, and had transferred to them all the regard and service that were owed to it. They were divine with its divinity, and descent from the tribal god when transferred to and centred in them, gave to their position of superiors among inferiors, of leaders

Individual pre-eminence: when developed and where seen

among led, the sanction of right as well as the lustre of divine ancestry. Round such chiefs a little court gathered, of which their more distinguished followers were the pillars. Minstrels were in their retinue, and sang their praises, and the praises of their kin, for the forefathers of the chief became subjects of song. As chiefs advanced to petty kings, the principal men of their following were in turn glorified, and common men sank into insignificance beside the royal house and the noble families. Each petty dominion became a focus of heroic song.

The chief's hall, the tyrant's court, and the castle of the feudal superior have been so many environments for the glorification of individuals, and centres for the diffusion of poetry celebrating these. The patronage of a chief gave a direction and a free spirit to heroic literature that it would not have possessed had it remained in the hands of priestly castes. What these can do in the way of epic production may be seen in the Indian epics. With the epoch of the chief began Heroic Epic. It was a progressive species for a long time.

Heroic Epic

Heroic epic is, indeed, a permanent variety in literature. From this time onward, there will be no lack of specimens of this variety. Poets of heroic epic have in a sense always been with us, but their productions belong to many stages of poetical development, beginning from the untutored poem of thin but sometimes nervous matter, and reaching to the poem of great technical skill and poetical decoration.

Rhythm was developed into metre during this period, and needed special devotion and practice. The poet was now a craftsman, and employed a form that was not at the command of everybody, and a diction that differed from that heard in ordinary speech.

I have given a rapid survey of the progress of epic writing. I have left *lacunæ;* I have not distributed time and emphasis; I have been one-sided in my view of literary *origines;* I have described generals cursorily, and left out important particulars, but I hope to have given an intelligible conception of the development of epic style.

Epic Poetry

The era of Epic Poetry followed on that of Heroic Epic. There were now guilds of bards, and legends were preserved, utilised, and grouped. He who could group and dock legendary lays, unify the reference, and give creative touches, breathe over them the breath of an original spirit, and provide full poetry, was a poet in epic poetry. Another, with less systematising power and shorter poetical flight, remained a poet in heroic epic. Heroic epic is the *sine qua non* of epic poetry. The poet of the first is a builder, the poet of the second a master-builder. A poem of the first sort is a chapel, a poem of the second, a cathedral. Epic poetry needs, externally, wide horizons, national life in some form or other, and movement of many men.

I have tried to trace our dignified tale about individuals down to the era of Epic Poetry. I call Homer an epic poet. I do not see why he should, with so great parsimony of phrase, be called an epic singer. Demodocus was one person, Homer another. The latter was something more than a composing rhapsodist of poetic ability. The man who arranged the Iliad, overlaid it with his own workmanship, and marked on it the sign-manual of his own poetic hand, made epic poetry. It is essential, indeed, to note two varieties of this, namely, natural epic poetry and artistic epic poetry. Homer wrote the one, Virgil the other. I propose now to offer some remarks on these two poets. This introduction is historical as well as critical, and it seems natural to preface it with some account of Homer as an epic poet. I shall take Virgil next, because Homer suggests Virgil. I shall have occasion, in the critical portion of the introduction, to mention most other epics that are not treated in the body of the book.

The Homeric poems. Their epic quality

It is not to be supposed that the Iliad and the Odyssey sprang into being without a fulness of time being reached. They are not primitive epics, except in a special sense of the term. They have too much literary art, and too many mannerisms of a school of bards to be primitive in the strict sense of the word.

They are certainly not like what are called the literary or art epics. They have not their self-consciousness, nor, if I may use the word, their far-fetchedness. There is not so much sameness in the ordinary narrative matter of a modern epic, as in that of an ancient. The Iliad is certainly picturesque and animated, but it has repetition and much of it. It has, it is true, no dreary flats, but tedium occasionally besets one who peruses it continuously. One could not say this of the Odyssey, which has a story of surpassing interest, and, better than the Anabasis, merits the name of the 'best story in the world.' Would not the Iliad, it may be asked, were we to take out of it the Hector and Andromache episode, the first book, the meeting between Achilles and Priam, etc., be shorn of its excellence, and its attractiveness repose on the homeric manner? Not so. The excellencies of the Iliad are very widely distributed, meet one, in fact, everywhere. All the same, the homeric manner--using the expression in the narrower sense, for in the larger, the homeric manner is just Homer, matter and manner combined—is a very powerful factor in producing the pleasure that all feel who peruse Homer attentively.

Homer's manner

What is the specialty of this homeric manner? It is not nobility, for every epic—genuine epic—has that. Well, Homer has solid vigour, clearly outlined action, an effortless style, and a mastery of love-compelling speech. A strong, straight speech it is, painted with simile, and adorned with the objectivity of epithet, full of life, and a something or other of primal virtue, that is not in, or, rather, that cannot be made to shine through words now. And the speech has the added charm of conveyance in a resonant metre of big flow, which can be ponderous or rapid as the occasion requires, and which reflects the gravity or gaiety of the thought. These facts are very imperfectly given by those who say that it is Homer's old-world manner that fascinates. The statement is very true, no doubt, but it is rather brief and somewhat dark.

Homer's Pegasus needs no spur. It passes over the plains, climbs the mountain sides, shoots aloft, travels round, and stands out on the azure sky, and prances in the brilliancy of the sun, all placidly, and naturally, and with most easy alternation. Homer is so engaging. He says his say and does not throw one off, now to this quarter, now to that, after a reminiscence or a coincidence. This constitutes one of his greatest charms to a modern. The effect he produces is not due to complexity or tumultuousness of imagery, but to the singleness of his simplicity, and to the strength of his lines of power. We may say, indeed, speaking of the Iliad, that it is not the deeds of war narrated that attract, but the art of the poet-narrator. And yet it was a big fray, a fray that had divine sanction and was honoured by divine participation, more heroic, more doom-fraught, and more a picture of life in little than other frays seem to be.

Homer's characters

Perhaps the prerogative of precedence enjoyed by the poet, as well as his unlaboured manner, has got something to do with our partiality for the fighting of these embattled chiefs. Anyhow, the homeric portraiture of characters needs no prerogative to commend it. Their awful and lovable attributes are skilfully interfused and naturally blended. We are not unaffected by the bovine force of Ajax and the outrecuidance of Diomede, but it is Achilles and Hector that affect us the most. We admire Achilles' manliness, his ebulliency, his haughty self-righteousness, his dogged, but not quite tearless resignation, and his tender gentility. We love Hector's patriotism, his loyalty, his moral manliness ; we admire the father, the husband, the hope and bulwark of his race. What a testimony to the worth of Hector, and to the impartiality of the poet, are the three laments that close the Iliad. Andromache misses the tender word he had left unspoken, Hecuba exults in the favour shown to her dead son by the gods, and Helen, Helen remembers his chivalry.

Achilles and Hector

The Iliad is a poem of great activity and of strong emotions. In it we follow the fortunes of a fight taken part in by many actors, and conditioned by the inaction and action of a hero of passionate individuality. When we think of the Iliad as a story, we think of the actors and their acting, in particular, we think of Pelides in wrath, of Pelides in the fight, of Pelides in tears ; when we close the book we say to ourselves, "What a man was Pelides." It is a tale limited to four moments—anger, turmoil, reconciliation, vengeance — and ending in an ethical sunset of warm and radiant humanity. The Iliad makes one's pulses beat, it makes one feel the emotions of a participant. One reads the Odyssey, lax and outstretched, as it were, and with a mind free from tension, whereas in the companion epic we feel a tightening of our attention, have a personal interest in the actors, and are conscious of a mimicry of the movements of the combatants, and a strong disposition to range ourselves now on this side, now on that. All this feeling, however, is due to strong interest and not to an intuition of vicariousness, which latter is a dramatic and not epic sensation.

The special effect of the Iliad

The Odyssey remains abidingly objective. Its reading is pure enjoyment tempered by compassionateness.

The special effect of the Odyssey

The Iliad is objective enough, for that matter, and all genuine epic must be such, but it is objective in a different way. There is more stirring action, more dramatic intensity in the Iliad, and one passes readily from spectator into quasi-actor. In reading the Odyssey we nearly always remain spectators, and passive gatherers of delight. When we think of the Odyssey as a story, we do not think of the feats of the hero, but of the lands he visited, the wonders he saw, the hairbreadth escapes he made, and not even the deed of vengeance wrought on the wooers, or the recognition and our satisfaction thereover, makes us forget the record of these ten years of wandering and adventure. Its variety is concerned with externals, is that afforded by adventure and shifting of scene, and is highly enhanced by the general romantic setting. The story, however, is not like an eastern tale of wonder, for, amid all the wonder, its sanity and rationalness are conspicuous, and we never lose our way in it, always retaining a hold on the individuality of the hero. Just after the slaughter of the wooers, before we read of the punishment of the faithless maids that dangled from nooses and wriggled with their feet for a little, but only for a little, the feeling of passivity that I have spoken of reasserts itself, and remains to the *deus ex machina* conclusion.

The epopee is not a genre that necessarily appears in every age. There was a time when it, or its anticipation, was produced galore, but, at other times, it needs a man of genius—an epic craftsman *par excellence*. The name epic, in the proper content of the term, implies something not primitive. Primitive epics are heroic poems. It is literary style, and scope and quality of story that give us epic ; it is thoughtful searching, an æsthetic setting

The content of the name epic

forth, and, in later epic, romanticism that give us the literary or art epic. Æsthetic setting forth does not imply a story with a purpose, but does imply one with a plot, for without this we cannot have even a good heroic poem. The epic has to present adventures and events æsthetically, but it has dramatic qualities, and, when to these are added elegiac and general poetic excellencies, as in the Æneid, its range of attractiveness is much widened.

Epic poets of Rome before Virgil

Before Virgil, Naevius and Ennius wrote historical epics, and between these and him there were fresh essays—*e.g.*, those of Varius in the first kind, and those of Varro Atacinus in both—in the historical epic, and also essays in the mythological. There had also been written epic tales—viz., by Cinna, Calvus, Catullus—with dramatic allurements, dramatic situations, and stagey passionateness. Virgil began his great poem at a time when, as regards metre, style, and words, the language was ready for the attempt, and he chose a story that had hold of the popular imagination.

Hostile criticism of Virgil

Virgil has been subjected to some most unjust and most minuscule criticism. I have never been able to follow the statements of those who belittle the Mantuan. Much of the depreciation is due to the fact that Virgil is not Homer. If it is true that without Homer there would have been no Virgil, or rather, no Æneid, what does that prove? Nothing. Simplicity, nature's beauty, and sheer power are admirable things, but so is grace, so is art, when reinforced by genius, and so is power that is vivifying, dramatic, and tremulous with emotion. I believe with Voltaire, that, if Homer made Virgil, it was his greatest work. Virgil has, with obvious exceptions, stamped his influence on all the epic literature that comes after him. I speak not only of manifest copying of incident, and disposition of fable, but of communication of tone.

If we had never known Homer, we had never discerned the homeric imitations, and why should our knowledge of their existence detract from our appreciation of Virgil, seeing that he professedly imitated Homer. He produced something with homeric echoes, it is true, but solidly distinctive as well. The resemblance only proves that he heired the homeric, which, indeed, he bettered. Let us forget Homer and read the Æneid as an independent bit of literature. We shall then be in a position to appreciate its power. We are not at all times bound to describe a poet in terms of his literary father.

Virgil and Homer

It must not be forgotten that Virgil dealt with a Trojan hero, and a tale that had had a development among his own countrymen, and that many homeric aspects are not so much virgilian copyings as national *rifacimenti*. Much that is in Homer is older than the poet and stock-in-trade of all heroic poets. Virgil exercised the same right as did Homer. His originality is not disproved by his procedure. Let us contrast the copyings done on Virgil of Silius Italicus. The Æneid is not a *contaminatio* of the Iliad and the Odyssey, as some would have us believe, with pathos and patriotism and intellectuality thrown in. The effect produced by the Æneid is altogether different from that produced by the Iliad or Odyssey. There is a conscious ethical colouring in Virgil. The special quality of his poem is a thoughtful and not a sensuous one. Homer gives us activity, manliness, isolated deeds, sorrow, and outbursts of sheer humanity. Virgil draws for us character, purpose, a passage to an end, weariness, and the still sadness that oppresses souls.

Homer sings, as sing he must, from impulse, and not from purpose, though he had to eat, I daresay. I think that too much is sometimes made of the impromptuness and *naïveté* of the Homeric poems, if it is meant, as would sometimes seem, that no plan, no reflectiveness, but mere eclectic haphazardness, as it were, and instinctive singing amassed and produced the verse. Naive ought to mean unconventional, and devoid of reflection, in the sense of devoid of thoughtful searching. Homer had art as well as Virgil, in fact, no man can be a poet without art, or, in this connection, I should say, technic. The rhapsodist poets had not only traditional methods of handling and poetic art, but had to write in a style that suited delivery. It is one thing to say that Virgil lived at a time when reflection and poetic artifice were recognised, another, and an erroneous thing, to say that he imposed art-forms on his story. Virgil made explicit what appeared to him implicit in the national history and strivings, read into them an order, a beginning, a middle, and an end. He voiced the thoughts, conscious and half-conscious, of his fellows. He idealised history.

The latter part of the Æneid

Virgil has been much blamed. He has been blamed for his limning of Æneas, and he has been blamed for the alleged lameness of his story, and the comparative feebleness of the latter part of his poem. Leaving out the 'tale of Troy' portion of the epic, and comparing narrative with narrative, we, to my thinking, ought to say that the latter part is as narrative superior to the first. The argument of the first six books is nobly weighted with the Descent and the Story of Dido, which are, however, both episodes. The later books are a better specimen of epic narrative than the earlier. They are in their way as good as Homer, and ought to be more pleasant to modern taste, unless a special effect is sought after. Their story is more compact, and has a more rolling volume than that of the Iliad or Odyssey. If they are at all tedious, it is when they reproduce the homeric form too closely.

The second part of the Æneid seems to me to be what Virgil says it is, viz., a record of the greater events of the story. So far as even running narrative is concerned, it is the better part of the epic. And it is more than an assemblage of heroic incidents. The plot has marked saliency and development. The landing, the compact, the outbreak of war, the alliance, the leaguered camp, the Trojan advance, the truce, the single combat frustrated and passing into a duel to death on the field of battle, are culminant points in a well-ordered and swiftly moving march of events.

Nor does it take rank only as a story, as a recital of events germane to a main issue. The tale of Silvia's pet stag, the episode of Nisus and Euryalus, the account of the life and death of the warrior-maid Camilla, the figured glories of the shield are embellishments of a master-poet. Lausus, Mezentius, Turnus himself, and the old Evander have, as personalities, attractiveness, and the first two, and last, have, in addition, a virgilian flavour. And

Pallas

Pallas, who, next to Camilla, was, I am sure, Virgil's favourite character, and whose name sounds to the reader in the finale of the Æneid, more like a dirge than a war-cry of vengeance, Pallas, who died ere his prime, after barely earning the first fruits of his youthful valour, surely Pallas has a more than common attractiveness. Over his fate, by mouth of Jupiter, Virgil utters the passive and active, the fatalism and freedom contained in his conception of life :—

> Stat sua cuique dies ; breve et inreparabile tempus
> Omnibus est vitæ : sed famam extendere factis,
> Hoc virtutis opus.*
>
> *Æn.* x, 467.

The story of the shield

The story of the shield in the eighth book is the story of Rome. It is a fine grouping of the psychological moments in the city's history, and a long-sounding pæan on its glories. The verse

* His own day awaiteth each ; short is the time of life to all men, and beyond recall : but to spread fame by deeds—this is valour's task.

is as magnificent as the matter is imaginative and pictorial. Its lines, to mention one quality, have, in virtue of their imaginative rhythm, all the effect on the ear that a historical procession would have on the eye, a difficult effect to produce, because the ear, unless to direct musical appeal, is not so impressionable as the eye, and is, moreover, somewhat barren of projecting power. Perhaps the sense filters through the sound and aids the impression. In that case it is a fine thing to have written poetry so interpreting and so permeable.

Æneas. Different conceptions of the heroic

It has been, and still is, fashionable, even among admirers of Virgil, to speak disparagingly or apologetically of Æneas as a creation of poetic fiction that we must be content to look kindly on out of homage to the genius of its creator, or at least as an amiable though occasionally lapsing saint, liable to accesses of battle-frenzy. He has even been called a 'milksop,' and a 'perjured adulterer.' Such criticisms are off the line; they are unsympathetic, they argue angularity. They prove that the critic either does not know the mind of Virgil, or has become prepossessed by some pet type of hero, the thought of which warps his judgment of another variety. In common life we have become emancipated, intellectually, at anyrate, from narrowness, and have become civilised in our conceptions of the heroic. We no longer look for barbaric or feudal elements in heroism, but in certain of our literary likes and dislikes we are still barbarians. How otherwise shall we explain it that the patriotic, the filial, the reverent Æneas is reckoned inferior to the, from some points of view, ruffling roisterers of Homer?

I suppose it is felt that the combination of piety, pessimism, and homerico-heroic in Æneas, is not a happy one. But in the hero's days there was enough of religious fear, and pessimism, or fatalism, to make possible the attribution of such a personage to them. The tinge of modernity, or domestication, in the hero's character, is not unjustifiable, and ought not to be unpleasing. Æneas had to perform a task that no hero of ancient epic had to perform. He had to transplant a religion and found a kingdom. He is made to feel a weight that the real Æneas never felt, and made prescient of a responsibility that the real Æneas never feared. It is the task allotted that accounts in large measure for the presentation of the hero. His character is a bit of an anachronism in the period of action of the poem. But all poetic and objective literature that concerns the past is more or less an anachronism, for is it not this much or that much of the thought of the present with the environment and matter of the past? The homeric dressing of epic is not the ultimate, nor, as I think, the best—it was not even the pre-virgilian—and the new epical wine of the human spirit could not have been always confined in homeric bottles. The literary epic has notes of many poetic moods, and is all the fuller and better a species for these. And if the individuality of the poet has passed into his creation, and Æneas, like Virgil, has the sense of tears, the epic poets who have succeeded the epic singers have all marked on their poems the imprint of their own personality, and could not, as poetic masters and creators, have done otherwise.

The heroic of Virgil's time

It is the literary or patriotic halo investing the ebullient Achilles and Wallace wicht that makes them acceptable to us as heroes. To the Romans of Virgil's time the fighting qualities of such persons, isolated from other qualities, and in a national poem, would have appeared the attributes of a centurion rather than of a national hero. At that time there was a disbelief in the permanency and utility of mere burning individualism. Vehement endeavour and self-asserting action had not, in the experience of the men of that age, had the recommendation of stability, nor did they have the sanction of the sober and ethical propriety of the national spirit. Virgil's hero reposed on the divine backing, was a waiter on Deity, and the delineation of such a person was at once a guide and homage to current public feeling, and, in that time of national hopes built on a politic if not perfervid individual, a hopeful augury for the future.

It is possible to be too philosophical in one's interpretation of a character like Æneas, but it is plain even to a cursory reader that, individually, he is meant to be a pattern of self-denial and sage acquiescence in the will of higher powers. He is also, typically, I should say, meant to be a prehistorical embodiment of the patience and reverent purpose of the best national sentiment pressing towards the realisation of its destiny and ideal.

Æneas a manly warrior

While Æneas is, to a certain extent, a type, he is also a warrior and must not be denuded of manliness. Virgil meant him to be a fighting man, meant to carry on the homeric tradition about his hero. On this homeric conception he grafted ideas of another sort. He certainly made Æneas a man with a mission, and a vehicle for the exhibition and glorification of certain virtues ; he imparted to him certain qualities of the ideal man of his own thoughts, and he saddened his visage over with the cast of the thought of his own day, but he did not mean to suggest to us that his creation was a seeker after a happy domesticity, balked of his quest, or a warrior and a hero in his own despite. Æneas was to Virgil the countryman, the comrade in arms, and the peer of Hector. Diomedes' view is the poet's :—

> Ambo animis, ambo insignes præstantibus armis ;
> Hic pietate prior.*
>
> Æn. xi, 291.

* Both (Hector and Æneas) excelled in courage, both excelled in brilliant feats of arms, the latter was more advanced in goodness.

The following words have no meaning, unless addressed to a great-hearted warrior :—

> Tu ne cede malis, sed contra audentior ito,
> Quam tua te fortuna sinet.*
>
> Æn. vi, 95.

Not only must we not denude Æneas of manliness, but we must not misrepresent to ourselves the nature of his mission, or narrow the conception thereof. He was not a mere religious missioner, and colporteur of his ancestral penates, but a conqueror and civiliser. He may be looked on as the introducer of a cult, but when he says on his oath before Latinus,

His mission

> Sacra deosque dabo ; socer arma Latinus habeto,†
>
> Æn. xii, 192.

he is not conveying a declaration of preference, or hinting at a theory of life, but uttering a highly-strung supplication, and using, I think, politic and conciliatory terms, which are to be taken loosely and not literally. He is rather speaking sentimentally than enunciating a formula that is to be his guide through life, or that gives the *raison d'être* of his voyage to Italy. In any case, the poet never dreamt of stating the whole mission of his hero in a supplication. The braveries, defiances, and gloatings attributed to Æneas by Virgil are not simply war-paint, but really the marks of a heroic soul abounding in courage. It is the religiously-ordered life, the reflective and self-conscious sentiment, and the abiding and intensely-realised purpose of Æneas that make them sometimes appear incongruous. The incongruity is more apparent in objective epic than it would be in lyric or drama. But, whatever Æneas is, he is not a poor little Trojan mouse with a mission.

* Yield thee not to adversity, but aye go more daringly forward, more daringly than thy fortune will permit thee.

† Rites and gods I shall supply ; let my father-in-law, Latinus, wield the sword.

It is not, indeed, as the poet of frays and blows that we are pleased to remember Virgil, but as the sad singer, the poet of a joy whose hand is ever at its lips bidding adieu. Antores, the Argive, died at the hands of Mezentius by a spear-cast meant for Æneas:—

Antores

> Sternitur infelix alieno vulnere, cælumque
> Adspicit, et dulces moriens reminiscitur Argos.*
>
> Æn. x, 781.

It is a squeamishness born of barbarian tastes and narrow prejudices that cavils at the epithet *pius* as applied to Æneas. The much-maligned *Sum pius Æneas* was addressed by him to one whose deity he divined, and whom he wished to propitiate by proclaiming himself god-fearing, for he straightway passes on to speak of his rescue of the penates, or Virgil may not have written the first book before the others, and, having fixed on the epithet *pius* as appropriate to Æneas, he may give it here, as a distinguishing item in the heraldic epical announcement. So that it has a reference to the hearer or reader as well as to the goddess. Epithets are constant things in epic, and Æneas is more self-conscious than other epic heroes. In any case the contemptuous superciliousness with which the designation is sometimes treated is quite misplaced. It has always appeared to me that *pius* has strong undertones of modern import. It has its well-known triple meaning—good, filial, patriotic—but there is more in it than these. These tones seem to me to say, as nearly as ancient fatalism and buffeted and somewhat passive individuality could say, "Whatsoever other men do, as for me, I shall serve the Lord." Æneas had the consciousness of right of the dictum quoted, if not its special aggressiveness.

Pius Æneas

* Hapless, by a wound not meant for him, he is laid low, and turns his eyes skywards, and in his death sweetly remembers Argos.

Æneas is the real, and not merely the titular hero of epic. Some lovers of paradox and framers of hasty and narrow generalisations will have it that Turnus is the real hero. Turnus is a homage to use and wont in epic, and doubtless the poet's recognition of the old Italian race, and the embodiment of its virtues, but Æneas is the real hero. Turnus is a marplot, an unthinking, irreligious, impulse-ruled semi-barbarian, the associate of tyrants and impious men. He is maddened by the gods. His bravery is the bravery of animalism and self-will, and he is not over-chivalrous.

Turnus

Virgil, working after Apollonius, introduced love into his epic. Apollonius' Medea, smitten of Eros, became enamoured of Jason's youthful beauty and heroic mould. Before she abandoned herself to love and unfilial conduct, she passed through a severe struggle. Her self-respect, and her duty as the king's daughter, alike forbade a facile acquiescence in the dictates of an overpowering passion. But Medea's heart had been too deeply wounded, and her whole emotional nature too completely captivated to permit of resistance. Such resistance as she made, by rebound, only increased her infatuation. So with Dido. Even before the intervention of Cupid-Ascanius, her woman's imagination had been won for the Trojan chief. Afterwards, neither her duties as queen-foundress, nor her self-imposed and self-consecrated loyalty to her dead husband, could stem the torrent of the desire that went out towards Æneas.

Dido. The Medea of Apollonius

It is common to rate Æneas, and through him, Virgil, for cruel treatment of Dido. But Æneas, to do him justice, took no initiative in the wooing. The initiative was all with the queen. First her imagination, and then her passion beguiled her. Æneas played the part of a human magnet. Perhaps Anna's services saved forwardness on his part. It was

Dido's initiative

not till the hunt that he became aggressive, and then the snug occasion and the sensual queen overpowered his passivity, and he sank the Trojan in the Phrygian. Of course Æneas must have been conscious that he was neglecting his mission, that he was toying with indecision, and trifling with a woman's tenderness. But the solace of womanly sympathy must have been welcome to the wave-worn hero, and was not Dido as beautiful as Dian? Dido, too, on her side, was neglecting a mission, and surely we are not to remember nothing against Dido and everything against Æneas.

Æneas' alleged insensibility

That impassioned appeal of the queen beginning with reproach, melting into tenderness, and ending in amorous breath did not dissuade Æneas from his recovered purpose. And why should it have done so? Æneas, convinced of neglectful dalliance, could not have acted otherwise than he did, and have at the same time remained true to the sad sincerity of his character. He cut a poor figure in the circumstances, as any man would. At least he made soft answer to the tempestuous queen.

His reference to the work cut out for him by the gods sounds callous and cruel after Dido's moving statement of her sacrifices, sacrifices, one can call them, of principle to passion. I suppose Æneas ought to have gone on sinning against the light that had been flashed in on his silken wantonness and unfatherly conduct. It is to my mind Dido's second appeal to Æneas, in which, by Anna, she entreated him to delay his departure for a little, were it only till the winds were fair, that she might learn to school herself into submission, it is this second appeal, I think, that makes defence of Æneas' action particularly difficult. It is always correct, however, to plead the high necessities of the epic. It was better that a woman should weep and die, than that Rome should remain unfounded.

Censure of Æneas is really a compliment to the art with which Virgil has drawn Dido. The poet of the *molle atque facetum* has developed, among other qualities, a dramatic power of surprising intensity. Any suggestions that Virgil has got from Apollonius only account for one half of the picture of the queen, that half which concerns the triumph of love over her former prepossessions. In the other half, that which concerns her behaviour after the scorning, he must be painting with memories of Greek tragedy present to his mind, as Nettleship points out, rather than with any definite recollection of the conduct of Medea towards Jason when the Colchians forced the Minyans into a compact that endangered her safety. Indeed, there is a strong tragic cast about the whole story of the queen. Dido is overthrown and punished by the blind forces that work the will of the gods for an act half involuntary.

Dramatic drawing of Dido

No one can read, or, better, recite, Virgil's verse without being conscious of a distinction that compels the attention and affection. This consciousness is due, broadly speaking, to the stateliness of the verse. There are other characteristics that will soon further rivet the attention and affection. These are the graceful and illumining diction with the special verbal delicacy of the poet, as well as the tender gravity of his language with its palpable surcharge of sorrow. We meet, too, as we read, with other characteristics that are national, and common to the prose and verse of the poet's fellow-countrymen, to wit, oratorical pomp and the proud brilliance of the full-throated Roman. It is partly this last characteristic that Sainte Beuve refers to, when he speaks of Virgil's influence causing to reflow in mediæval times, after long drought, *le large fleuve de la grande parole*.

Virgil's metre: its distinction

But there is something of greater rarity and subtlety

in the Virgilian harmony. All high poetry has its metrical forte, its special rhythmical flavour, and, I think, spiritual impressiveness. Virgil's metrical specialty is not the fitness of words to thought that we may find even in prose, or the simple suiting of sound to sense, but something not rational or imitative, something more perfect in the direction of harmonious adaptation and rhythmic realisation. It is difficult to define this in words, for we now touch on the very ontology of poetics, and at such a point one is apt to grow dithyrambic. There are several good translations of Virgil, each presenting a facet of the Virgilian manner. But nothing like the totality or purity of this manner is presented in any. No translation, of course, can do this service for an original, and still less can it do so for a poet like Virgil, whose whole individual nature, so to speak, is in his verse. The manner of a poem largely depends on its metrical quality, and Virgil, in the matter of harmony, is not only a hexametrist in regular succession, but a hierophant, mitred and endowed with utterance by nature herself. Milton's verse, with all its majestic volume and severe music has not to my ear, a vocality equal to that of Virgil, with its something of sorrow, its echo of thoughts too deep for utterance, its pure and human stateliness, and its suggestion of personality.

Its vocality

It is the expressive, the speaking quality of the Virgilian melody that engages one's attention and wonder. It has eloquence, and seems by predestined appropriateness to convey thought. The Spirit of the World in melancholy mood must chant some such melody as Virgil's. Mr F. W. H. Myers well describes this quality of the poet's verse, when he says in his remarkable essay on Virgil: "His thoughts seem to come to us on the wings of melodies prepared for them since the foundation of the world."

Its moral and emotional quality

The moral and emotional quality of Virgil's metre grows on one. The metre has a dying fall of pathos that often sounds, refrain-like, amidst all its stately nobility and golden roll. It has a wondrous and individual charm, which the poet's own intonation must have converted into a very gospel of harmony. The outward features of the *technique* of the metre may be searched for and set down, but its full effect is not due to any trick of style, but to the natural systole and diastole of metrical emotion. Virgil's poetry is epical threnody, often overflowing the narrative into pathetic comment or sorrowful exaltation. His poetry is epical threnody, but we must have emerged from boyhood, and experienced more than one disillusion before we can understand to the full its word-and-song philosophy, or hear with responsive ear its notes of world-sorrow. Then we find in it the reflex of our sorrowful reminiscence and sombre anticipation. We seem then to hear in it an almost audible wail over the tender grace of a day that is dead, and a half-articulate lament over the perishable happiness of a day that is to be. The Æneid is weighted with psychology, and a psychology that has not many joyous notes. Now and again there float to our ears muffled murmurs of bliss from prophesied communities that are descendants of the saintly good—communities, for individuals as recipients of happiness count for almost nothing in Virgil—or from a few typical personages who have been adjudged worthy of permanent joys in the unseen.

Its general excellence

Virgil was indeed skilled to make one realise his conceptions by striking language and rhythm. Witness the hallowing pomp that lives in the rhythm of many of the allusive and prophetic passages in the poem. Witness the chanting dirge over mankind or individuals that sounds in much of the immortal Sixth Book, a dirge that speaks in tones of melodious and melancholy philanthropy. We find also a striking dramatic appropriateness in the language of the poet's smaller efforts. Stateliness never leaves Virgil. His Muse is always matronly and self-contained, never hysterical, like Lucan's.

An objective tale has aspects that reveal to us the poet's notions of what is most desirable in life. These do not sketch an ideal to be striven after, but only answer the question, what is the best lot in life? An answer may also be given to the deeper question, what is life? The question is, of course, not to be formally propounded nor pointedly answered. That would be unepical. Is there a lesson of life portrayed for us in the Iliad? I daresay there is in the Odyssey, and it is perhaps materialistic in its advice, preaching something like the superior attractiveness of home life, *pace* Tennyson's dantesque conception of Ulysses, but I do not find a lesson obtruded in the latter epic, and do not find one at all in the former. If lesson of life means the picture drawn, then I think Mr E. Myers gives us it, with his 'Gain of a Friend,' 'Quest of Honour,' 'Untimely Death.' The Iliad is simply a story, and says nothing about an end in life, either explicitly or implicitly, but merely registers some facts that concern select men, and experiences that occur to all. There is a lesson of life behind Virgil's lines, and it is 'Duty,' 'Self-Sacrifice,' 'the Nation before the Individual.' Virgil is not formally didactic, but he may in a sense be said to teach resolution, and enthusiasm, and that tearful determination born of a baffling that is no baffling, but only education. For a nobly ideal tone, for the presence of that presentation of literary grace that makes the grace a direct moral force, that makes beauty of style to have a strong sentimental effect on the reader, Virgil is unsurpassed and unsurpassable.

Lesson of life in epic

I have considered Virgil here, as I said, that I might

place my remarks on Virgil in juxtaposition with those on Homer. But there are certain epics that I ought to describe early in this introduction, and these are the Kalevala and the Indian Epics.

The Kalevala

The Kalevala, the great poem of Finland, is an example of an epic that owes nothing to civilisation. Indeed, it reads more like a primitive description and resolution of creation than an epic. There appears in it a universal co-operation of nature with the mood of man, and the song-men of the Kalevala are just those who would have spoken of the sun as their brother, of the moon as their sister, and of rivers and trees as kinsmen. Imagining expatiates without let, there is quite a flux of personification. We see the musings and beliefs of nature-children who have passed from a savage state onward, without being drawn into the progress of the world, without being made to realise that man's activity is more engrossing and more important than the face of nature. Nature lay before them like an open book, and they read it narrowly and in detail. Necessarily there is in their nature-talk much that is crude and misty.

Its argument

In the poem is told the shadowy story of one Wainamoinen, a mighty magician of Kalevala ('the land of heroes'), of wondrous birth, who went to Pohyola ('Northland'), to get to wife the daughter of Louhi, the lady of the land. He had before this courted Aino, by permission of her brother Youkahainen, whom he had vanquished in singing. The maiden, however, had rejected his addresses and drowned herself. Youkahainen, the rival minstrel, shoots Wainamoinen as he rides along the coast, and he tumbles into the sea. He floats, swims, and is borne by an eagle to Louhi's territory. She consoles him in his piteous condition, and tells him that the hand of her daughter is to be given to him who shall make the sampo, a talisman of some sort. This Wainamoinen cannot do, but names his brother Ilmarinen, a worker in metals, as a likely maker. The latter does make the object, but is for the nonce refused the hand of the maiden. Louhi sends home, at his own request, the weary Wainamoinen in her own sledge drawn by her own steed.

On the road home he meets Louhi's daughter, or the Maiden of the Rainbow, as she is called in Rime VIII, and solicits her hand. She intimates her preference for the single state as follows :—

Bright and warm are days of summer,
Warmer still is maiden-freedom ;
Cold is iron in the winter,
Thus the lives of married women ;
Maidens living with their mothers
Are like ripe and ruddy berries,
But the most of married women
Are like dogs enchained in kennel,
Rarely do they ask for favours,
Not to wives are favours given.
Crawford's Trans., p. 99.

However, on being pressed to wed, she prescribes him three seemingly impossible tasks that must be accomplished by a successful wooer, two of which he performs, and in the performance of the last wounds his knee. After some trouble he gets the blood staunched by magic words, and the wound healed by magic balsam. He then resumes work at the third task, which was, to build a boat from the fragments of the maiden's distaff and the splinters of her spindle, and to move it into sea without so much as touching it. For the completion of the boat-building he needs to know certain magic words. He seeks these in the land of Puoni ('Death'), without success, and at last learns them and much more, from the giant Wipunen, who swallowed him and thus passed on the knowledge. Wipunen is not only a Cyclops, but a sort of Iopas as well. He sang :

> How the moon was first created,
> How the sun was set in heaven,
> Whence the colours of the rainbow,
> Whence the ether's crystal pillars,
> How the skies with stars were sprinkled.
>
> Crawford's Trans., p. 254.

Wainamoinen goes home disconsolate over his rejection and his old age, but obligingly appears at the house-warming of Ilmarinen, and sings wedding-songs. He afterwards sails with Ilmarinen and Lemmikainen for the sampo. There are some harp-songs of his given in a later rime, and in the last he is censured by the two-weeks-old child of the virgin mother Mariatta, and sails away to the sunset. Lemminkainen, brother of Wainamoinen, and Kullervo have parts of the poem to themselves. The story is very loose.

I have read the Kalevala in Mr Crawford's translation. His metre, a reproduction of the original, resembles that of Hiawatha.

The Indian Epics

Both the Indian epics, the Rāmāyana and the Mahābhārata, exhibit the vice of a too lengthy action. In fact, several epics might be quarried out of their materials. In the Rāmāyana there are proofs of the existence of genuinely heroic stuff that might have given an epic whole with one conspicuous personality, had it come into the hands of a poet who knew how to select, and who possessed a sense of epic construction. Rāma is too mild, or rather, too much drawn to rule. It is deeds on the part of the individual, and broadly human preconceptions on the part of the poet, that should define an epic hero. Both poems are too biographical. It is the biographical that regulates the heroic, and not the heroic the biographical. We have to follow Rāma and the Pāndavas into heaven, not because heroism militant brings them nigh it, but because it is good to round off human life with a translation. Both poems have been spoiled by accretions, and emasculated by brahmanising.

The Mahābhārata is an example of an epic of growth with little continuity, or at all events, without the informing unity in continuity of a great artist. It extends to over 200,000 lines, and must have been the work of generations. There is no central event in the poem. It is a chronicle of family matters, of feuds between the Pāndavas and the Kauravas, with attachments thrown in, and with interlardings of morality, metaphysics, and precepts of kingcraft. One has only to read Prof. Monier Williams' sketch and criticism of the Rāmāyana and Mahābhārata, or to bethink him of a satisfying reason for their great popularity, to be convinced that the poems, whatever objection may be taken to their form, possess a matter that is powerful and attractive.

Epic action. Its length and loftiness

An epic, as we understand the term, should have a lengthy and satisfying story. Without length it is impossible to have the long vistas of action and the variety of character that such a poem requires. And the story cannot be commonplace, but must satisfy the grand emotions of the soul. The traditional reputation and the internal necessities of this class of poem, unite in tying the story down to the description of big, if not momentous action. We have only to interrogate our memories. All our recollections of epic are recollections of actions that vitally concerned a section of humanity, and the names of the great heroes of epic are synonyms for brave and noble actors. It is impossible to exhibit the character-play of the high personages typical of epic in a petty action. Such actions enshrine nothing but commonplace actors of earthy mould and paltry behaviour. A lofty action lifts actors, it lifts a poet's manner, and sustains his spirit at the high general level of epic. An epic action is not likely to be simple, for its interlacing of conflicting energies demands a modicum of complexity.

An action that is lofty and long, and that has some complexity, is a requisite of an epic poem. The ramifications of a long action will, however, bring the reader into touch with much that is subordinate in tone, with much that is ordinary. The largeness of such a poem must for mere relief's sake admit these things, and the life of epic being human life, or humanised life, must, to be true to its pattern, exhibit a representative amount, though not a plethora of the human mood. The show of epic cannot and must not be all splendid, and its field of action has and must have its byways of calm as well as its highways of effort.

Its variety

Any great action of sufficient length and sufficient pitch can be treated epically, provided it have movement and human or humanised striving. The story unfolded in the action may be as heroic as is desired, provided that its heroism do not exceed credibility, or, as we should rather say, transgress the limits of traditional liberties, and that sanity, poetical sanity, I mean, which is not the same as prosaical, rule its conceptions and animate its plot. Even in episodes, where more freedom may sometimes justly be claimed, there must appear traces of the dominion of sober wisdom—sober in exaltation, for soberness, as a pure intellectual quality, and exaltation are not contraries. Not that the poet is to be limed to earth, or that his poetry is not to be dyed in the tint that his imagination may colour it with, but because in episodes we ought to see some fulfilment of the real

There must be sanity in the action and in the episodes

necessities of a genuine story, and not pure play of the fancy.

Advantages of a national, and at the same time untouched subject

A national subject presents many obvious advantages to an epic poet. It supplies him in a definite manner with the ready-made and not unpliable objectivity that is the basis of epic narration, it engenders patriotic feeling, and thus increases the range of the emotional imagination, and it enlists beforehand the sympathies of the reader. Suitable subjects of this sort are the most susceptible of epic treatment, and fortunate is the would-be epic poet who finds an untouched one at his hand. To him a virgin theme of national and historical significance is, to say nothing of the unreachable precedence genius may thereby win, an excitant of effort and an earnest of success. It presents him with an unused warp of poetical story on which to weave a texture of his own planning and colouring, it furnishes real outlines of character with shadowy interiors, over which he will have a creator's opportunities and rights. It gives a good poet a prescriptive right to knock at the door of the Temple of Fame. The history of poetic greatness will repeat itself:—

> Erunt etiam altera bella,
> Atque iterum ad Trojam magnus mittetur Achilles.

Homer the first great poet of his subject

We may be fairly sure that no poets of great parts forestalled Homer, otherwise, in virtue of their being poets, they would not have been lost in the long night. I use the name Homer for the poetical draughtsman that sketched the main contour of the Iliad, whom no one that can diagnose literary proprietorship, or gauge intellectual autocracy, will ever believe to have been a ghostly *eponymus* of the Homeridæ, or a convenient expression for a corporation of bards that wrote, and not all at the same period, epic rhapsodies with some centripetal quality to be thrown on a common stone-heap. Homer had the advantage of handling a great theme inadequately handled by predecessors, and was poet enough to give effect to all its potentialities.

Contrast Homer's good fortune with the evil fortune of his continuator, Quintus Smyrnæus, who follows his poetical sire with not so unequal steps. Quintus is not Homer, but Homer would not have banned his work.

Quintus Smyrnæus. His subject

Quintus wrote the τὰ μεθ' Ὁμήρου in fourteen λόγοι. It is a sequel to Homer's account of the beleaguering of Troy, and introduces to us fresh Trojan champions, Penthesilea, Memnon, and Eurypylus, son of Telephus. Achilles overshadows all in the first few books. Neoptolemus is pre-eminent in the last half. The former kills Penthesilea and Memnon, the latter, Eurypylus. Antilochus, Achilles, and the Telamonian Ajax die out of the story. Deiphobus, with access of heroism, plays the patriot among the Trojans till his death. Philoctetes is brought back from Lemnos, and kills Paris with a poisoned arrow. We are told, as we know them from Virgil, of the woes of Troy :—

> The woes of Troy, towers smothering o'er their blaze,
> Stiff-holden shields, far-piercing spears, keen blades,
> Struggling, and blood, and shrieks.

There is an extra book telling of the faring of some of the Greeks after the fall of Troy.

Quintus and Homer

The movement in Quintus is more historical than it is in Homer. His poem might be called the second part of the siege of Troy, told in heroic verse *à la* Homer. The story of Homer is more compact than that of his continuator, has a more discernible clue, and is timed and dominated by one individual. There is not the same unity in diversity in the poem of the lesser Smyrnæan. In the Iliad Achilles is always in or near our thoughts, as he frowns from the background, or works in the foreground. Neoptolemus dominates only the last part of Quintus' poem. The Posthomerica has not so good a story for epical purposes as the Iliad, and its poet had for predecessor one whom it was hopeless to equal, and to whom, even if the successor had been able to approximate to his master, there had been secured the homage of centuries with its *nec viget quicquam simile aut secundum* prejudices. Quintus copies Homer and copies him to some purpose, and to copy Homer well is to be a good poet. He sometimes appears to me to out-homer Homer, a fault that is sure to be laid to the charge of an imitator. We, however, require an epic poet to be more than the possessor of poetic ability. We exact from him initiative, and architectonics in general. I might quote many passages from the poet illustrative of his homeric vigour and simplicity, and, it must be admitted, of his independent power. I shall give some quotations and make a reference or two.

Illustrations from the poem

The Achilles who weeps over the fair face of the unhelmeted Penthesilea has some affinity to the Achilles who wept before Priam :—

> Μέγα δ' ἄχνυτο Πηλέος υἱὸς
> Κούρης εἰσορόων ἐρατὸν σθένος ἐν κονίῃσι·
> Τοὔνεκά οἱ κραδίην ὀλοαὶ κατέδαπτον ἀνῖαι,
> Ὁππόσον ἀμφ' ἑτάροιο πάρος Πατρόκλοιο δαμέντος.*
>
> Posthom. i, 718.

The poet, with fine discernment and an exquisite sense of situation, makes Hecuba, on hearing of the death of the son who had brought woe on herself and his country —though Hector is present to her remembrance—weep for Paris, her unforgettable boy. Priam, the while, un-

* And the son of Peleus groaned mightily, as he sees in the dust the sweet strength of the maid ; gnawing pains devoured his heart therefor, as much as erewhile for the slaying of his mate Patroclus.

conscious of the wailing, is made to shed tears at Hector's tomb to the memory of his manly son. It is a fine scene in the ninth book, when, after the speech of Deiphobus, the spouse brings a bundle of arms to her husband ; the children fetch their father's weapons ; and an old man, buckling on his son's armour, exhorts him with words and display of his scars :—

> *Καὶ στέρνα τετυμμένα δείκνυε παιδὶ*
> *Ταρφέα σήματ' ἔχοντα παλαιῆς δηιοτῆτος.**
>
> Posthom. ix, 123.

Machaon, alive, bloomed on earth, and, dead, lay under it. So said Nestor, and the requiem is as pretty as tender. Earth to earth. He sprang from its bosom, and to its bosom he returned. The earth-born becomes the earth-embraced :—

> *Αὕτως δ', ὡς ἀνέθηλε, καὶ ἔφθιτο.†*
>
> Posthom. vii, 44.

Ossian's Fingal

As regards length and variety the story in Ossian's Fingal cannot be called satisfactory. The fable of the poem is fragmentary and rambling, and has a very shadowy portrayal of character. Such of it as relates to Fingal is empty of narrative interest. It is simply the account of a sojourn of Fingal in Ireland, and has not as much real matter as is to be found in one book of a full-bodied epic. As far as the manner and scope of the telling go, the story appears a spun-out incident of the king's life, and an epic must be something more than the account of an incident. It must contain story, a goodly assemblage of the facts of human life that are of human interest, in particular, those that concern man militant. Fingal is little more

* And showed his son his smitten breast, with the scars of former fights running together.

† Just so died he, as he flowered.

than a record of moods of exaltation with a little narrative thrown in.

The record of the struggle and the fights against the kings of the world would have furnished suitable material for an epic. If the Ossianic style had been wedded to a suitable story such as might have been furnished by some parts of the war against Rome, we might have had an additional epic of moving story, of bold figures, and of lyrical and tender, but not enervating pathos.

Difference between national and historical

The difference between national and historical, in the narrow sense of the latter, is that between antiquity, or rather the storied past, and a time of documents, of authenticity. Whenever the national, by the fact of its being comparatively recent, passes into the historical of dated fact and obtrusive detail, it is unsuitable for epic purposes. When we leave the men of doughty deeds or the men of nation-making and chivalrous exploits, and come to civilised men of action whose life is stripped of all wonder, we have left the region of the heroic and are in that of the prosaical. In the expression 'national hero' the adjective really connotes a long bygone past, and always has a reference to nation-making times. When the national, by reason of an actual greatness, or the magnitude and reverberation of a shock with the external world, becomes the property of all peoples rather than of one, then national, and historical in the noble sense of the word coincide in their application.

History as epic matter

History, as history, is quite unsuitable as epic matter, and it is only when a poet in his verse commends it to us—providing much else at the same time—as the cult of hero- or patriot-worship, as did Camoens, that he is likely to produce the epic illusion. The Lusiads, indeed, is historical epic of a special sort. A poet who chooses a definitely historical subject for epic treatment may or may not be acting wisely. Much will depend on the capabilities of the subject for such treatment. If it can be made to appear in a sort of historical twilight, then the choice has much to commend it. In any case the supposed poet will, ere he earn success, have to draw heavily on his poetic resources. If a person from a definitely historical epoch be made the hero of an epic, he can only be treated epically by one who has lived long enough after the events, to allow them to become faint in men's memories, and only then, with success, by one who has great poetic gifts, and a measure of the epic afflatus. Imagination will else be impeded, and galvanised vitality and ludicrous masquerading be the results obtained.

Difficulty of historic epic. Lucan

The writer of a historic epic will always labour under disadvantages. Witness Lucan. It is easy to find fault with this poet, but the difficulties in his way were serious, and it would not be true to say that his poem is not a successful essay in epic. Lucan did not live long after the time he celebrates, and yet, by force of poetic genius, he has produced an original and living poem. Now, if Lucan had not been a genuine poet, for, *pace* Quintilian, he was certainly this, he would never have produced a poem of outstanding worth and epic cast, but would, like Silius Italicus, have unintelligently written his poem from a recipe, and produced an unoriginal and therefore lifeless product. It is easy, as I say, to rate Lucan for unepical characteristics, but the fact remains that he is the most original epic writer of the post-Virgilians. He put his originality and its distinguishing mark, namely, poetic bravery, into his Pharsalia, and produced a positively great poem. It is difficult to poetise on recent, or, indeed, any history. Clio is not Calliope. She is diffuse, voluble, unimaginative; she cannot versify herself into her sister. She unrolls events rather than arranges them.

Her movement is too lineal. She builds no solid rounded poetical fabric, but projects mere specimen scaffoldings.

Events in epic are not simply recorded, more or less critically, but are illustrative of character conceived and planned beforehand, are hinges of a story. Epic is not history, and should be mingled with pleasing fable, and imaginative matter generally, and, now at least, lyrical outbursts. History, not as history, but as a magnificent setting and halo-giver, lends distinction to an epic, painting round it a glorious horizon, and shooting over it vivid lights of reality. Does not the Iliad, a poem that treats a historic subject epically, shed an after-glow on the heroico-epic Odyssey?

The Araucana. Its subject

The Araucana of Don Alonso de Ercilla is an epic with a historical subject. Its writer preferred to be historical above all things. It has the defects of such a poetic ideal, namely, lack-lustre style and ungrouped content. Its subject is the fighting of the Spaniards to overcome the rebels of Arauco, a small state among the mountains in the east of Chili. To relieve the sameness of the narrative, the author has introduced much matter and many devices in his second and third parts. He tells of the contemporaneous siege of San Quintin and of the battle of Lepanto. Ladies, the daughters of caciques, with long stories, are brought into the poem. The cave of the magician Fiton is described. It is here that Ercilla sees the battle of Lepanto in a magic sphere. The poet on being asked by his soldiers tells them the true story of Dido. In this the well-known legend is rationalised and emptied of all poetry. We meet with some good speeches in the poem, and there is some fine hurtling rhetoric in the sixteenth book, where Caupolican, Peteguelen, and Tucapel harangue the meeting of caciques. Our author knows the art of writing a fairly engrossing narrative. It has rapidity, even if it be fitful, and animation of incident, and it lays a grasp on the attention of the reader.

Arauco is a small subject at best, and the poet has to supply episodes, and even to decline upon padding. At the end of his work he brings in matter quite extraneous to his subject, and that savours of personal touting. The subject is small, as regards amount of epical stuff, but viewed as history, and written in the order of chronology, it furnishes material for thirty-seven cantos. The narrative decidedly lacks distinction and stoops to commonplace incident, or it is the lack of distinction that throws into relief the commonplaceness. Ercilla has vigour, and the dash and facility of the born narrator. His narrative reveals qualities of soul. It cannot, considering the aim of the author, be free from the prosiness of a chronicle. It is, indeed, a rhymed history. It is not at all likely that a man who begins a poetical story with the intention of producing history, and scrupulously correct history, will end by producing, in spite of himself, a poem of epic concentration and high poetic worth. The battle-pieces in the poem are such as we should expect from one who, like Tasso, could wield the sword as well as the pen, and whose right arm had contributed material for his epic.

Its style

Ercilla has not his countryman Lucan's swelling style. He cannot sing himself and his readers into enthusiasm, as can Lucan. At the same time he has not his exaggeration and his frantic attempts at sensation-picturing. Though Ercilla expected an acknowledgement for his poem that he never got, yet he was modest in purpose. He sent his book forth, like a servitor in humble garb, *como criada en tan pobres pañales*. He has lyrical outbursts, pathetic snatches, but nothing like that pervading touch of power that ought to belong to a narrative poet of epic mould.

I should like to give just one or two specimens of sentiment from Ercilla. He thus eulogises love, meaning, by the term, the passion that inspires as well as inflames :—

Citations

¿ Qué cosa puede haber sin amor buena?
¿ Qué verso sin amor dará contento?
¿ Dónde jamás se ha visto rica vena
Que no tenga de amor el nacimiento?
No se puede llamar materia llena
La que de amor no tiene el fundamento ;
Los contentos, los gustos, los cuidados,
Son, si no son de amor, como pintados.*

Arauc. xv, I.

This is his version of 'Call no man happy till he die' :—

Nadie puede llamarse venturoso
Hasta ver de la vida el fin incierto :
Ni esta libre de mar tempestuoso
Quien surto no se ve dentro del puerto :
Venir un bien tras otro es muy dudoso,
Y un mal tras otro mal es siempre cierto ;
Jamás próspero tiempo fué durable,
Ni dejó de durar el miserable.†

Arauc. xxvi, I.

It is placidly tame. Life means toil and souring change :—

¡ Oh vida miserable y trabajosa
A tantas desventuras sometida!
¡ Prosperidad humana sospechosa,
Pues nunca hubo ninguna sin caida!

---

* What thing can be good without love? What verse will give pleasure without love? Wherever has been seen rich vein that does not have its birth from love? No matter can be called complete that has not its base in love ; pleasures, delights, passions are but pictured if they be not of love.

† No one can be called happy till he see the end of life, so uncertain, nor is he rid of stormy waves who is not anchored within the harbour. It is very doubtful if one good follow on another, and it is always certain that one ill comes after another. Never was happy time lasting, nor ever did luckless time cease to be.

¿Qué cosa habrá tan dulce y tan sabrosa
Que no sea amarga al cabo y desabrida?
No hay gusto, no hay placer sin su descuento,
Que el dejo del deleite es el tormento.*

Arauc. xxxiv, 1.

Cervantes on the Araucana

In estimating Ercilla's position, perhaps we ought not to overlook Cervantes' opinion on the Araucana, to wit, that it and two other poems are the best heroics written in Castilian, and able to compete with the most famous of Italy, *son los mejores que in verso heroico en lengua castillana están escritos, y pueden competir con los mas famosos de Italia.* I do not know anything of the other poems. The critics say they are of little value. This will the more redound to the credit of the Araucana, or possibly throw doubt on the judgment of Cervantes.

The Henriqueida

The Portuguese have an historic epic called the Henriqueida. It recounts incidents in the life of Henry of Burgundy, the founder of the Portuguese monarchy, ending with the capture of Lisbon, and is written by Francisco Xavier de Menezes, Conde da Ericeira. It has the orthodox twelve books. Its author was an admirer of Boileau, and a man who had paid much attention to epic poetics, as is evidenced by his Advertencias Preliminares. He has not written a successful and capturing epic. The pupil of Boileau was not likely to do so. He advertises too much his rule of thumb. He writes, as it were, from a recipe, which he would fain make into a theory. His poem is, notwithstanding, a good deal better than the French poem of the same name. Its illusion is pleasing and fairly credible, and, its style being mild-mannered, it is devoid of that

* O miserable and toilsome life, subject to so many misfortunes! O human prosperity, a thing suspect, for never was there any without fall! What thing will be so sweet and so savoury as not at last to become bitter and sour? There is no delight, there is no pleasure without its alloy, for stoppage of delight is torture.

pretentious exaltation, which, in Voltaire's poem, throws incongruities into relief, and predisposes the reader to derisive laughter.

De Menezes did not take his argument into his soul. He writes epic with a map of the route spread out before him. His poem is too manufactured and eclectic. He has copied so many that he has left no room for himself. He imitates largely, even down to an *aposiopesis*. He is rich in references, alluding, among others, to Archimedes, Galileo, Clorinda, Protesilaus, Clœlia, Camilla, Tomyris, Penthesilea, and the wife of Mithridates. He can insert an allusion to Herostratus, but has not vitalised his poem into an impressive and duly subordinated whole. He has invention, technic, a quantum of general poetic power, but positively no inspiration from the Muses. The contrary is his own opinion, for, at the beginning of his twelfth book, he both exhorts the heavenly Muse to possess him, and declares his consciousness of her inspiration. He ends his poem thus :—

> O espirito fogindo ao vituperio
> Parece que ainda teme ao varaô forte :
> Naô voa ao Ceo no cego parasismo
> Mas dece a escurecer o negro Abismo.*

Compare this with

> Ast illi solvuntur frigore membra,
> Vitaque cum gemitu fugit indignata sub umbras.†
>
> Æn. xii, 952.

The poet brings relatives into his work—his mother Joana, noticing the anagram Aonia that her name gives, and his wife, another Joana. He also mentions his father, and does not altogether repudiate for the Menezes a connection with Menoitiades. After reading in the

* It appears that the spirit fleeing disgrace still fears the sturdy hero : in its blind perturbation it does not take flight to the sky but goes down to darken the black abyss.

† But the other's limbs are relaxed with cold, and his spirit flies down to the shades, groaning and reluctant.

Henriqueida, one feels strongly the force of the contention that an epic must have original treatment, that is, that, granted the necessity of a certain resemblance to specimens of the same class, the manipulation and presentation of incident must be original. Even a belated epic must have, if not the freshness of literary types just arrived at maturity, yet a creative art directed by imagination and intellectuality.

The effect of a national theme on its poet

A national theme has a stiffening effect on a poetical narrator. After every lyrical or imaginative flight his story will bring him back to solid earth. He will be too much interested in the exposition of definite action to stop long to preach. Such preaching as he indulges in will not be formal preaching, but rather an invitation to contemplate the excellence of the actors, or a eulogy of worth that assumes, but does not mention an imitative instinct on the part of the reader. He will be under no temptation to spin a whole canto of dolorous lament over an accident of life, or a fact in the human lot, but will content him with a pathetic aside of more or less length, passing into elegy by following out a suggestion got from his story. The poet of art-epic does well now and then to supply with the aid of imagination the universal aspect of a particular event, he does well now and then to chant the lyrical moment in an objective fact, he even does well sometimes to delay his story by an interlude of personal import, but of more than personal validity.

The Æneid national: not so the Argonautica

It was a strong savour of nationality that helped to give the Æneid its popularity, and that still to us foreigners lends it much of its preciousness. The poem is the retrospective poetisation of the doings of the nation, with notes of swelling prophecy thrown in. It has its value as the high poetical record of a patriotic poet.

It is, to be sure, national, and has supreme national value in another regard, in regard, namely, that it is a sort of crowning mercy of Roman literary effort. The Argonautica of Apollonius is, on the other hand, not a national poem. It is an epic that no nation has appropriated or patronised, a poem of the cabinet. No patriot pulse ever beat harder at its perusal, no man ever rose from reading it with finer intuitions of national character.

The Argonautica

The Argonautica is a poem of pale intellectuality and blank vigour. We may be curious, but are hardly interested readers of it. I do not see how, when recited, it could have secured for long the attention of an audience, even of an audience of erudites. To the reader it has the objectivity of a reflection in a mirror, an outwardness that is manufactured and passing, that is not felt by the thoughts, or deposited in the memory. Jason is not an Achilles. He feels fear. It is true that his surroundings are odder and weirder than those of the flamboyant Pelides, but none the less is it true that these did not help the Alexandrian to set down and describe genuine heroic action. Jason's prowess, if in part a natural ferment, is also the calm and calculating virtue that is shown by a heart fortified by a belief in the offensive science adopted, in this case, that of witchcraft. Beowulf, though a moody man, fights the fire-drake without pre-arrangements or safeguardings.

The depicting of Medea

It is in the depicting of Medea's passion that the poet shines. This is a passionate, detailed, and psychological account of the development of love in woman, and of its symptoms, one of the most charming love-studies ever written. Medea's heart, at the thought of Jason, leapt in her breast as leaps a ray reflected in perturbed water :—

Πυκνὰ δέ οἱ κραδίη στηθέων ἔντοσθεν ἔθυιεν,
Ἠελίου ὥς τίς τε δόμοις ἐνιπάλλεται αἴγλη

Ὕδατος ἐξανιοῦσα, τὸ δὴ νέον ἠὲ λέβητι,
Ἠέ που ἐν γαυλῷ κέχυται· ἡ δ' ἔνθα καὶ ἔνθα
Ὠκείῃ στροφάλιγγι τινάσσεται ἀΐσσουσα·
Ὣς δὲ καὶ ἐν στήθεσσι κέαρ ἐλελίζετο κούρης.*

Arg. iii, 754.

It melted within her as melts the dew on roses in the morning warmth :—

Οἷόν τε περὶ ῥοδέῃσιν ἐέρση
Τήκεται ἠῴοισιν ἰαινομένη φαέεσσιν.

Arg. iii, 1019.

Love lets not Medea sleep, when sleeps even the mother of sons just dead :—

Καί τινα παίδων
Μητέρα τεθνεώτων ἀδινὸν περὶ κῶμ' ἐκάλυπτεν.†

Arg. iii, 746.

It is true the love is all description, that is, the heroine is not made to live her passion, save in puppet-life. The poet is always behind the representation. There is no flinging forward of the character and the passion of Medea into real objective life, as happens in the Æneid, when Dido's ardency puts on individuality and outwardness in spite of the formula of divine instigation, and her passion becomes stamped indelibly with the mint-mark of humanness and independence by the utterance that voices its intensity :—

Siquis mihi parvulus aula
Luderet Æneas, qui te tamen ore referret,
Non equidem omnino capta ac deserta viderer.‡

Æn. iv, 328.

The maiden snow of the beautiful witch did not per-

* Her heart moved ceaselessly within her breast, as in a room leaps a sunbeam reflected from water that hath been newly poured into a cauldron or pot, for it darteth here and there, shaken by the swift whirling. So too fluttered the maiden's heart in her breast.

† Deep, unconscious sleep was enfolding even a mother of dead boys.

‡ Did I see a little Æneas playing in the hall, whose face might recall thee though gone, I had not indeed seemed so smitten and abandoned.

mit of such an outburst, but we look in vain in the Argonautica for its parallel.

Nationality in the Iliad

The Iliad is not so strongly national as the Æneid. Indeed, its theme is sometimes spoken of as ideal, with the implication that there is some sort of thesis to prove, or mirror to hold up. It is said that Greece beheld its best, its ideal self incarnated in the youthful manhood of Achilles. There is a considerable straining in this attitude, there is an affiliation of homeric sentiment to modern. It is the case that Greek local national feeling was not strong. Nationality in the large sense of the word was too big a concept for Greeks. Over against their deficiency in this sentiment we must set their possession of a strong racial feeling, stronger perhaps than that most peoples possess. This latter feeling would easily induce a patriotic emotion outflowing towards the Iliad. We know, as a fact, that the patriotic interest taken in the Iliad was extreme. There is certainly in the poem itself, no abstract characterisation, but quite the reverse. It is a tale of the doings of choice men in a great cause, adorned by the naturalness, the pathos, and the poetry of a great poet.

Ideality in epic, but naturalness withal

In every well-wrought epic there will, it is true, appear ideality. No character-drawing can approximate to perfection without exhibiting this quality. I should feel disposed to say that a national and ideal handling gives the very best result in epic. A theme cannot be heroic and poetical without ideality, which, I take it, is the result of the noble and imaginative treatment of the theme. But, between the possession of ideality, and the possession of that quality which would make a poem approximate to what the French call a *thème à thèse*, there is a great difference.

No epic can be successfully written with a rarefied

theme, or a hero that is fantastical, or a bit of a lay figure. If Achilles is a type of race, it is not because he has the race in his blood and realises it—that is not the view the poet takes—but because his action leads to such an inference, because the count of mighty heroes must include him. He is a type, by second intention, one might say; the race is a-making in him and his action, is in him awaking to self-consciousness.

The execution of an epic, which, be it remembered, is a lengthy poem, that should fictitiously centralise in an individual qualities that are not demanded by the story, that should exhibit anything like an imposed abstractness, that should, in fine, embody motive-grinding or adjustment of any sort, would be a task of great difficulty. Such a poem, though perhaps not formally didactic, would soon lose all epic stamina.

There should be no thesis in epic

A writer with such cravings should adopt the psychological novel as the vehicle of his message. An epic hero is not a study in concentration, he does not thread his way through a maze of entangling circumstance, he is not a worker-out of moral problems, or a master of impossible situations. He is a worker in the open. He may be the saviour of his country, but he is not the saviour of society. Epic action is the action of heroic humanity invested with a tinge of glory.

Aristotle makes no account of a glorified theme in his remarks on epic. He does not say that a poem of this sort should be the record of a grand transaction, be it national or simply momentous. Indeed, so far as his analysis of the plot of the Odyssey goes, we might infer that commonplace themes could be treated by an epic poet. But this analysis is rather a quintessential abstract than an analysis proper, and it is the totality of a recognised epic that ought to give a definition of the poetic variety. Aristotle

Aristotle and the theme of an epic poem

lays stress on characterisation in an epic poem, and thereby suggests status and importance in the persons to be characterised, and he plainly thought epic action to be of some magnitude when he said that a poem of this class could furnish material for several dramas. In any case, many an epic has been written since Aristotle's day, and the variety ought to be defined and discussed only after a consideration of these.

A suitable fable with masterful individuals needed

To exhibit his assemblage of excelling individuals, a heroic poet has need to choose a suitable fable. He must not choose one where men acting are overshadowed by events happening. Some fables are naturally, or by maladroit handling, too explosive to be epical; events follow one another thick and fast, giving the action a superimposed and fatalistic cast, and the actors a puppet-like character. Lucan, for example, is always getting ready some thunder-clap or other, and in his onward movement startles and jolts us excessively. An action that is strongly but not frantically progressive is very fitting for this class of poem, wherein, also, we need actors that in a measure spin the action out of their own body and mind, that are at all events creative in their energy, and not mere incident-driven passivities. These actors must stand out clear against the background of incident, fate-borne, it may be, in a last analysis, but still free, if only in initial choice, men fit to mould events to their purpose, or even to give fate a ringing fall.

An epic poem proper has to do with civilisation

While the seeker after an action capable of epic treatment ought to make the presence of the interest supplied by spirited individuals a prerequisite, he cannot stop short with the attainment of this single object. If an epic poet is advantaged by having an argument of historic colour, and national reference, and large issues, and a spice of ideality to boot, it is plain that an epic poem must celebrate a time in which civilisation has made considerable advances. Of course, by civilisation, I do not mean refinement or education, or anything of that sort. An epic poem proper is a poem of civilisation, of national existence ; a heroic poem, in the limited sense of the term, can celebrate almost any stage of human life. An ex-savage of manly body and mind may make for the latter poem an excellent protagonist. It is true that a heroic poet is able to endow the past, and sometimes not incongruously, for this type of poetry is not bare realism, with a fulness that was only potentially in it, and thereby to give his poem a largeness of atmosphere that will produce the illusion of breathing the ample air of epic, but such retrospective enrichment has its limits.

The difference between epic and heroic

The difference between the two classes of poems is to be found in the strict interpretation of the term 'heroic.' A heroic poem is a poem about a hero as an individual agent, and, in a less prominent degree, it may be in a very small degree, about his following. Subjects of this content were the only possible ones in early times, but might be leavened by any humanities of thought and incident in the gift of the poet. When we see in a subject the accomplishment of a higher aim, when a hero is celebrated as first among peers, or as a national entity, we have an extension which approximates to the extension seen in the epic poem. How nearly this point is reached will depend on the poetic force and story-telling power of the poet, for both a fully developed heroic poem and an epic poem mean more than poetic annals about individuals, and one individual-in-chief. It is to give a good working definition of an epic poem to say that it is an embellished heroic poem.

The epic poet is a great embellisher. He weaves a richer and more intricate pattern than the heroic poet. Weaving a larger web, he has, in virtue of his ampler material, more scope, and indeed more necessity, for artistic disposition. His bigger story lends itself to greater possibilities in character-drawing, and to the more liberal presentation of entertaining contrasts between major and minor personalities. Narrator, as he is, of a longer tale of noble endeavour, he can mix the epic and dramatic in more telling proportions than the heroic poet. He is not only in a better position, from the vantage-ground of the possessor of a lengthy fable with principal and auxiliar heroes, to display the excellencies of full-bodied narrative—the onward sweep of events, their eddying dispersion, the calm and chastity of the pauses of fate—but better able, from the dominating effect of his wide expanse of story, to indulge in some digression, say, in lyrical outbursts, without imperilling the epic quality of his poem. He has in the nature of things more halting-places in his poem than his brother-poet has in his, more occasions for chorus-like comment, more pegs on which to hang reflections, more opportunities, in fine, of furnishing high poetical fare.

The epic poet a fuller poet than the heroic

Our poet must, necessarily, to make an orderly whole out of his many coherent parts, exercise a more compelling, a more informing power over his complex and abounding material, than the poet of a simpler and less full story.

In what I have said about an epic fable I should not care to be thought to allege even faintly that a suitable story epically handled will frank a mediocre poet to success. There are epic poets who have discerned and realised the possibilities of stories that, could we forget the transformations, would seem to us unsuitable, who have converted what in other hands would have been unworkable, or ordinary incident into surpassing circumstance. Who else but their respective poets could have so sung of

There is much virtue in the touch of the epic poet

Achilles' wrath, of Ulysses' wiles and wanderings, and of Man's disobedience? The epic touch is in the application of the poet, and is not to be infallibly found in one feature or another, but is to be discerned pervading a poem as a strong essence is to be discerned pervading a composite perfume. All the same there are themes that no amount of epical afflatus or general poetic power would ever develop into epic poems.

An epic poet must have poetic versatility

In my remarks I have been chiefly thinking of the worker in literary epic, whom the progress of poesy has converted into a many-sided poet with a lyre of numerous strings. Camoens, Tasso, and Milton were distinguished lyric, as well as epic poets, and no one will ever now succeed in writing an acceptable epic, who has not, in addition to distinctively epical gifts, great poetic sensibility and large poetic powers. Even though a poet were to hark back to the far past for a subject, we should, to use a figure of Sainte Beuve, ask, for reasons that concern form as well as thought, that the golden point of the arrow be dipped in a potion of the living present.

An heroic poet, on his side, may write a poem crowded with incident and adorned with much that is poetical, and, from lack of nobility, style, and inspiration, fail to produce an epic. I do not think any circumspect and unbiassed critic will dignify with the name of epic the heroic poems of Barbour and Blind Harry.

Barbour's Bruce

Barbour's Bruce, in spite of the historical cast, is gossipy, and the events are often humdrum, too humdrum for epic. They are arranged inartistically, as they would come from the mouth of a voluble story-teller who loosely adhered to history. A judicious suppression of matter, and a heightening of the interest in certain parts, would have added much to the value of the poem. There is, I say, a lack of plan in the work. It might be called Incidents of the Manhood and the Kingship of The Bruce. Every good story of length has a forward movement, and a more or less definite amount of cumulative momentum, but Barbour's poem does not impress one in respect of these qualities, and the emphatic pauses and consummation, such as they are, are there, somehow, because so they occurred in the order of events, and not because the poet exercised selection and sought effect.

It is stated by the poet of himself early in the first book that he says *nocht bot suth fast thing*. Would that in the interest of his story he had feigned something, and, with an imagination released from durance, had better realised the epical possibilities of his fine subject. Barbour is a shackled singer and reverences outward conformity too much. His admiration for his hero, though intense, has a certain abstractness about it. In this regard I hear a fuller tone in Blind Harry's poem, for the Minstrel gives us a more emotional, a more elegiac presentation of his hero. There is a want of soul and style about this :—

> Bot oft failzeis the fulis thocht ;
> And wyB mennys etling
> Cummys nocht ay to that ending
> That thai think it sall cum to ;
> For god wate weill quhat is to do.
>
> B. i, 582 (S.T.S.)

An epic poet would not so phrase it. The following has a trumpery particularisation about it :—

> Bot off all thing, wa worth tresoun !
> For thar is nothir duk ne baroun,
> Na erle, na prynce, na king off mycht,
> Thocht he be neuir sa wyB na wycht,
> For wyt, worschip, price, na renoun,
> That euir may wauch hym with tresoune !
>
> B. i, 515.

I am confident that no such unheroical strains as the following will be found in heroic poems that have a good claim to be regarded as epic :—

Thar may no man haf worthyhede,
Bot he haf wit to steir his stede,
And se quhat is to leif or ta.
Vorschip extremyteis has twa ;
Fule-hardyment the formast is,
And the tothir is cowardiB,
And thai ar bath for to forsak.

B. vi, 333.

They will not be found in the Poema del Cid or in the Roland.

Barbour calls his story a romance, but it has such solidity and scope that it must be considered under some other rubric. It is, outwardly, and in real intent, a heroic poem, and for this reason should have its epical quality appraised.

It has not the roundness of story, the distinction of style, and the touch of genius that heroico-epic poems have. Patriotism and hero-worship have given it its heroic flavour, but soothfastness has, at the same time, pauperised invention, chilled imagination, and lent it that matter-of-factness that is fatal to its inclusion among minor epics. The Bruce is a long metrical narrative, not devoid of poetry, desultory but delightful. Its poet is a good teller of detached stories. He has trumpet-tones, the light and shade, and the humour that belong to good narration, as well as the passionate patriotism of a perfervid Scot, but he has not written an epic, not even a quasi-epic. His matter overflows into details and shapelessness, and his metre has a plebeian hop about it. Barbour was a manly man as abbots and archdeacons should be, but was unable to see his subject poetically and transform it into a heroic whole.

A capable modern ought to find The Bruce a first-rate

heroic subject. It has national quality, antique and hallowed dignity, and would admit of a measure of romance. Such a national epic would have to introduce Wallace, both for patriotism's sake, and for the sake of the good material. Its action would begin, say, after the battle of Falkirk; it would stop with the battle of Bannockburn: to carry it farther would be to make the poem a chronicle or a heroic biography. On the eve of the latter battle, a Wallace reference might come in by way of episode. The proposed poem would have, as detachable portions, such themes as Lament over Wallace, Penance of the Bruce, Death of Edward I, *Malleus Scotorum*, etc. It would at least contain an *aristeia* of Bruce, one of Edward Bruce, and one of Douglas. There would be descriptions of the battle of Bannockburn, of single combats, of fights many, and of gests many. There would be apostrophes to Scotland and to Freedom, and such like poetical fare. We should have Wallace episodes, such as a Battle of Stirling, and a Journey to France.

The story of The Bruce a fine subject for an epic.

The poet of this poem would have the rare chance of introducing three grand figures, directly or episodically, namely, Bruce, in the foreground as the protagonist, Wallace as the martyr and inspirer, and Edward, as a foil, and more. Barbour would not be in the way. He would be a pioneer like the prehomeric poets. One could quarry out of his and Blind Harry's matter. This epic would certainly possess enough attractive story, and would present plenty scope for reflection. The poet could be as elegiac as he pleased, and with effect, over Wallace. I do not wish to write a recipe for an epic, and to incur the ridicule attaching to a serious recipe-maker *à la* Pope, but the subject is patently a fine one, and the writing of a poem worthy of the theme should not be so very unfeasible a task for a poetical paladin.

The wonderful in this projected Bruce would not necessarily be the mock supernatural of witchcraft, for, *pace* Boileau, I think the Christian religion of the epoch might be made to yield something of regular supernatural for purposes of embellishment. Its introduction would certainly not be an easy matter, for Tasso's wonderful, even what may be called his legitimate wonderful, is sometimes sensibly extraneous, and it is only his art that reconciles us to it. And the man who wrote a Bruce now would write like a nineteenth century man, and not as did one of Tasso's century. A holy bishop might prove useful ; supernatural and religious phenomena could be utilised ; in short, the means to the end proposed are in the finding of poetry and reverence.

Although I should end the poem referred to with the battle of Bannockburn, the pilgrimage of Bruce's heart ought to find a place in it. It is a fine story, this, with its

> Ane caB of siluir fyne
> Anamalyt throu subtilite.
>
> B. xx, 304.

Our poet, in his last book, would doubtless feel constrained to laud his hero, and, with the personal intrusion that is permitted in modern epic, could easily fit in the gem.

Blind Harry's Wallace

The rustic enditing of Blind Harry merits praise and enthusiasm. It is not an indiscriminate collection of gests in chronological order, for it has vigour of language, and reflection, and descriptive power, and mounting fervour. It is true, however, that the poem exhibits commonplaceness, and trumpery wording, and that the poet drops ever and anon into sorry and petty detail. He has the garrulity of the chronicler.

The hero of the poem is takingly described. He is strong of arm, quick to resent an affront, and such a dealer of blows as were the Roncevalles and Nibelung heroes :—

> He gat a blaw, thocht he war lad or lord,
> That profferyt him ony lychtlynes.
>
> W. i, 348 (S.T.S.)

> Bathe bayne and brayn he byrst throw all the weid.
>
> W. iv, 467.

> Wallace tharwith has tane him on the croune,
> Throuch bukler, hand, and the harnpan also,
> To the schulderis, the scharp suerd gert he go.
>
> W. iii, 364.

Outwardly he is pleasing, in manner reserved and debonair, and, in condition, a victim of double-faced Fortune. This is just the popular conception of the hero of Scotland, for which, indeed, Blind Harry is responsible, and, if not true to life, deserves to be so considered.

In the Wallace of the poem is depicted the natural man. He has enough of earth to make him interesting and real, and enough of chivalry and nobility to make him admirable. He is no son of heaven and religion, like the pious Æneas, fatalistic, fate-worn, and sombre-souled, a puppet in his purposes, and a puppet in his amours, but strong-willed and full of initiative.

The heroico-romantic our substitute for epic.

It is from the heroico-romantic that in our day we are most likely to receive a pleasure akin to that engendered in us by the perusal of epic. Poems with subjects of this stamp can be readily written by a qualified poet, and he is not such a rare appearance as the many-sided and solid poet of epic song. The same theme, too, can be readily put again into similar poetry, for the romantic manner is adaptable to many points of view. To most epic themes that have been treated by strong poets, there would seem to have been established a predestined and inalienable right of priority, a priority not merely of precedence, but of pre-eminence. As far as each one theme is concerned, Nature appears, after service rendered, to have broken the mould that formed a poet for its treatment.

Much of Scott's poetry belongs to the above class. It is the romantic handling and the rapid manner of such poems, joined to a marked poetic sentimentality, that give them their impress and vogue. It is the very singleness of aim their structure evinces, and the comparative isolation of the individuals appearing in them, that render their production so possible, and that speed readers over their lake-surfaces so quickly, and, in a fashion, so pleasurably. The voyager on the broad sea of epic has not such immediate and pronounced court paid to him. He must assume the poet's standpoint, do some assimilating work at least; he must take his pleasure rationally and with healthy slowness, following the movement of a naturally flowing, even though artistically guided and deflected story. The emphatic romance of heroico-romantic poetry, not overborne by weighty story, and the less soaring spring of its inspiration, are features that markedly separate it from epic.

Heroic poems with national attachments and epic colouring serve very well as a substitute for the more commanding species, and with them we must needs be content until some one—for, I suppose, the epic repertory is empty—ventures on the, till now, untrodden, perhaps untreadable ground ranged over by the various poetic masters. Perhaps, however, the capacity of the poetic temperament that affected the grand style of epic has become atrophied through disuse.

There was a deal of practice in epic poetry to be had in the days of the Old Epic Period of more than one nation, when each cycle of legend and fact had, it is likely, at least one prime poet, who had many competent continuators. For the making and equipment of such poets not so very much versatility was needed. There were needed familiar, or comparatively recent, or still echoing story, simplicity, the knack of recital, some fibre-stirring poetic power, and a desire to live on the lips of men. There was then, as now, needed for a poem of epic dimensions, ability to focus the story. Nowadays we should ask, in a complete epic poet, great versatility. Who is likely to be sufficient for the telling required, and the manner of it, for the dexterous blending of high and solid fact with a not too killing amount of romance? He had, in fact, need to be a phenomenon, but, as all great poets are phenomena, we should not despair of his advent. John Keats, in his unfinished epic Hyperion, had too nebulous a subject to give us an earnest of striking success. Had it been possible for the poet to finish his poem, it might have proved an agreeable specimen of the mythological epic, conceived in the Greek spirit, and executed with modern decorations. One of its chief claims to veneration would have been its powerful verse-music.

Former and present requirements of an epic poet

What are sometimes called short epics, but which in reality are short heroic poems, like either part of Beowulf, or, if of modern workmanship, poems of heroico-romantic quality, like Southey's Roderick, or mere poetic essays in description, like the Raptus Proserpinæ of Claudian, are said to be convenient vehicles for displaying intensity of character, and tragical trend, and concise pictorial grouping of incidents and appearances. This is true enough, said of such poems, but no reason for their usurpation of the name epic. The names heroic—in the case of the Beowulf

So-called short epics

we might perhaps say heroico-epic—and heroico-romantic, are good enough for two of these varieties. As to Claudian's and such like poems, I am unable to see what right they have to the honourable appellation now under definition. Surely every narrative poem that describes beings of some standing, and is written in a fervid and pictorial style, is not to be called epical.*

Heroic poems, like the so-called Teutonic short epics, are rather epics *in posse* than epics proper, and register the advances made in the production of this species of poetry. They prove also that, if we add to the qualifications of the heroic poet, a larger utterance and a prouder purpose, we come within sight of a very satisfactory epic poet. A short poem is not an epic, nor, for that matter, is a long poem, if it is merely a congeries of story, and ill-adapted, or forbidding poetical *tours de force*. An epic poem must be a consistent entity and unity.

Firdusi's Shahnameh

The work of Firdusi may be called a congeries of heroic tales. The Shahnameh consists of heroic tales in which appear only a few figures. They are powerfully told, but there is too little body in each story. The poet is an epic annalist, or rather, for there is a compactness and a looking to a moral in the stories that is foreign to mere annals, we should say that he is a poet of poetical history, with heroic rallying-points, written in a severe, an epic manner. No series of tales can ever be proved to be an epos, which, as a literary variety, is a rounded whole, and not an arrangement of history in heroic procession. If the poem as it stands be called an epic, with Rustum as its main hero, the name epic is a misnomer, for it is on this supposition

* Claudian's poem is a painted tale, smelling of the lamp, with some scenic and still-life beauty, but nothing that can appeal to deep feeling. It is a tale of arrested growth and poverty of scope, and possesses little or no intensity to atone for the circumscription.

nothing more than an epic biography, and intermittent at that, of a hero who lived for æons. Rustum might have been made the central figure of an action of national moment, but there is no branching out, no clustering in the onward march of the story.

Firdusi has vigour, pathos, command over expression, has a pointed style, and the general mark of power that gives individuality and charm. He is now stately and towering, and now pathetic with the pathos of simplicity. His characterisation of men, and action, and things, in and through each other, is masterly, and his utterance is inviting and gnomic. He has passion, and elegy, and human abasement before fate. Rustum is as stormy and passionate as nature, and as tender as woman. His chivalry is as warm and benign as the sunlight. His bravery and strength are dæmonic. He could have

ta'en
Achilles by the hair and bent his neck.

The matter of the Book of Kings, to have epic contour, needs an interior action to which a good deal of the content might be attachable as illustration, or embroidery, or national glorification. I mean that a portion of the matter of the poem might have been treated in this way, for the incorporation of the whole of the heroic action of the poem in a so-called epic would be fatal to the assumption of any such poetical status. Camoens' national stories are grouped round a centre. They are pendants to, and retrospects from, and anticipations of a narrated action that has a beginning, middle, and end, and in which the sentiment of nationality has reached its head.

If some great national act promoted and accomplished by Rustum had been made the subject of the interior action, then we might have had from him, in episode, recitals from Iran's glory-book. Allusiveness, and a moderate personal intrusion of the poet, as song-master and fame-bestower, might have accounted for as much more of the outlying heroic as it was desirable to include in the work. I do not say that, if thus written, the poem, or the part of it chosen for manipulation, would have been more effective. It would have gained, and it would have lost. The detachedness of the figures gives them distinction, and has led to concentrated effort on the part of the poet. Certainly the historical gallery would have been less rich in finished, and distinctive, and seducing pen-portraits, if epic system and subordination had been followed in their arrangement. On the other hand, such method would have set a great light in the poetic firmament, and the simultaneous brilliance of this and the lesser lights would have dazzled and pleased us, and made everything resplendent with the splendour of the great concave. The unity that is in Firdusi's tales is the unity that is got from their being the work of one man—with overlaying of earlier material no doubt—and the account of one people. The other unity that is attributed to them, that got from the witness borne to a constant and predetermined flux and reflux in human doings, is a philosophical, and not an epical unity, and may be discerned everywhere by an eye that can see the one in the many, that can take in the linked causality of the dramatic movement in any national history.*

Epic and romantic narrative

The chief difference between epic and romantic, considered as modes of poetical narrative, is to be found in the solidity of the matter of the former mode. Man as man, as an agent along the broad lines of human effort, is the epic theme, everything else is embellishment, elucidative and ornamental, or, it may well be, the high thought and

* I have read Firdusi in the German translation, and my knowledge of the poem must be as imperfect as it is second-hand. I fancy my reader has read Mr Arnold's Sohrab and Rustum.

vocal humanity that speak to us from the deeds of the actors, and that are set forth to us by the poet as interpreter and elegist. In romantic, man is pretty much a lay figure—a happy-go-lucky hero, a showy paladin, a personified abstraction, or a mystic name—in the service of the poet. He is pulled about by the caprice of the writer, and not accommodated to the necessities of a solid story; he may be nothing but a greedy doer of numerous deeds, or whimsical, or mystical, or allegorical, anything but grandly and sanely human.

It is only of the long poetical narrative of romantic fibre that one need predicate qualities. The short romantic poem embellishing a romantic situation, or illustrating a romantic idea, or adumbrating romantic dreaminess, need not concern us. It is too limited in scope, too marked in its individualism, too remote, in fine, from epos to be referred to in any comparative estimate of these two modes of narrative poetry.

The short romantic poem

The old epic manner, with its stately simplicity and sharp uprises of swift imagination, disappeared in its purity with the disappearance of singleness of aim and impressionability, and the growth of the reflective imagination. Poetic sensibility, as a whole, has become more complex, and differentiation in poetic style has set in and grown more pronounced. Thus it has come to pass that the epic manner can now no longer be what it once was, and that epic material, having suffered, theoretically at any rate, a certain circumscription from the appropriative labelling of what was once embryo romanticism, may now formally and with advantage be re-inforced with a quantum of the definitely romantic.

The change in the epic manner

The epic manner can well admit of a transfusion of allusiveness and self-consciousness. The presence of a certain diversity in the action, of a sort of parallelism of two actions, epic and romantic, is not a disadvantage. It is the strong tide of story that bears on, and throws together into harmony, the admixture of facts and imaginations, of the actual and the wonderful, and no one who has not the power of projecting a story that will with plastic outwardness assert itself and rivet our attention, can hope to supply a band to such poetical masonry.

The wonderful in the new epic: its adaptations and restrictions

While seriousness is the predominant characteristic of epic, and the wonderful so far as it concerns the work-a-day—not the select—religious or solemn beliefs of men, is, in virtue of this seriousness, admissible into, and even suitable to this stamp of poetry, a place in it, in latter-day epic chiefly, can also be found for the wonderful that, as in Lucan and Tasso, is a substitute for, or eking out of the supernatural, provided that this latter variety adorn the action and be not an introduction of the fantastic for its own sake.

It is, indeed, the effect of this second wonderful on the story that will justify or condemn its amount, or quality, or both. The type of the wonderful must, of course, in a measure, suit the date of the story. But attention to this suitability is not all that is required. The appearance of this substitutionary wonderful is in itself almost an admission that the supernatural is machinery, and necessitates, for the proper affiliation of this supernatural to the action, the creation of a poetical atmosphere that will supply a unifying verisimilitude. Good poetry and a sense of poetical situation will even atone for any chronological overlapping in the use of the wonderful.

The fibre of the story must not be weakened by the wonderful, nor its sequence spoiled, nor its sobriety infringed on. These things happen when the wonderful and the fantastic are brought in for the mere pleasure of the thing, to regale a reader's appetite for whimsicality that does not overstep credibility, or to prove the poet's capacity for the accumulation of the preposterous, and, when these things happen, we have romance with epic externals, and, it may be, epic scope, but without epic solidity and sobriety. Again, we must be able to pass from the sober to the wonderful of the argument, and *vice versa*, by easy and willing transition, and not by a leaping movement of the mind.

The poet of romantic epos cannot altogether abandon verisimilitude, or push the fantastic into burlesque. Caprice or a studied volatility may torment a story into all sorts of windings, but some semblance of probability and natural sequence must be preserved, and the strange and the playful must not pass into what is artistically absurd and nonsensical.

The poet of heroic and the poet of romantic epos

The chief difference between the poet of heroic epos and the poet of romantic epos is to be found in the aim of each poet, and in the effect his poem produces on the reader. The aim, of course, will have had its result in the selection of material, and will determine the handling of the same. The heroic poet aims at more than amusement. He has a strong sense of the dignity of life and action. He also has to establish for himself a reputation. He feels that he owes a duty to the world and to his country. He is usually a man of higher moral fibre and severer outlook on life than the poet of romantic epos. The reader feels that it is good for him to have read the poem, and is filled with patriotic sympathy and admiration for heroic character.

The imagination of the latter poet works under no such chaste restraints. He can invent without being tied down by fact, or tradition, or the requirements of dignified handling, to invention on particular lines. A general resemblance to reality is alone imposed on him. Within his limits he may distort facts, impart a different complexion to action, change a scene capriciously and by large leaps, play fast and loose with probability, use lavishly and abuse poetic machinery, play the madcap with fancy and just miss burlesque. He must stop short of comic business. His work is nothing massive or compelling reverence ; it is a fairy palace, not a cathedral or a national monument. His reader feels that he has danced to the poet's piping, that he has been amused and mildly thrilled, that the obverse of the presentation has generally worn the aspect of gaiety, but that there have been suggestions and partial glimpses of a reverse of sombre aspect.

There is a largeness about epic that does not appear in romantic, unless, *minus* seriousness, in romantic epos.

Comprehensiveness of epic

Humour may find a place in an epic poem. Virgil and Homer admitted it, and so have some of their followers in this *genre* of poetry, and a delineation of a full life of the senses, which epic, although some rarefaction of matter has set in in later epic, professedly is, ought not to exclude manifestations of this mood of a sentient being. Romantic has less breadth and more limitations than epic. It is not necessarily weak in its limitations, for strength comes from concentration. It certainly does not always minister to merriment, for a romantic poet may be as serious as Dame Melancholy, and pure romance is an affair of weirdness, of mystery, of twilight, and of gloom.

A romance, having less scope than an epic, has less variety, and, being shorter in story, has more concentration and not so many opportunities for relaxation and leisurely survey. It may be, and is, more pictorial, but has not so much life-like largeness of men in action. It has detail, but not the many-sidedness of the large and outward life. If a poem is short, things may get crowded and the poet perforce practises concentration, which leads to concussive exertion on his part. A greater effort is made in romance and the wings droop sooner. Epic spreads out a pleasing tale with no set lesson to teach or special impression to make. It has its own rapidity, what may be called objective rapidity. Of subjective rapidity, Lucan, a fast and furious writer, has enough.

Epic action ready-made

It is not to be forgotten that, whatever arranging and embellishing power an epic poet may and must exercise, he does not invent an action, but treats one ready-made. Indeed, if he has held to the thread of an objective tale of deeds and men, he is not likely to have been misled and strayed by the romantic vein he may chance to possess. A story of deeds and men, I say, of men working and deeds wrought in some well-known sphere of activity. I do not think, for example, that a polar expedition could be made the subject of an epic. It has too little attachment to common life, and would be therefore difficult of treatment. It tells rather of a warring with the elements than of human interaction. The imagining in it would degenerate into mere description, or would be too wild and prosopopoetic. The gods for good or ill, would, I am afraid, be out of the poem. A subject presenting free scope for imagining on heroic lines, and the dignity conferred by the use of the supernatural are undoubtedly factors that help to produce pleasing and powerful epic.

Actors and acting in epic

Many actors will, as a rule, appear in heroic action. Epic heroes are not isolated units in an empty world. To conduct any enterprise of life—and epic deals with the great enterprises of life—to a successful conclusion, there is need of co-workers. The long and complex action of epic postulates a sufficiency of actors.

As I have just said, the action is ready-made, and therefore the parts in the action are, in a way, marked out beforehand, and the poet cannot capriciously exalt and depress rôles and neglect the status of his characters.

No *outré* character can be introduced ; no *lusus naturæ* in manner or deeds, for epic, that is, sane action, is not accomplished by such products, but, inside this prohibition, there may be as much dramatic play of character as is in the bestowal of the writer. It is the drama of character exhibited in epic that fascinates. The characters are forcefully robust, or, if not this, rationally conducted and naturally endowed entities.

Divine promptings were listened for by these men, but were mainly recognised as preliminaries and illuminants of action. They represented the falling of scales from the eyes, or, at most, a fillip to a will that had paused before obstacles.

The acting in romance is not so independent. It is exploited by the writer, and so is often toying and indecisive, goalless, mystic, or, if not this, animated by intangibility and insipidity of motive, and resulting in minor and evanescent advantages.

Actors in history, unless glorified, are matter-of-fact men. However enthusiastic it may be, their acting has the fatal taint of plodding, and plodding is unpoetical. They have not the detachedness of the self-guiding heroes of epic. There is always a certain amount of posturing and self-assertion seen in the latter. In historical action the logical nexus between events that preceded and those that will succeed is always in evidence, and logic is not poetry. The torch-race of humanity, if celebrated in verse, would need its narrative clipped into sections, and each section bordered, and tinted, and set in various reliefs, ere it gave an epic cycle. An epic action must be framed off so as to present an independent grouping, and those who appear in it must not do so as agents in succession to other agents, and as pioneers for posterity. Whatever similarity there may be between the acting of epic heroes in general, the part that each plays in the action of his own poem must not acknowledge causation, but have something primal, something promethean about it.

The Gods in epic

Epic heroes are not overshadowed by gods. The former have as much right to exist as the latter, in fact, the gods are theirs, inasmuch as the gods are in the epic for them, and not they for the gods. The gods are part of the heroes' world, and must appear in any full delineation of the same, as felt influences, as advisers, as dispensers of destiny, but not as benumbing powers.

The gods give dignity to epic. There is no denying that. As participants in an action they contribute not only to its forwarding but also to its glorification. The divine will always remain a factor in epic poetry, for high poetry aims at high effects, and if, in poetry with a modern theme, we, with all our present resources, introduce the divine as a sanction, or as an indication of seriousness, how much more should it appear in poetry relating to the large issues of bygone times, times in which the divine voice as a monitor and arbiter was listened to and reverently accepted.

Tradition, too, has placed them in possession here. No successful epic has ever been written without supernatural of some sort. Lucan's supernatural is of the most apologetic stamp, and his parsimony of the divine, a consequence indeed of the subject, has given a result that ought not to make us approve of his choice of a theme in which the divine was bastardised into a lower variety that made up in violence for what it had lost in dignity.

The gods are a utility in this class of poetry ; they are an ornament ; they are a tradition. They first came into it—when they were not themselves the sole or main actors therein—by necessity, as facts in the life of man, as much so as fighting and hating, and have remained in it, they or their substitutes, because successive epic poems have fixed the cast of this sort of poetry, because heroic is convertible with antique, and the antique without the supernatural is maimed. In short, epic poetry has in its life defined itself, and it remains for us to examine and approve the natural selection that has operated.

Heroic poetry treats of Man

Heroic poetry from the time that it can truthfully be called literary, and not a sort of mixture of anthropomorphism and theogony, has treated of man, and man's world, material and mental. A story of endeavour, of resistance overcome, of something accomplished, of means used in the accomplishment not dissimilar to ordinary human means, but higher in degree—such is a definition of a heroic poem, and it is correct for any of its periods, but perhaps of the highest development of the *genre* to which the name epic poem is appropriate, we might, more succinctly and sympathetically, if somewhat grandiosely, say that it is a story of circumstance and scope, well told, and told in the grand style. The main scene of the action is earth, and men are the chief witnesses and participants, though scenes from a parallel supra-terrestrial action may be shown, and divine spectators and co-workers be introduced. In Milton's poem, though many of the agents are divine, yet the agency is human, or, rather, humanised.

The heroic has an affinity with the antique

No man is a hero, in the poetical acceptation, to his fellowmen. He may be a saint, a superlatively brave or superlatively clever man, but a hero—no. There is as much difference between an ordinary great man and a hero, as between Cæsar the perpetual dictator and Divus Julius. A hero is a great man beatified, and beatification is an affair of years, of many years. Therefore heroic subjects must always, it would seem, be antique subjects. Those early bards who sung heroic strains on subjects that concerned their own times, or nearly so, subjects that were familiar as the known and the credible are familiar, were able to dispense with the hallowed past and the consecration of centuries, for epic was in the air, and in it they lived, and moved, and had their being.

But must have modernity as well

Assuming that it were possible for a poet to write an epic poem without putting something of his day and generation in it, it would not be advisable to do so. The far-awayness of epic poetry can only be in the subject, the poetry itself cannot be far away. Some trick of thought, to say nothing of expression, will reveal its date. All epic poets have written for their contemporaries. It is facts in his own experience that inspire a man. A poet speaks first to himself in his poetry, then to his fellows, as counterfeits of himself, and he can never, if he tried or desired it, shake himself free of his age. Modernity is unavoidable, nay, rather to be courted, even if it be only the modernity that appears in poetic interpretation. Somehow there must be built a bridge between the time of the poem and the time of the poet. And in no other way than by the sounding of a modern note, can interested listeners, or even the fit audience, though few, be secured.

The language of epic poetry

Epic poetry is of the spirit, and the epic poet will have the epic vocabulary. It is not given to every poet by melody and verbal representation to make words into things, and epic poetry, so far as bare conception of the variety is concerned, is not so much an affair of apt words as are other varieties. At the same time, when word-power, joined to a mastery of metre, puts at the disposal of a poet the magical touch that moulds vocables and rhythm into a higher unity, in which the original mixture of imagination and harmony becomes speaking music, he can work the triad of sound, style, and story, and thus command the whole gamut of our emotions. The environment of sound that belongs to an epic is an important aid in the differentiation of one epic from another. Poetry, in its essence, is speaking sound. The need for a special dialect in epic has long since disappeared, and any affectation in vocabulary outside of the large liberty of poetry would be hurtful. The language ought to bear some relation to dignity of subject, and, as far back as the time of early epic, distinction marked the heroic style. There must certainly be a vocabulary of choice.

The amount of mythology and mythological language permissible in our variety depends on the date of the subject, but a mixture of heathen and Christian mythology, as we find it in the Lusiads, is not to be commended. There will always be room for the language of the minor mythology that concerns nature and natural appearances, for all those expressions that have been appropriated by the poets. The twilight of the gods is not an accomplished fact in poetry, and all the human coin of the pagan fancy may be used in it.

Epic, by tradition, and by the fact that it is poetry, must use figurative language. It has come down to us with a language bearing on it the impress of early wonder. Language does not need to have formal similes to be figurative. The presence of epithets may constitute it such. Epic never had the artless manner of the ballad. Epic as epic always had a higher aim than the ballad, and this aim was reflected in its superior tone. The balladic manner was merely the literary expression of the capacity for lilting that was in every human being, *plus* pathos.

Figure comes naturally to poetry. Poetry in its characteristic manifestations is noble and emotional, and finds in figure a meet expression of the supernal quality of its thought. The impalpable things of the imagination that take to the air in figure and poetry, are, of course, not the proper ingredients for epic poetry, as such, but find some place in the work of the modern epic poet, who has got to be a master in the poetic art.

Poetry is more than ever a necessary medium for epic. In spite of the incursions that the one may make into the domain of the other, prose is more differentiated from poetry than it was long ago. Poetry was earlier in the field and exercised a long suzerainty. It was the medium for the epico-historical, for philosophy, and for science, as well as for the imaginative. By and by the applicabilities of poetic form were measured, and poetical topics defined. Poetry precipitated prose, and, in the reaction, the latter, exhibiting antagonism, eschewed the appearance of verse. Now, however, prose—largely, no doubt, as a result of internal development—has become aggressive and expansive. It craves the spirit and power of poetry; it renders homage to poetry; it calls the rhetorical the poetical, and coquets with metrical form.

Epic should have metrical form

Modern epic, which has reposed so much for its success on good and full poetry, must necessarily have metrical form. Metrical adaptability of thought is really part of the poetic inspiration, and gives the difference between the speaking and the silent poet. The fine frenzy of the poet's soul receives coherence and reason from metre.

Epic has a uniform, flowing metre, in measured or rhymed bars. The metre is homogeneous. It would be inexcusable to introduce lyric modes, though lyric inspiration and expression are present in the modern epic. Epic is older than lyric. Lyric, as lyric, is a thing of moods, of sudden glimpses, and, as such, is foreign to early poetisers.

Poetry and Metre

I believe that all real poetry is, and cannot avoid being, metrical. Prose has its own domain, where poetry cannot enter without loss to the subject treated, but poetry can live and thrive in regions where prose would be asphyxiated, and even on ground that may be said to be common to both, poetry has the additional charm of a rarer literary felicity. Prose cannot perform the effect, and can certainly never accomplish the flights of poetry. Prose, when it becomes surcharged with abundant and striking imagery, soars into the region of verse, and the contention of some, when stated explicitly, is, that prose can take this height without doffing her terrestrial habiliments.

I am writing on the understanding that it is the business of poetry to minister a refined delight, and I shall, for simplicity's sake, suppose myself to be speaking of a proposed adventure of poetry and prose, into a region which is poetry's by prescriptive right, but which also has been trodden by prose, and with marked success, namely, the region of the imagination. Why is the work of the poet here likely to surpass the work of the prose writer? Because he works in a better medium for this class of work, and under better conditions. The former, and we are speaking of a man of pronounced poetical temperament, receives an access of energy and insight in his imaginative work, and with his thought floating on the musical swell that flows and recedes, and flows but to recede again, must produce a harmony of sound, not to be approximated to by the latter, who sends his thought tamely from pillar to post and from post to pillar. His imagination is subjected to nobler impulses, and he, his eyesight purged from the blinding effect of a too narrowly circumscribing, and almost tangible horizon, must see farther into space, and catch more remote and more spiritual analogies, than the man who is content to gaze all round instead of gazing beyond. A poet with his singing robes about him, will in imaginative work produce, as regards richness and totality of effect, a far finer result, than the same man with clipt wings essaying prose-flights that just miss being poetry, or than another man, not a poet, and therefore of a narrower and less piercing vision, writing prose-raptures that deserve, perhaps, the name impassioned.

We might even take higher ground and say that metrical form is a source of, a distinct incentive to, poetic inspiration. The man who is master of metrical form thinks a more complicated mode of thought than the man who writes prose, and the web that his thought weaves will be shot with more varied colours, and will exhibit a much richer pattern. I do not think it is an exaggeration to say that poetry sprang from metre, and has stood on metre to reach the higher things of the imagination.

I should be disposed, then, to claim metrical form as essential to the epic. Narration in the epic poets from Homer downwards enshrines a very special use of the imaginative faculty. Can a man who reads a prose version of the Odyssey feel the life, the beauty, and the nobility that is to be met with in the original? And the supposition that prose can give the sensations of verse, is only made more incredible by the substitution of any of the great modern epics, for, as a matter of fact, the Greek epic, from its antique severity and the simplicity and detachableness of its imagery, lends itself more readily to a prose rendering than the more richly imaginative modern epic. Just imagine the perusal of a prose Paradise Lost. How certainly we should miss, should we not, the fine flights, the noble sublimity, and the entrancing harmony of the poem? Take even an epic of a lower order, the Nibelungenlied. I cannot think that, chronicling epic though it is, anything like its effect could be produced by a prose version. I am not referring particularly to the tale of doom told in dance-music, but to metrical quality *per se*, and to the identification that one establishes between medium and matter.

Those who reason on prose-poetry ought not to confuse the pathetic with the poetical, nor emotional rhetoric, nor even the time-beat of strongest feeling, with the winged and ordered harmony of genuine poetry. Which of the prose-poets is not intermittent in his metrical passioning, or, what is worse, does not dump us down repeatedly in a bog of prose? There are quiet reaches in poetry, no doubt, where thought is stilled into inaudibility, but even in these, music, so to speak, still echoes and keeps melody from dying. Has prose, leaving metre out of account, got anything approaching to the imaginative penetration and the dower of ideal beauty that poetry has? Poetry, for the poet is more clairvoyant in spiritual matters than the prose-writer, gives an outlet to thoughts that, owing to tumultuousness or beauty, could not endure the shackles of prose. It is the dress of metre that tones these down to intelligibility and expressibility, and they cannot be made to assume a more earthly attire. The form of poetry is as important as its matter, for the form is in a sense a part of the matter.

Epic prevailingly impersonal

An epic poet writes calmly and self-containedly. He keeps outside of his story, and only lets his personality appear in the recognised pauses, but an allusion may be so worded and a simile so dressed as to interpose personality. Such infringements of epic impersonality are easily forgivable, if the matter is appropriate and the poetry good, and even old Homer sometimes forgot himself and apostrophised his hero. I am not so sure that the chanted lay of an epic singer was so impersonal as it looks when indited.

And without hurry

There ought to be no hurry in epic. Sometimes hurry is met with in short epics, but there our sort of poetry is not seen at its best, nor in full revelation. By hurry, I mean haste in the telling of the story; rapidity of manner, which is legitimate and admirable, is not to be brought under this word. Our poetry is so hostile to hurry that it has protected itself against it by the patronage of repetition—by recurrent expressions and recurrent commonplaces in ancient, and by recurrent asides in modern epic.

The episode

The episode is a feature in the writing of epic poetry. It is a relief when one direction in an epic action is for a time abandoned in favour of another of similar convergence. More characters are thus introduced, and the old ones, when re-introduced, have acquired an access of vitality and interest. This change of route procures variety for the poem, and is provocative of energy on the part of the poet, who takes another tack and profits by a different array of suggestive circumstances. It is a good thing to delay the movement of such an action, partly because a persistence in one direction would lead to monotony and the use of questionable expedients, partly because an epic action is many-sided, and demands, and will have its effects enhanced by, an illumination of its various sides. Cross movements in moderation are beneficial in epic, but the criss-cross of Ariosto is distracting, and ought, in serious work, to be avoided.

Clearness of epic

Let us have no hurry then in epic, and no obscurity. Story-telling about a life in the open, lived by men whose characters appear, and burningly appear, in their behaviour and words, exacts no profundity from the teller, and ought to cost no labour to the reader. The clearness that had to belong to the recital of the epic singer, ere he could give delight to his audience and win applause for himself, has remained one of the abiding characteristics of the poetry in question.

Ethics

There are some who say that all poetry is ethical, that ethics is in it plainly. This affirmation is due either to love of paradox, or to the assumption that we are always in the 'sermons in stones' mood, or to persistent tradition—in spite of Aristotle, who believed poetry to be first of all a pleasure-giver. I shall say of epic that there is scarcely anything that will so damn it as direct didactics. In fact, it is not possible to obey the epic afflatus and to be didactic at the same time. Others say—and the latitude of the statement is so large that it need not disturb any enthusiasm opposed to its unexplained content—that poetry is ethical, because to impress the imagination powerfully is to teach excellently, the imagination vitalising, and even suggesting, good conduct. Seeing that epic does not in any special sense act constantly and powerfully on the imagination, unless it may be in poetical asides, I am confirmed in my conviction of the irreconcilability of the didactic and the epic.

Original treatment is a desideratum in an epic. As a matter of fact, all the great epics do exhibit originality.

Original treatment in epic

It is only minor writers of epic who hardly exhibit a spice of this quality. They have an exemplar and some poetic facility, and they shadow their predecessor with literalness and slavishness, producing a result that is generally incongruous, and often grotesque. All the great epics have, I say, originality. They have points of resemblance, it is true—they have similarity of manner, to wit, a nobility that is now staid, now brilliant; they have kinship in matter, that is, they treat of heroic individuals and heroic action—but in the thought, in the air of the poems, there are felt at work different poetic souls, each with a distinct individualism. To this fact is due the variety that is felt in each separate poem. It is to the poetic thought rather than to the architectonics of the story that the special stamp of each epic is due. Of course the nature of the story counts for a good deal in the effect produced.

What is an epic? Let us define it first by examples. It is a poem like the Iliad, like the Æneid, like Tasso's

Jerusalem Delivered, like Milton's Paradise Lost. In

Definition of an epic poem

these circumstances the thing defined is graspable enough. No exactly hard and fast standard can be fixed. I should, for my part, set down this as a satisfactory definition :—*A story of circumstance and scope, well told, and told in the grand style, and, to secure this grand style, in metre.* This is to define an epic positively and generally. Many pointed characteristics were revealed to us when we considered this sort of poetry negatively, but the qualities that must be present before the standard of the exemplars is reached, may all be got out of the definition by a process of comparative deduction. More or less will the putative epic approach to the standard. There are many prominent features in this poetry, and one individual epic, though having all these, may have them, some in major and some in minor degree, and, notwithstanding, be upon the whole a noble epic. The heroic poem is a subordinate species, with the same traits, but under development, or in milder manifestation. It may include anything from the somewhat thinly-stocked lay of the epic singer that confers and seeks renown, to the well-filled heroic poem that misses the distinction and inspiration of epic proper.

It follows that a good heroic poem may be a better thing than a poor or minor epic, which, indeed, may only from its outward shell, deserve such a designation. One would rather be the author of the Bruce than of the Henriade or the Henriqueida. I do not seek to inhibit the application of the adjective epic to designate, or refer to, the genus heroic, for this would be a somewhat doctrinaire, and not perfectly necessary inhibition, but the term epic has acquired a certain connotation, and the use of the term, without any caveat, in common parlance, as convertible with heroic, has its disadvantages. An epic poem is a heroic poem, but the *vice versa* is not true. It ought to be emphatically recognised that the term epic has, and, when regard was paid not to stages of growth in a poetic variety, but to the fact that the Homeric epics were the first works of the kind within the ken of literary criticism, always had a nobler content and a more echoing resonance than the term heroic. Convenience, precision, and correct literary delimitation require the admission, and, on occasion, the express statement of this fact.

So much that is epical is excellent, that the attributes are deemed convertible. This is erroneous and bewildering. It is this misuse of the adjective that ought to be chiefly objected to. The landmarks of literary varieties ought not to be removed. Confusion, and cross-classification, and mongrel description are the result. Dante's sublime poem is as excellent as its encomiasts will have it. Why not then be content with the adjective excellent, why substitute for it epical, and thus throw us on to a wrong plane in our deliberations on the poem? The Divine Comedy does not perform on the mind the effect of epic. Why bring Spenser's Faery Queen, and Tennyson's Idylls of the King under the rubric of epos? The one is an allegory on the beauty of holiness, with mundane references, the other, a song of the soul militant that includes a threnody over the mishaps of men.

Features and excellences of epic, lyric, and dramatic poetry

Some writers seek to belaud the epic variety of poetry by belittling the other varieties. The fame of great epics, the very dimensions of the poems, the totality of the view of life to be found there, together with their mixture of poetical modes, have, each and all, contributed to the glorification of this variety of poetry. Add to this that the epic poet professedly caters for our entertainment, and sets himself to please his reader, as the old epic singer set himself to please his hearer. A story is more entertaining than a thesis, and, when this has itself great interest for us, and is, in addition, lit up by the lambent light of that narrative style that softly illumines the life-like reality of varied objectivity, much of the magic of epic is explained.

Each variety of poetry has its own virtue, and gives its own pleasure. Much of the attractiveness of modern epic poetry depends on its incorporation of the features of other varieties. Perhaps I should not say incorporation, for, to take one feature, epic was always dramatic, and its characterisation must remain such. Anyhow, there are more lyric movements and lyrico-ornamental matter in the pauses and body of epic verse than used to be there. We settle down to the reading of an epic as we settle down to the enjoyment of a long voyage of pleasure. We promise ourselves equable weather and a pleasure that can be taken in instalments, and is not prohibitive of other pleasures. The action in epic is never so intense as to hurry on the poet by its own momentum, or to forbid digression into a byway of the main story. The plot has finality, and points of interest, and *dénouement*, but it has not the living nexus, or the rise and fall in situation, or the dominant crises of the drama. A tragic plot is a thing of stormier impetuosity and with more self-development. Its incidents are derivative and generative in a sense in which those of epic are not, and it presents or suggests a vicariousness that quickens the interest of the spectator or reader. The movement in drama is more like that of a tempestuous transit than that of a voyage of pleasure.

Although several dramas can be quarried out of an epic, it does not therefore follow that epic is the better variety of poetry. The fact of the quarrying is true enough, but the materials got from it are simply outlines, suggestions, and a little predestination. To say nothing of the dramatic dress with which they have to be invested, all the distinctive part of the dramatist's task remains to be done after their selection. The dramatic poet is a craftsman differing much from the epic or lyric poet in his proper work and aim. He has, as poet of his *genre*, less of pure poetry, poetry on the wing, than the lyric and perhaps than the epic poet, but more realisation, less of the graces of verse, but more moral thunder. There is, however, no reason why the dramatic and the lyrical should not be intermixed. The amount of the intermixing will depend on the temperament of the poet. Lyric colouring, lyric garnishings, lyric interludes are not a disadvantage to a drama.

The work of the dramatic poet can have all the vigour of pointed writing transfigured by metrical expression and the figurative embellishments of poetry. Peculiarly his are those flashes of spiritual insight that pass before the dramatic sense when in the leading-strings of high poetic imaginativeness. It is the special business of this variety of poetry, at least of its noblest sort, and this is my term of comparison, to thrill us with pity and fear. The pleasure derived from the perusal of dramatic poetry is two-fold. There is its special poetical charm with a distinct logical leaven in it, and there is also its therapeutic attractiveness.

It is a fierce light that beats on the drama and is reflected therefrom on the witnesses or readers of the action. In lyric, the poetry of suggestion, the imagination, not being tied to a story or a thesis, is unloosed, and may give us anything from a warm glimmer of emotion to shooting stars. It is a detached and impulsive form of verse, and ministers to our delight by joyous singing, by soaring enthusiasm, by the fusion of feeling and metre, by delicate poetical intuition. In lyric it is always a case of man speaking to man, of feeling calling unto feeling.

CHAPTER I

THE LATER ROMAN EPIC

It is the famous line, *Victrix causa deis placuit sed victa Catoni* that gives Lucan a place in the memories of most men. And yet this poet was once widely read and often quoted in more than one country. That was, however, at a time when literary education was in a certain sense more thorough, because more restricted, than now, when there was not so much ephemeral, if also inviting, literary fare to be tasted. One could then make the most of education and reading along a particular line, and thereby gain a wide and historical acquaintance with a nation's literary life. Then, too, Lucan had not lost his traditional rank among the worthies of Latin literature, a rank indicated by his membership of Dante's great group (*la bella scuola*), which group our own Chaucer had in mind when he wrote the line, *Virgile*, *Ovyde*, *Omer*, *Lucan*, *and Stace*. Lucan was indeed a favourite author in mediæval times, and long retained the place in classical education he has now lost.

The Pharsalia. Lucan once more read than now

The poet of the Pharsalia has merits that will always entitle him to the attention not only of curious but also of serious students. A certain earnestness, which, though marred by stageyness and unreality, is everywhere present in this epic written for a purpose, and an undeniable moral grandeur will always gain for Lucan a

His merits will always command attention

measure of attention and even enthusiasm. It was the same qualities, joined to an epigrammatic showiness of expression and a noble largeness of utterance, that gave to this poet during his short lifetime unquestioned precedence in the recitation-rooms of Rome. He is far from exhibiting the strength, the finish, and the reposeful purpose of the writers of the golden age of Latin literature, for his was a precocious, though sterling talent, too early wooed and applauded into artificiality and rhetorical exaggeration. He was not permitted to reach the fulness of a natural flowering-time, but was encouraged, when a mere boy, to ape sententiousness and straddle after effect. In spite of all drawbacks Lucan deserves study for intrinsic merit as a poet. And he deserves study, not only as a poet, but as the foremost writer of the Latin literature of the decadence.

His projected epic foredoomed to imperfection

Lucan essayed the impossible. He tried to write a poem of the epic order on the closing events of the struggle between Cæsar and Pompey. His poem, as epic, was foredoomed to imperfection. No man has written, or can write, a satisfactory epic on a historic occurrence *quâ* historic occurrence, and to make such an attempt is to argue oneself lacking in epical discernment. Let us recall to our minds the character of some of the best known epics. The epics of Greece are prevailingly ideal; Virgil's epic is a compound of legend, patriotic reminiscence, and universal pathos; Milton's epic is quite unhistoric in theme; the epic of Tasso treats of a romantic poetical episode that has been woven into the prose tapestry of human history, and the poet treats it in the epic manner; the Portuguese epic is a picture-gallery of the storied past of Portugal, escaping by its long perspective the dangers that beset the epical treatment of a decade of history, and its poet is an epic craftsman. This wrong-headed attempt of Lucan, however, to describe epically what he rightly felt to be one of the most momentous periods in the world's history, lends an additional interest to the examination of an epic poem produced under such conditions. For Lucan, in epic style, is nothing if not unconventional. He discards all the conventions of the epical machinery. No doubt he employs some substitutes, inferior, belittling substitutes one must characterise them, but what I say is true in the main. He has the mark of mere modernity on him, and is by that much an unpoetic soul.

Historic fact as material for epic poetry

History, as history, is not the domain of the epic poets. And the reason of this is not far to seek. These poets have either themselves lived in a credulous and god-haunted time, or they have been able after suitable choice of subject to recall and live into such a time, and by imaginative sympathy recreate it for others. The primitive epic singer found his subject in the air, the later epic poet first proved his title to the name by a happy choice of subject. Epic poetry without invention and imagination is inconceivable. Its narrator must either be the medium that voices the beliefs of the popular imagination, or be able to set forth with imaginative truth some legendary, or historico-legendary story. What room is there in history for invention and imagination? With a historic subject the flood of a poet's inventiveness is dammed up. He can only invent within the limits of the literally true. Documentary facts are stubborn things, and are, unless their antiquity or old-time character permits of an imaginative or romantic setting, stones and not bread in the hands of the purveyor of epical fare. How much more is this the case with remembered facts. Facts of the ordinary sort admit of degrees of presentation, that is all. What we had a right to expect from Lucan in the shape of definite literary production was a historically accurate poem containing sane reflections poetically dressed, or a drama of history, presenting, supposing the Latin genius capable of such presentation, characters whose motives and actions were of national and human import. But the poet of the Pharsalia accomplished neither the one nor the other.

To Lucan his chosen theme was politically pleasing. He harked back to a time when liberty, as he deemed it, was, though moribund, still militant, which frame of mind is not the best preliminary for the writing of an epic. Pompey represented for him this period of freedom and senatorial predominance; Cæsar was for him the subverter of antique custom, the leveller of the senate, the first of the autocrats.

Pompey and Cæsar

Pompey was a dull hero. Not that the man was altogether uninteresting as a personality, or that he did not do things worthy of commemoration, but he made such a poor show at a critical and inspiriting time. He was not of heroic mould. One cannot associate shilly-shallying with heroism. There is a strong temptation to suspect that circumstances made Pompey, for he certainly never could bend them to his will, nor even courageously grasp what they placed within his reach.

I suppose this man of many successes could never have been what he was, unless he had possessed commanding ability. The conqueror on three continents must surely have been something more than a master of ceremonies regulating the movements of a military machine moving on to assured victory.

Pompey was not an engaging personality. As morals went in his day, he was an eminently respectable person. He had not kicked against the pricks of public opinion as Cæsar had done. He had a large following, but few friends; he could not win over men to himself as man. He had over and over again played the part of a military and civil *deus ex machina*, but, after the playing, was nothing but an official hero and quondam state plenipotentiary. He had gained battles all over the Roman world, but was only a general of soldiers, and not a leader of men. He did not gain success against Cæsar, and did not deserve to do so. He claimed to be a superior person, but not with the attractive self-consciousness of Scipio. Pompey's claim was an affair of pose. For selfish ends he rubbed shoulders with the crowd, but with the air of a demigod condescending to be an individual. In fighting with Pompey, Cæsar had to deal with a man who had outlived his reputation, if not his capacity—*magni nominis umbra*.

Cæsar was the very opposite of Pompey. His life had contrasts—the lights and shadows of his personal character and fortunes, and not only crowning victories, but ambitions carefully planned and won. He did not wrap himself in mystery, nor invest himself in an affected aloofness that was really irresolution waiting to be wooed or compelled. He could gain the sympathies and command the admiration of his associates; he earned the goodwill and impressed the imagination of the populace.

In political insight he was in advance of his time. He wished to make Roman citizenship the reward of merit, and not a caste privilege or national right. He wished, and by his acts proved that he wished, to break down the middle wall of partition between Roman exclusiveness and the outside world. Cæsar, in spite of the free flinging of his youth, had simple tastes. He was courageous; he was not the bondslave of passion; he could see before and after, and guide both himself and his fortunes. If sometimes cruel in act, he was only politically cruel, not naturally.

Lucan's sentimental and declamatory matter led him to deify Pompey. He need not on that account have bedevilled Cæsar. He must have known Cæsar's real character. The gentleness and clemency of the great dictator are matter of history. Cicero, his contemporary, makes warm mention of it; and every now and then in Lucan's poem the real historical personage displaces the poetical lay-figure, and stands forth in dignity and sentiment the peerless man he really was. Cæsar was, it may be added, a much more epical character than Pompey. His birth was mysterious, he had attachments to the legendary past, he was identified with a phase of national regeneration, he passed through victory to death, he underwent the transfiguration of a national apotheosis. The besmirching of Cæsar is the greatest blemish in the characterisation of the Pharsalia. Neither poetry nor partisanship entitles a writer to blacken greatness. And Cæsar was a great man. His contemporaries acknowledged the fact, and succeeding generations have ratified their opinion. Pompey was, one is tempted to think, a pinchbeck great man.

Lucan's subject-matter

The subject-matter of Lucan's epic is, as has been said, the events of the final struggle between Cæsar and Pompey, the *bella per Emathios plus quam civilia campos*, and their immediate sequel. The first event mentioned is Cæsar's passage of the Rubicon, the last, his beleaguering in the palace of Alexandria. The whole of the poet's real matter might have been presented and decently dressed within the limits of one or two books, and it says not a little for Lucan's imaginative fertility that he has spun out and amplified a somewhat meagre array of facts into the ten books of what is, upon the whole, a most pleasing poem.

The First Book. The apostrophe to Nero.

The opening of the Pharsalia is fine, and suitable both to its theme and the type of poetry. To the novice in Lucan the early introduction of the apostrophe to Nero is displeasing, and its effect marring. It contains expressions which in fulsomeness of phrase outstrip the laudations usually proffered in the panegyrics of imperial eulogists. It is, notwithstanding, quite in the poet's sky-striking manner :—

Te, quum statione peracta
Astra petes serus, prælati regia cæli
Excipiet gaudente polo, seu sceptra tenere,
Seu te flammigeros Phœbi conscendere currus,
Telluremque nihil mutato sole timentem
Igne vago lustrare juvet : tibi numine ab omni
Cedetur, jurisque tui natura relinquet,
Quis deus esse velis, ubi regnum ponere mundi.
Sed neque in Arctoo sedem tibi legeris orbe,
Nec polus adversi calidus qua vergitur Austri,
Unde tuam videas obliquo sidere Romam.
Ætheris immensi partem si presseris unam,
Sentiet axis onus. Librati pondera cæli
Orbe tene medio : pars ætheris illa sereni
Tota vacet, nullæque obstent a Cæsare nubes. *

P. i, 45.

I suppose this is honest flattery, although some see subtle irony underlying it. Doubtless, before Lucan wrote these lines there had been more than one tiff between him and his imperial master, caused by the latter's jealousy of our poet's growing reputation and patent superiority. But Lucan is hardly likely, at this period of his life, to have foreseen or even suspected—it is hardly the business of a contemporary to infer—the impending outrages of Nero's principate. He was

* Thee the palace of the sky, preferred to earth, shall welcome, mid the plaudits of heaven, when, thy watch over, thou shalt, late I trust, seek the stars, be it thy pleasure to wield the sceptre, or mount the flame-bearing chariot of Phœbus, and roam with wandering fires over the Earth that fears nothing though the sun is changed. Every deity shall yield to thee, and nature shall leave it in thy choice what god thou wilt be, or where thou wilt place thy world-throne. But thou shalt not choose thy seat in the Northern sphere, nor where the warm pole of the opposite South sinks away from us, whence to look with slanting beams on Rome. If thou rest thy weight on one side of the vast universe, its axis will feel the strain : maintain, mid-sphere, the equilibrium of the sky, and may all that portion of bright heaven keep free from clouds, and, round Cæsar's seat, may no clouds obscure our view.

probably in serious mood when he wrote this bit of poetical fustian, the more so as the sentiments were not commanded, since Nero at this time, and afterwards, was more desirous of being acknowledged as the most versatile product of nature, than of being deified, and absurdly vain though he was, would only regard homage like Lucan's as a strongly-worded tribute to the representative of the deified Cæsars, or, it may be, as an earnest of the personal deification that was to be his when the first of men had in due course become the youngest of the gods. There are, however, passages in the Pharsalia where we find such vehement denunciations of tyranny that we are tempted to suppose them written under the influence of some personal smart or other.

The causes of the war

Lucan, in the style that becomes him so well, deplores the civic madness that drove Roman to fight with Roman (*pila minantia pilis*), while the world was still unconquered, and Crassus' defeat still unavenged, and, proceeding to recount the causes of the civil war, tells how Rome thought, by a tripartition of power, to stay ambitious passion, but only more strongly engendered that of two at least of the rivals, a passion that after Julia's death broke the brittle bands of a state compact, and strode surely to war. This war, according to the poet, was made easier by the steadfast and majestic supineness of Pompey, and the tireless and ruthless energy of Cæsar. In the body politic, we may well believe Lucan, there existed much of the irritation and viciousness that often lead to war. Rampant luxury had driven out antique staidness and simplicity; o'erleaping ambition and political feuds had produced a state of general unrest; a longing for the forceful realisation of wishes, and for the chance advantages of a civil war, precipitated the strife.

The real action of the poem begins with Cæsar's bewilderment by the banks of the Rubicon. His hesitation is projected into space, and allegorised into a remonstrant Spirit of Rome that half pleads for, and half dictates, a pause. The story moves on with much rhetoric and no little aptness of phrase and simile past the passage of the Rubicon and the seizure of Ariminum ; past Curio's arrival, * and Cæsar's speech of bold self-justification and bitter denunciation of Pompey ; past the fine description of the lull in Gaul after the temporary uplifting of the nightmare of Rome's occupation, when the bard was left to sing his songs of the brave (*fortes animas belloque peremptas*), and the Druid to his sacrifices and his cult of immortality—moves on to the panic at Rome and the collapse of all resistance, to the apparition of Sulla's ghost in the field of Mars and that of Marius by his rifled tomb on the Anio, to Aruns' augural hocus-pocus and the matron's vision of the battles and murders to come. This matron, foreseeing Pompey's death, says :—

The action of the First Book

> Hunc ego, fluminea deformis truncus arena
> Qui jacet, agnosco. †
>
> P. i, 685.

The second book carries the story of the epic on to the flight of Pompey to Epirus. At the outset Lucan laments the presence in Rome of portents of disaster. He thinks their effect was enervating. Let the future overtake us suddenly, says the poet, that amid all our fears we may not lack hope.

The Second Book

* Curio said to Cæsar, *Tolle moras—semper nocuit differre paratis* (Away with delay—lingering has always ruined readiness), P. i, 281. Of Curio, a man *venali lingua*, Dante says, *ch'a dicer fu così ardito* (who in speaking was so bold), Inf. xxviii, 102. In the poet's hell he is punished for his evil counsel by having his tongue slit backwards right down into his gullet.

† I recognise him, as he lies, a headless trunk, on the river's sand.

A striking picture is drawn for us of the dumb grief that held the city. Rome, on the eve of war, is compared to a mother on the eve of a death in the household. The result is sure, the sufferer is indeed in the article of death, but apprehension has for the moment choked the wail in the throat, and palsied the arm all but uplifted to strike the breast.

In the exaggerated account of the supplications of the matrons, we have a touch in which Lucan shows to advantage as the poet of patriotic sentiment. One of the most frantic of their number bids the matrons beat their breasts and tear their hair, bids them wail on, so long as the contest is undecided; the time will come, she says, when the victory of one or the other combatant will force them to feign a joy they will not, and ought not to, feel. This, on a time of civil war, is a sentiment taking enough, and of an original turn of thought. There is rhetoric in it, but the rhetoric is not hollow. A little further on, the same sentiment is given expression to, when the men setting out for war (*pietas peritura*) patriotically, but vainly, entreat the gods to let loose the barbarians on Rome, that she may not have time to turn her hand against herself, and supplicate Jupiter to at least so far hear them as to strike down leader and led, while still guiltless.

There is a long digression in this book on some events of the Sullan and Marian wars. To make Marius the instrument of the god's vengeance is a not inept conception. The narrative is, for realistic effect, put in the mouth of a sympathetic narrator, an old man who remembered the past and feared the future. The poet has obviously sought after, and has made the most of, an opportunity of exercising his descriptive faculty. He strains after odd effects with his wonted overdone vigour, and misapplies his talent by the depicting of horrible and insane oddities of bloodshed and death. As a result of the Sullan massacres, Tiber, according to Lucan, was so gorged with corpses, as not to be navigable, and the blood of the slain so swelled the bulk of the river as to cause an overflow. The river struggled to its mouth and passed, a blood-streak, over the blue sea.

Brutus and Cato

It is in the second book that Brutus and Cato are introduced to the reader—the former, the type of the young uncompromising republican, ready to slay the coming victor, but, in the meantime, willing to subordinate his judgment to that of his kinsman and exemplar (*virtutis jam sola fides*); the latter, the spokesman of Lucan's personal feelings, the exponent, one might say, of the right that was on Pompey's side. Cato, as Lucan depicts him, felt himself impelled to take action, and believed that on the side of Pompey, his only place in the circumstances, he would be a make-weight to support such republicanism as still remained in Pompey's doubting soul. Cato, in any event, was willing to be the scapegoat of the wrath of the gods. This character, in the poet's hands, is a too conceitedly self-conscious one, even for a Stoic, and the colouring is of too lugubrious a shade, but in many ways it suited Lucan's pen, and has been powerfully and pleasingly traced. Cato was just that embodiment of antique affection and reverence, and had just that moral mightiness and elevation which suited, the one, Lucan's political principles, the other, his swelling style.

Marcia

The Marcia episode has no right to a place in genuine epic, and hardly any to one in so-called historic epic. Lucan, however, could not have missed such an opportunity for the display of high sentiment and mock-moral posing, as the return of Marcia to her stoic and sententious lord afforded. And if we take Lucan, at a proper valuation, as a young-eyed poet of warm, if somewhat simulated feeling, we shall be disposed to admire the animated and didactic description of Marcia's remarriage.*

The rest of the second book is taken up with an account of Cæsar's steady advance and Pompey's precipitate retreat. Cæsar, in fact, met with no resistance, save at Corfinium, where Domitius, an ancestor of Nero, tried to make a stand, but was forced to surrender by his troops. To him Cæsar presented his life, somewhat rantingly disclaiming all intention of profiting by this clemency in the event of a Pompeian victory. Cæsar's demeanour in this book is, as befitted Lucan's conception of him, grandiloquent, and truculent. Notwithstanding, our poet's setting forth of the action in the second book is really a eulogy of Cæsar's resolute and soldierly activity. Pompey does not appear to advantage. He makes a speech to his troops full of tall words and boastful enumeration, which has no effect whatever, not even an immediate one. There is in the second half of this book a noticeable amount of legitimate rhetorical and poetical expansion.

The Third Book

In the third and fourth books Lucan describes the resistance of Massilia and the operations against the Pompeians in Spain.

Pompey on his voyage to Greece is visited in a dream by the spirit of his first wife, Julia. The spirit advises him of impending disaster by dwelling on the bustling activity she had witnessed in the lower world against the approaching influx of doomed combatants, and, not content with this doleful prediction, proceeds to remind

* Dante's Cato says in the Purgatorio of Marcia :—

> Marzia piacque tanto agli occhi miei,
> Mentre ch'io fui di là, (diss 'egli allora),
> Che quante grazie volle da me fei.*
>
> P. i, 85.

* Marcia so pleased my eyes, when I was yonder, that all the favours she asked of me I gave her.

him how fortunate he had been in the lifetime of herself, his first wife, and how unfortunate he was fated to be as the spouse of a wife that had already brought disaster and death to her first husband. Neither by day nor by night, said the spectral visitant, would he be able to free himself from the relations into which he had entered with Cæsar and Cæsar's daughter.

The management of the Julia episode evinces genius but not the sanity of genius. It is so like Lucan to have a good idea, and to torment it in its development into distortion. How differently Virgil treats the appearance of Hector's ghost. What a purification of the soul by pity and fear is in its management.

The leading Pompeians had fled the city before Cæsar's arrival. The senators that remained were servile to Cæsar's least-expressed wishes. The tribune Metellus alone opposed the masterful procedure of the conqueror. When the latter was in act to seize the treasure stored in the temple of Saturn, Metellus barred his passage into the building. This was not an incident that the poet was likely to miss making capital out of. Metellus, accordingly, after some inconsequent remarks of Lucan on the power of lucre, stalks into the narrative, and addresses Cæsar in stilted, but not so ineffective, remonstrance against his purposed robbery. Cæsar's reply is couched in that language of hollow largeness which it pleases Lucan, as a political sectary, to constantly attribute to him. Metellus was told by the conqueror that to touch him would be to do him too much honour. The tribune was dissuaded from his opposition by Cotta. The digression on the sources whence the wealth laid up in the temple had been obtained, which follows the recital of Metellus' act of resistance is happily conceived, and embodied in terms of pleasing allusiveness.

There is one theme of description that now duly offers

itself to the pen of the poet, who is not slow to take advantage of it, namely, the enumeration of Pompey's allies. The digression is entertaining enough as a specimen of Lucan's manner, but it is too long drawn-out, extending, as it does, over more than a hundred and twenty lines. The geographical area covered by the description is a wide one. We have mentioned the Alpheus, Strymon, Mæander, Ganges, etc.; Athens, Troy, Parthia, Libya, etc.; Phœnicians, Arabians, Ethiopians, etc., and even Arimaspians. It is not to be supposed that so many peoples—as numerous, says Lucan, with careless inconsequence, and actual self-contradiction, as those led by Xerxes or Agamemnon—flocked to Pompey's standard, or that so many lands were emptied of inhabitants, but the poet had need of pegs on which to hang descriptions or references, and he provided himself with as large and varied an assortment as possible. We have reference within reference, allusion begetting description and description allusion, and all the various features of the poet's *cacoethes pingendi.*

The men of Massilia were faithful to the senate, and bade defiance to Cæsar, or, as Lucan puts it, refused to take part in a fratricidal war, to intervene in a quarrel between gods, professing their preference of the hardships and fate of Saguntum to such a course. Cæsar replied to the defiance in ultra-bellicose strain, saying that war was his food, and inaction his disaster, and proceeded to invest a town that disdained to give way before Fortune *virum toti properans imponere mundo.*

An oak-grove of awful shade, and sacred to the gods of the Druids, was cut down to furnish timber for the purposes of the siege, Cæsar's axe being the first to break the spell of sanctity that hallowed the forest. The inhabitants of Massilia, after Cæsar's departure for Spain, not only beat off the besieger's attack, but in a successful sally fired their siege-works. They were, however, vanquished by Decimus Brutus, Cæsar's admiral, in a naval battle off the town.

The naval battle off Massilia

The account of this battle contains some of Lucan's most marked efforts in the way of producing surprise effects, quite an array of incredible and fantastical bizarreries. One Tagus, a Roman, was pierced back and front by two darts, whose points touched. The blood, its circulation for the moment arrested, rushed with access of force on the blocking steel, and spurtingly expelled the darts, thus ending the man's life in a thoroughly Munchausen-like manner. Another man was pinned by the bowels to the side of a ship. A third, named Lycidas, was caught by a grappling-hook, but, ere he was dragged away, his comrades seized his limbs, and to the tune of 'Pull friend, pull foe,' he was rent in twain, and literally died by halves. A fourth victim was jammed between two colliding prows, or rather spitted, for his bones did not prevent the brazen prows from griding the one on the other. And so on. It is not expedient to tell of the various shapes and pathetic situations of the slaughter. The poet whirls along in breathless haste, his pen throwing off picture after picture in rapid succession, many of these displaying vigorous strokes of portraiture.

The Fourth Book

One half of the fourth book is occupied with an account of Cæsar's campaign in Spain against the Pompeian generals, Afranius and Petreius. At first the fighting was indecisive, and Cæsar was buffeted and baffled by the season, the weather, and famine. The soldiers of the rival camps fraternised, and Lucan sings the praises of concord, but Petreius, a sturdy Pompeian, and a literal-minded soldier stopped this exchange of courtesies, expelling from his camp and massacring Cæsar's soldiers. The speech which the poet puts in his mouth for the occasion is spirited, but the feeling is too heightened, and the glitter is the glitter of the school rhetoric. Petreius' soldiers, obedient to his exhortation, rushed at their opponents, and the men of both sides, like tamed beasts that have but just tasted blood, slaughtered each other with bitter hostility. Then a scene of peace became a scene of strife, and the pathos of reconciliation gave place to the pathos of fratricide. The poet has wrought events up to this climax, the situation is too conveniently antithetical. Finally Cæsar, by cutting off the Pompeians from a water-supply, a circumstance the poet makes the most of, forced them to surrender. He treated them with the marked clemency which became him, and which he always exhibited. Even Lucan in this book calls him the leader of the better cause. At the end of his account of the surrender of Afranius after privations that made delicious a draught of water from the stream, the poet has a fine aside on the joys of contentment and peace :—

> O prodiga rerum
> Luxuries, numquam parvo contenta paratu,
> Et quæsitorum terra pelagoque ciborum
> Ambitiosa fames, et lautæ gloria mensæ,
> Discite, quam parvo liceat producere vitam,
> Et quantum natura petat.*
>
> P. iv, 373.

Meanwhile, Caius Antony is being besieged by the Pompeians at an island near Salonæ, on the Dalmatian coast. Famine forces him to attempt escape from the post. Two rafts laden with fugitives have already escaped, but the third is caught from under the waves by a chain stretching from the shore to the island, and, thus entangled, is dragged to a place favourable for an attack. Vulteius, the captain of the raft, persuades his comrades to kill one another. His speech to this end

* O Luxury, lavish of substance, and never content with simple fare, O Appetite, covetous of foods sought over land and sea, O Pride of the Sumptuous Table, learn ye with how little one may sustain life, and what is the amount of nature's requirement.

has about it a stoical exaltation and fine fervour that are really capturing :—

> Vita brevis nulli superest, qui tempus in illa
> Quærendæ sibi mortis habet : nec gloria leti
> Inferior, juvenes, admoto occurrere fato.*
>
> P. iv, 478.

It is in this book that Curio dies out of the epic. He had gone to Africa to uphold Cæsar's interests there. This he did for a time successfully, defeating the Pompeian general, Varus, but was enticed into an ambuscade by Juba, and slain along with a large portion of his troops. Curio had been won over to Cæsar's side by the great man's personal influence. He was undoubtedly a man of great ability, and, in Cæsar's opinion, capable of fulfilling important trusts. Any blemish on his character was probably magnified by malignant Pompeian gossip. Lucan eulogises him flatteringly, and dismisses him stingingly. He was once, says the poet, the most promising of Roman citizens (*haud alium tanta civem tulit indole Roma*), but, while others bought the state with success, he sold it for gold (*emere omnes, hic vendidit urbem.*)

The Fifth Book

In the fifth, sixth, and seventh books the poet concerns himself with the preparations for, and with the actual undertaking of, the great battle of Pharsalia. Ever since Cæsar had at the Rubicon drawn the sword and thrown away its scabbard, he had with burning energy fought and followed the Pompeians. Pompey was mustering forces in Epirus, as a preliminary to the stand that was to hurl back impetuous Cæsar. Cæsar's fortunes, Pompey, no doubt, thought, were soon to ebb, and his own power was to overflow the West, and submerge all his rival's recent successes. It had

* There is no shortness to be found in the life of the man who has time therein to seek his own death, and the glory of dying is not staled, youths, by running to meet imposed doom.

been bad policy on his part to allow himself to be dispossessed of Italy. He had thus narrowed the arena of contest and staked the issue on one battlefield instead of on two. But Cæsar's celerity had benumbed Pompey's faculties, and perhaps the once ever victorious general built much on the power of his name in the East.

The Pompeians convened a senate in Epirus, for Rome, so the poet makes them argue, was where they were, just as Rome had once, under the leadership of Camillus and in the favour of his star, been lodged in Veii. The senators thus assembled appointed Pompey their leader. Appius, a prominent Pompeian, went to consult the oracle at Delphi, where he forced the unwilling Pythia to submit herself to the obsession of the divinity. Appius went to Delphi to furnish copy to Lucan regarding Delphi and all that its oracle suggests. Phemonoë, the priestess of Apollo, passed through convulsive agony, as, surcharged with the secrets of all time, she with difficulty disentangled and proclaimed the somewhat dark future of the individual inquirer. Deiphobe of the Sixth Æneid is a much more impressive person than Phemonoë. Lucan comments on the slender ray of light thrown by the god on the immediate future of Rome itself, and ridiculously concludes that the gods, perhaps, shrank from involving Magnus in ruin, or were afraid that, through the oozing-out of some forewarning or other, due punishment might not be meted out to Cæsar by Brutus.

Cæsar before he left Italy, had to quell a mutiny of his soldiers who, in the tone of remonstrance addressed to their commander, anticipate the standpoint of Lucan in regard to the civil war. The poet, after a shameless attribution of baseness to Cæsar, makes him, in a speech that arrested the action of the mutineers, deliver himself, puppet-wise, of sentiments that are, strictly taken, inconsistent with the baseness attributed, and too high-flying for a man of Cæsar's sanity and tact :—

> Non illis urbes, spoliandaque templa negasset,
> Tarpeiamque Jovis sedem, matresque senatus,
> Passurasque infanda nurus.*
>
> P. v, 305.

> An vos momenta putatis
> Ulla dedisse mihi ? Nunquam sic cura deorum
> Se premit, ut vestræ morti, vestræque saluti
> Fata vacent. Procerum motus hæc cuncta sequuntur.
> Humanum paucis vivit genus.†
>
> P. v, 339.

Cæsar's fleet was becalmed on the passage from Brundisium to Epirus, and, after a landing had been at length effected in Epirus, it was some time before Antony was able to transport across the strait the remainder of the forces. It was during this trying interval that Cæsar recrossed the sea in a small boat in the face of a tempest, to ascertain the cause of the delay of his subordinate. Lucan, after some sensible remarks on the humbleness and happiness of the estate of Amyclas, ‡ the boatman, follows the voyage of the daring general. Before embarkation, and on the voyage, Cæsar, by the poet's ordinance, enlarges on himself and on the situa-

* He would not have denied them (the soldiers) cities, and temples for their spoiling, and the house of Tarpeian Jove, and the wives of senators, and their married daughters doomed to nameless wrong.

† Do you suppose that you have counted for anything in my success? Never does Divine Providence lower itself in such wise that Fate attends to your danger and your safety. All your lot depends on the actions of the great. The human race exists for a few.

‡ Of Amyclas Dante says (Parad. xi, 68) :—

> Nè valse udir che la trovò sicura
> Con Amiclate, al suon della sua voce,
> Colui ch'a tutto 'l mondo fe paura.

Nor did avail aught (that is, increase the acceptability of poverty among men) the report that he who caused fear to all the world found her (poverty), at the sound of his voice, free from care with Amyclas.

tion, in rhetoric suggested by Cæsar's traditional utterance on the occasion in question.

The fifth book ends with Pompey's sending of Cornelia to Lesbos. It is not likely that Cornelia was so apprehensive of disaster, as her tearful leave-taking would make us imagine. Strong feeling usually checks utterance, a reasoned-out and voluble analysis of this feeling and of one's apprehensions is certainly foreign to emotional situations. The occasion for an effective leave-taking has not been psychologically chosen, and effect is not gained by opening up vistas of emotion. Let us place the farewell of Cornelia beside that of Andromache, and we shall realise how absurd, and that for more than one reason, is the former.

The Cæsarians and the Pompeians were now face to face. The sixth book records the beginning of hostilities, and the preliminaries of the great battle. Cæsar, as soon as Antony had joined him, proceeded to his task. He attempted with an inferior force to blockade Pompey in his position at Dyrrhachium, but experienced a mishap that had almost proved a disaster. Discerning the necessity for another plan of campaign, he retreated into the interior as far as Thessaly, to the scene of the coming battle.

The Sixth Book

Lucan speaks of Cæsar as of a gamester anxious to throw for everything or nothing. In his comparative way he speaks in exaggerated terms of the toil spent on the lines at Dyrrhachium :—

> Tot potuere manus adjungere Seston Abydo,
> Ingestoque solo, Phrixeum elidere pontum,
> Aut Pelopis latis Ephyren abrumpere regnis.*
>
> P. vi, 55.

He will have it that Cæsar's army was saved at this

* Just so many hands would have joined Sestos to Abydos, and with piled-up mound wiped out Phrixus' sea, or have broken off Ephyre from the broad realms of Pelops.

place from annihilation only by the humanity of Pompey.

He makes much of the exploits of Scæva, a centurion of Cæsar's army. Single-handed, this soldier prevented the Pompeians carrying a tower which was the key of the enemies' position. The burlesque unction of Lucan's description of this man's fighting is most striking ; absurdities jolt on one another. He chose his weapons with a large indifference. Corpses, stones, stakes, all came handy. He was even of a mind to project himself on the enemy. His sword became so blunted by clotted gore that it broke, and did not cut the limbs it struck. He was feathered all over with the darts that had pierced his person. One was shot into his eye ; he wrenched out the dart, and the eyeball with it, and trampled on both.

Scæva

Pompey was urged by his captains to take advantage of his success and cross over into Italy, but refused to introduce the horrors of war into his native land, and followed Cæsar into Thessaly.

In this book there is a tract of descriptive geography, eighty lines in extent, and the rest of the book, some four hundred lines, is taken up with the doings of the witch Erichtho. Sextus Pompey consulted her on the events of the immediate future, and, to give him the information he desired, she raised a corpse to life. The portion of the narrative devoted to Erichtho is most vigorous, and of sustained imaginative force and fertility. It is a poetical glorification of witchcraft. Erichtho herself is a creature of power, of virile purpose, and action. Her surroundings are appropriately pictorial and realistic. However fantastic some parts of the account may be, the whole forms a series of intellectual *tours de force* that could only have been conceived by a man of uncommon ability.

Erichtho

The seventh book is the book of the battle. The

poet makes a very good beginning with the dream of Pompey on the eve of the battle. There are both point and pathos in the conception. Pompey dreamt that he was in his own theatre, listening to the plaudits of the multitude. The poet finely says that perhaps Destiny, knowing that the sleeper was never again to see his country, indulged him with this last sight of the imperial city.

The Seventh Book

Then follows an apostrophe to the sentinels, bidding them not rouse with the blare of their trumpets the sleeping Pompey, doomed as he is to a morrow of care, and a night of troubles that will murder sleep. All this is appropriate and pleasing, but straightway the poet, in conjuring up the scenes of mourning that would have attended the death of Pompey, had it taken place in Rome, lapses into his usual vein of exaggeration.

Pompey's reluctance to join battle was overcome by the reproaches of his followers, and, so Lucan says, by a speech of Cicero, who, it would appear, was anxious to get back to Rome to defend sorrowing clients. The speech is of a character with that of the other speeches of the poet's puppets. Pompey, who, according to the poet, would have preferred a Fabian policy, abdicated his rights as a general, and yielded to the persuasions of others, or, as the poet puts it in a speech of rhetorical argumentation, to the compulsion of irresistible fate, deprecating the while all responsibility and blood-guiltiness.

The preparations for battle and the omens that preceded it are described, and speeches are put in the mouths of the commanders. Cæsar's speech is a masterpiece. It is full of proud self-confidence and prescient of victory :—

Sed me Fortuna meorum
Commisit manibus, quorum me Gallia testem
Tot fecit bellis. Cujus non militis ensem

> Agnoscam? cælumque tremens cum lancea transit,
> Dicere non fallar, quo sit vibrata lacerto. *
>
> P. vii, 285.

It has a correct statement of Cæsar's case. It appeals to sound instincts of the soldiers. It rightly magnifies the importance of the moment. It is fortified by glimpses of great motives for fighting, and by legitimate depreciation of the enemy. It flatters the soldiers, teaching them to repose on their past deeds, and congratulating them on their present form. It breathes tolerance. It recommends mercy, but inculcates firmness.

Pompey's speech is not nearly so effective as Cæsar's. It follows Cæsar's, and, to some extent, the risk of repetition must have weakened Lucan in its composition. Besides, Pompey is not represented as in valorous mood before the battle. The speech, however, has some fervour, some partisan vaunts appropriating the country's patriots, some imaginative conception of a rightful cause, but too much self-assertion :—

> Si Curios his fata darent, reducesque Camillos
> Temporibus, Deciosque caput fatale voventes,
> Hinc starent.†
>
> P. vii, 358.

In the flight that Lucan takes previous to the description of the battle an exaggerated estimate is given of the importance and results of Pharsalia. There is a good deal of fine-sounding inconsequence in this flight. The poet even says that to have had freedom and to have lost it is worse than never to have had it at all. But there is one compensation the gods have

* But Fortune has put me in the hands of my friends, whose deeds my many wars in Gaul made me witness of. Of what soldier shall I not recognise the sword? and when the quivering spear passes across the sky I shall not hesitate to tell by whose arm it was hurled.—(*Cf.* Tasso, G. L. xx, 18, quoted in this book.)

† If the fates in these times were to give back the Curii, and the Camilli, and the Decii devoting their head to its doom, with us would they stand.

vouchsafed, and that is the enrolment of mortals (*Divus Julius . . . Divus Nero* (by anticipation)) in their own august ranks, which statement may simply refer to the deification of Cæsar and his successors, but sounds very like irony.

The Cæsarians charged over the open space separating them from the enemy, paused midway when they saw the Pompeians meant to act on the defensive, then, unmoved by the sight of embattled relatives and fellow-citizens, threw their javelins, Crastinus showing the example, and advanced to the attack with drawn swords. The poet would have us believe that the Pompeians were so morally shocked and sorrowfully unnerved by the fratricidal fury of their opponents as to contribute by their supineness to the loss of the battle. The defeat was, on this supposition, due to the commendable shrinking of the Pompeians and to the relentless enmity of fortune. Pompey fled the field a discredited general, and a beaten and broken man, and no apology of Lucan's can hide the fact.

Cæsar is made to roam the battlefield like a very demon of cruelty. He inspects the swords of his soldiery, watches the faltering and the faint-hearted, and rejoices over the bloodthirsty. He leeches the wounds of his men, puts weapons in their hands, and directs the manner of the striking. He gloats on the field of battle over the corpses of the slain.* And this of Cæsar the Clement, the man who pardoned his opponents before they asked him. Brutus is made to run madly through the enemy in the disguise of a common soldier, Cæsar being his objective point. Domitius, Corfinium Domitius, is singled out for special honour, a man whose

* It is true that Cæsar only buried his own dead. (The Pompeian dead had only the heaven for a covering (*cælo tegitur qui non habet urnam*). Compare Sir T. More's Utopia :—'The way to heaven is the same from all places, and he that hath no grave hath the heavens still over him.')

historical record does not justify the distinction. But this mention would soothe a tyrant's vanity.

In the eighth, ninth, and tenth books the poet tells of the death of Pompey, of Cato's march to Leptis, and of Cæsar's doings in Egypt. After the battle of Pharsalia, Pompey, completely demoralised, fled to the sea-coast, and took ship at the mouth of the Peneus for Lesbos, whither he had sent his wife Cornelia. Thence he made for Cilicia, and thence, by advice of Lentulus, he sailed to Egypt, where he was murdered off Pelusium by order of Ptolemy, moved thereto by Pothinus.

The Eighth Book

It would appear that the courage with which Pompey bore up against misfortunes in the hour of unsuccessful battle deserted him during his flight. At any rate, Lucan, who described him in the seventh book as of constant mind in adversity, speaks of him in the eighth as frightened at the rustling of a leaf. The favourite of fortune was completely cast down by her ruthless desertion of him. He probably felt how hopeless any further effort of his would be, after the failure of the supreme one he had just made. He must, taught by recent events, have realised how unlikely Cæsar was to tolerate the existence in the world of any power at all co-equal with his own, and have discerned clearly enough that Cæsar, however much he might be disposed to deal leniently by himself, could not, unless he were to forfeit all claim to prudence, make any terms with the party to which he was indissolubly fettered, and which was as yet only in a tottering condition and not ruined. He had before him a high wall, and behind him his enemy.

The poet is melancholy all through the book. Cornelia receives her husband at Lesbos, in a lachrymose, ranting, and hysterical manner. She even wishes that she had been Cæsar's wife, so that the misfortune she was doomed to bring as a dowry might have missed her husband. The Lesbians are too profuse in their protestations of goodwill. Pompey ceases to be moody, only to be boastful. In his instructions to Deiotarus, he drags in a bit of self-glorification, and speaks as if he had imitated Alexander in his eastmost march.

At the council in Cilicia, Pompey recommends that application for aid be made to Parthia. The speech is grandiose in tone, but declines on this humiliating recommendation. Lentulus' reply, if not devoid of Lucan's vices, is manly and Roman :—

Juvat ire per orbem
Ducentem sævas Romana in mœnia gentes,
Signaque ab Euphrate cum Crassis capta sequentem ?*
P. viii, 356.

Pompey's death seems to supervene in the narrative rather abruptly. Lucan is indignant over the conception of such an audacious deed on the part of effeminate Egyptians, and over its execution with the assistance of a degenerate legionary in the service of Egypt.

Towards the end of the eighth book there is a fine statement of the *gesta* of Pompey, which the poet proffers as an inscription for a tombstone. It is effective as a whole, and has a pleasing movement of metre and thought. The exploits are well grouped, and the ending has due spaciousness and consummation :—

Dic semper ab armis
Civilem repetisse togam ; ter curribus actis
Contentum patriæ multos donasse triumphos.†
P. viii, 813.

After Pompey's death Lucan concentrates his attention

* Is it thy delight to pass over the world leading savage nations against the walls of Rome, and following standards that were captured along with the Crassi near the Euphrates ?

† Say that after war he aye resumed the civic gown, and that, content himself with three courses of the conqueror's chariot, he bestowed many triumphs on his country.

on Cato. From the Stoic heaven into which the poet translates him, Pompey breathes his spirit into Brutus and Cato. Cato had hitherto been a lukewarm Pompeian. It was pious hope, and not enthusiastic partisanship, that had made him take this side of the quarrel. Henceforth, if we are to believe the poet, he was animated by more zeal on behalf of his party. He had always been devoted to republicanism, but his greatest motive to persist in this devotion is now the memory of Pompey. As a matter of fact, Cato was a single-minded man of indomitable purpose who had embraced Pompey's cause because, in the circumstances, he could not act otherwise, and whose determination and legitimate distrust of Cæsar's aims pushed him into the action that would best checkmate or harass his opponent.

The Ninth Book

Cato, following the movements of his chief, had repaired to Africa. He was there joined by Cornelia and Sextus Pompey. Cneus was already with Cato. Cornelia exhibits wild hysteria over her husband's death. She is troubled by her inconsistency in surviving him. The two sons of Pompey give vent to insane expressions, the one of grief, the other of vengeance. With Lucan enthusiasm and hyperbole are almost identical.

At the make-shift obsequies performed by Cornelia in honour of Pompey, Cato pronounced a eulogy. This eulogy has received much notice and is worthy of it. It does not represent the speaker's real opinion of Pompey, but it suits his lofty and statuesque character. It has many well-pointed and happily-chosen antitheses :—

Nil belli jure poposcit :
Quæque dari voluit, voluit sibi posse negari.
Immodicas possedit opes ; sed plura retentis
Intulit : invasit ferrum, sed ponere norat.*

P. ix, 195.

* He demanded nothing by right of war, and, what he wished men

It is couched in moderate language, and yet is as rhetorical as the occasion and the speaker demand. Macaulay says of this eulogy that it is a 'pure gem of rhetoric,' and 'not very far from historical truth.' It is not quite easy to acquiesce in the latter description. Pompey was a man whose reputation was probably greater than his merit.

Cato, after quelling a mutiny with words that do not accord with the sentiments of the eulogy of Pompey—he says that the second tyrannical triumvir is dead, and that only one is left (*unum Fortuna reliquit jam tribus e dominis*)—embarked to join Juba. Impatient of the delay caused by a sea voyage, he determined to disembark, and journey to his destination overland. At this point of the story we come across striking exhibitions of Cato's character, such as his truthful exposition to his soldiers of the dangers they were to incur on their march—he refuses to hide facts, *tectoque metu perducere vulgus*—his chivalric, if somewhat ferocious, Sidneyism in refusing the present of a draught of water, and his manly and stoical reply to Labienus, when the latter bade him consult the oracle :—

> Estne dei sedes, nisi terra, et pontus, et aer,
> Et cælum, et virtus. Superos quid quærimus ultra ?
> Juppiter est quodcunque vides, quodcunque moveris.
> Sortilegis egeant dubii, semperque futuris
> Casibus ancipites : me non oracula certum,
> Sed mors certa facit : pavido fortique cadendum est,
> Hoc satis est dixisse Jovem.*
>
> P. ix, 578.

---

to give him, he wished them to have power to refuse. He possessed boundless wealth, but he brought into the city more than he kept ; he laid hold on the sword, but he knew when to lay it aside.

*What abode of Deity is there, unless the earth, the sea, the air, the sky, and virtue ? Why seek we the gods elsewhere ? Jupiter is whatever you see, whatever thought you are stirred by. Let waverers seek divination, those who are always afraid of future mishaps. 'Tis not oracles that give me certitude, but certain death. The coward and the hero must die ; let it be enough for Jove to have said this.

Cato was a man who, in spite of fortune's buffets, persevered in a preconceived and prescribed line of conduct.

The march across the desert infested by the Gorgon-born serpents has a hundred lines devoted to it. The hardships of the soldiers are described, and their deaths, some of which are ludicrous in the extreme. One poor wretch, bitten by a virulent species of serpent, swelled so frightfully that his increasing bulk absorbed his limbs and, as it were, his identity, producing a huge mass that his comrades were afraid to touch, and that they left unburied in its ever-increasing inflation.* With the assistance of the Psylli, a tribe of serpent-charmers, the soldiers of Cato managed to complete their march.

The poet returns to Cæsar towards the close of the ninth book, and does not leave him again. In his pursuit of Pompey, Cæsar arrived at Asia Minor, and visited the ruins of Troy. The poet has a finely imaginative description of this scene, enough, I think, to make any poet's reputation. The proper names are finely introduced. The allusions are appropriate and the whole matter very poetical :—

Cæsar at Troy

Sigeasque petit famæ mirator arenas,
Et Simoentis aquas, et Graio nobile busto
Rhoetion et multum debentes vatibus umbras.
Circuit exustæ nomen memorabile Troiæ,
Magnaque Phœbei quærit vestigia muri.
Jam silvæ steriles, et putres robore trunci
Assaraci pressere domos, et templa deorum
Jam lassa radice tenent : ac tota teguntur
Pergama dumetis : etiam periere ruinæ.
Adspicit Hesiones scopulos, silvasque latentes,
Anchisæ thalamos ; quo judex sederit antro :
Unde puer raptus cælo : quo vertice Nais
Luserit Œnone : nullum est sine nomine saxum.

---

* This soldier's name was Nasidius. His death, and that of his fellow-soldier Sabellus, are referred to by Dante, Inf. xxv, 95.

Inscius in sicco serpentem pulvere rivum
Transierat, qui Xanthus erat : securus in alto
Gramine ponebat gressus ; Phryx incola manes
Hectoreos calcare vetat. Discussa jacebant
Saxa, nec ullius faciem servantia sacri ;
Herceas, monstrator ait, non respicis aras? *

P. ix, 961.

Hard on this description we have a presage of immortality on the part of the poet :—

Nam si quid Latiis fas est promittere Musis,
Quantum Smyrnæi durabunt vatis honores,
Venturi me teque legent : Pharsalia nostra
Vivet, et a nullo tenebris damnabimur ævo.†

P. ix, 983.

Cæsar is shamefully slandered by the poet, in that the latter declares that the sorrow Cæsar manifested on

* Impelled by wonderment o'er ancient song,
He seeks Sigeum's shores and Simois' stream,
And that Rhœtean tomb ennobling all,
And shades of heroes silent save in song.
All round him lay the memory of Troy,
Now sunk in ashes. Phœbus' mighty walls
He traces. Barren woods and sapless trunks
Conceal the palace of Assaracus,
And with their time-worn roots begird the fanes
Of Gods. In thickets Pergamos is lost;
Its very ruins are no more. The rock
Where hung Hesione now met his gaze,
And covert woods that saw Anchises' troth
And spousals. Next, the cave where Paris judged,
The spot from whence the youth was reft to heaven,
The mount on which the nymph Œnone played.
Each rock bore storied name. Unwares he crossed
The stream of Xanthus creeping o'er the sand.
The grass was tall, and thoughtless marched he on,
Till Phrygian native dared him to profane
Dead Hector's dust. "Why, know you not," he said,
"These loosened stones that look not now divine,
Here stood the altar of Hercean Jove?"

† For, if one may promise aught to a Latian Muse, during such time as the honour of the bard of Smyrna shall endure, so long shall future ages read of you (Cæsar) in my lines. My Pharsalia shall live, and by no generation shall I be condemned to oblivion.

the reception of Pompey's head was feigned and not real. This is one of Lucan's most rancorous allusions to Cæsar, and is a most wanton perversion of truth. He continues in depreciatory mood into his tenth book, where he vilifies Alexander the Great, calling him *Pellæi proles vesana Philippi*, and *felix prædo*. Cleopatra comes in for her own share of passionate invective. She is called Dishonour of Egypt, Destroying Fury of Latium (*dedecus Ægypti*, *Latii feralis Erinys*).

Cæsar espouses the cause of Cleopatra, and reconciles her to Ptolemy. He is entertained at a splendid banquet, where he asks information about the sources of the Nile. The royal officials plot against Cæsar, who is besieged in the palace. The poet makes Cæsar gain possession of Pharos, and soon after the mention of this event the poem abruptly ends.

I have considered Lucan's poem at some length, it may be thought at too great length, but this poet's qualities are best brought out by a detailed examination of his narrative, for the Pharsalia has not a plan that one can outline in a few paragraphs, or broad features that need discussion under but few heads. It is a compilation of rhetorical efforts gathered round a spun-out story.

Lucan's treatment of his historic subject

Lucan's subject is a historic subject, and a historic subject of the near past. No more unpromising theme for lengthy treatment can be offered to a poet than the near past. He may make it the occasion of some lyrical outburst, but to weave its matter imaginatively into an objective poem that will, as such, earn real and lasting renown is, I fear, beyond accomplishment. If he give full freedom to his imagination, his lying will be evident to every one's memory; if he curb his imagination, or stay it by a drag, his poem will lack ideality.

Our poet had to deal with untransmutable matter, and too little of it. He painted his patches of epic stuff in high colours, he doubled, tripled, and quadrupled their number. To entertain the reader he dissipated his attention over a multitude of points that did not deserve diffuse treatment, and ransacked the purlieus of the subject for the wherewithal to amuse.

The men of his poem have no field for heroic action, as a substitute for this action he makes them speechify and vapour. This leads to a sameness in the presentation that is distinctly tedious. The large life of a genuine epical subject lends variety to its treatment. A multiplicity of action is presented to the poet, and from this he picks and chooses what suits his taste, and imposes on it a variety that follows the movements of his own sane intelligence.

Even if Lucan had had abundance of epical stuff to work with, he could not have made an epic, for he was unable to adopt the sympathetic attitude to tradition and antique fancies that success in such a work implies, nor had he any feeling for the heroic in action, for which his substitute was tempestuous activity. The poets of that age had lost the art of depicting men. They placed puppets on the scene, and, making up their minds to be terribly in earnest, they neglected calm action, and described a rapid action that had febrile rather than natural qualities.

Human activity was disendowed of its major share in epical narrative, and description substituted in its place.

He used description, as was then the custom

The lost art referred to, dearth of matter, and the desire to open a new vein, had all to do with the substitution. This description appeals to the eye rather than to the feelings. It does not by the mere touch of an epithet set off a salient feature and leave the imagination to fill up the suggestion, but it lavishes store of petty details. It does not connect a landscape with gods or men, but it is an effort in minute observation. It does not merely tint an emotional description with the colour that learning adds, but it makes a point of manifesting its erudition. With Lucan, however, erudition was not pushed into the display of pure pedantry, as it afterwards was. And in all his description, whether of pleasing or revolting details—for the devotees of description painted the ugly as well as the beautiful—there is always some ripple of style to entertain us.

Lucan declamatory and oratorical

Lucan is strong in declamation. He even mistakes it for truth. This was to be expected. The age was one of declamation, and the poet, by training as well as by birth, was the child of his age. The Pharsalia irresistibly suggests to us the recitation-room, and it is from this standpoint that we can most easily understand some of its demerits, and best appreciate its exalted style and trumpet-tongued earnestness.

Quintilian says that Lucan was rather an orator than a poet. This opinion is intelligible enough, and the rhetorical side of Lucan's poetry would predispose a student of oratory, like Quintilian, to its adoption. The surroundings amid which our poet made poetry must have endowed him with many of the attributes of an orator. But, while his poetry exhibits some of the qualities of oratory, namely, a love of brilliance, a seeking after effect, and a pervading pompous storm and stress, it is conspicuously lacking in many of the characteristic qualities of this art, such as logic, proportion, judgment. These latter virtues, are, indeed, in their poetic equivalents, as necessary to the narrative poet as to the orator. And Lucan has no method, no sense of fitness, no wise discrimination; his poem has not epic, still less dramatic unity. But he was poetical. His feeling was much too deep to be only oratorical, and he had intuitions of beauty in nature and conduct that are not those of an orator as such; his expression has an 'art for art's sake' ring about it that oratorical talent could not of itself have communicated; and, generally, he swings himself with far too great frequency and facility off the plane of the actual into that of the ideal to have had genius that would have responded with docility to the curb of the orator.

His sincerity and intellectuality

Although we miss in Lucan the chaste restraint, the sanity, and completeness of Virgil's genius, we are yet drawn to him by many admirable qualities of heart and mind. He is animated, however overdriven its expression in words may sometimes be, by a fine sincerity, the pulsations of which we feel everywhere, now throbbing out regrets for a day that is gone and a liberty that is lost, now beating to the vehemence of a young man's assertion of the nobility of virtue. His poetry sparkles with intellectuality. It exhibits vigour, originality, and novelty of expression and metre, although the repeated manifestation of these qualities in verse that swells on the same tone grows monotonous both to mind and ear. His words crowd appositely on one another, and his phrases convey here a conceit and there a positive beauty that make us pause and retaste our pleasures. These are momentary pleasures, I dare say, not to be remembered when the occasion is past, neither suggesting new outlooks on life, nor surprising the deep thoughts of the mind itself, being more an affair of verbal arrangement than of ideas. All the same, a style that gives such pleasure is an evidence of genuine power, and Lucan can be read for the charm of his own literary individuality.

His subjection to words

One must admit, however, that he is led about by words. They suggest to him developments of thought and tricks of narration. He relies on them for variety, shifting his vocabulary merely to secure an effect. He makes words and phrases take the place of ideas, but, more than that, he wills to deviate from the beaten track, and, for the mere sake of novelty, torments his language into queerness. Often he succeeds in making a telling phrase, but often only perpetrates an oddity, using, as he frequently does, metaphorical language that puzzles the understanding.

The Thebaid of Statius: its subject

The subject of the Thebaid is the events of the expedition of the Seven against Thebes. Œdipus, after his self-inflicted punishment, gave place as king to Eteocles and Polynices, his two sons. By arrangement, each of these was to rule alternately, and for a year at a time. Polynices, during his brother's tenure of royal power, wanders through the waste places of Aonia. He suddenly bethinks him of visiting the court of Adrastus, king of Argos. There he meets and quarrels with Tydeus in the vestibule of the royal palace. Adrastus makes peace between them, and afterwards recognises in them his sons-in-law sent by fate. Tydeus and Polynices, now fast friends, marry, the one, Deipyle, the other, Argia, the daughters of Adrastus. But Polynices becomes unquiet. He wishes to reign at Thebes. The year of his brother's rule has all but elapsed, but there is no sign on Eteocles' part of a desire to quit the throne. Tydeus undertakes an embassy to Thebes to expostulate with Eteocles on his retention of the kingship beyond the prescribed term, but his mission is fruitless. On his journey back Eteocles tries, by means of an ambush, to get him assassinated. An army is mustered to place Polynices on the throne of Thebes. Its leaders are these seven champions—Adrastus, Tydeus, Polynices, Amphiaraus, Hippomedon, Capaneus, and Parthenopæus. All are killed in the war save Adrastus. Eteocles and Polynices are killed in a duel. Creon succeeds to the throne, banishes Œdipus, denies the last rites to Polynices and the Argives. Jocasta commits suicide. Antigone and Argia burn Polynices' body on the pyre of Eteocles. The Argive matrons who had followed Argia to Thebes request the interference of Theseus, who marches against Thebes and captures it. Creon is killed. Such is, briefly, the story told in the Thebaid. The action is much delayed by digressions, but is taken up and hurriedly finished in the last two books.

Tydeus

A large portion of the second book is occupied with the story of the valiant deeds by which Tydeus defeated Eteocles' attempt to assassinate him. It is a good example of Statius' manner. After a tempestuous speech, in which he denounced the conduct of the king, Tydeus forced his way through the royal bodyguard, gnashing his teeth and throwing terror into the souls of the female onlookers. He was followed by the fifty men of the ambush, who overtook him at the place most suitable for the accomplishment of their cowardly purpose, a gorge between two hills, wooded, and threaded by a difficult path that was dominated by a perpendicular crag, where the sphinx used to perch when it puzzled men to their doom. Tydeus, advancing along the path through the forest, saw in the moonlight the sheen of the armour of the ambushed warriors. His few words of defiance were interrupted by the flight of an arrow that grazed his shoulder. Impelled by a sudden inspiration, he hastily scaled the sphinx's crag, and became, for the time being, master of his fate. Thence he reft a huge rock, too large for a team of bullocks to move, and hurled it on his foes, killing four and frightening away the others. Emboldened by the success of his act he leapt on to the plain, and with the alertness and reach of the hundred-handed Briareus, to whom he is compared, dealt death on all sides.

There is much of Statius in this piece. The sphinx

has fifteen lines of descriptive digression to itself. There are exhibited facility in narration and readiness of phrase; the flow of verse is unrestrained. Tydeus swells both in word and deed all through the contest. He is passionate to the verge of the bombastic. We have epical strokes, epical war-whoops, epical retorts, and whimsical deaths.

Tydeus, after killing his last man, says with pointed bravado:

> Ite sub umbras
> O timidi paucique.*
>
> Theb. ii, 667.

Too few, and this after the despatch of forty-nine, for one was spared to carry Tydeus' denunciation to Eteocles. Statius seems to have felt that he had exaggerated Tydeus' prowess, for he makes Minerva appear at the close of the combat and remind Tydeus that it was not in his own strength that he had accomplished his deliverance.

Two similes from the second book

The second book has many similes. I shall notice one, remarkable for its vigour. Eteocles has been visited over night by the phantom of Laius, wearing, for realistic and reassuring effect, the aspect of the seer Tiresias. The phantom warns him of his brother's preparations, and encourages him to resist all overtures. The king awakes with a start and,

> Qualis ubi audito venantum murmure tigris
> Horruit in maculas somnosque excussit inertes,
> Bella cupit, laxatque genas, et temperat ungues,
> Mox ruit in turmas, natisque alimenta cruentis
> Spirantem fert ore virum: sic excitus ira
> Ductor in absentem consumit prœlia fratrem.†
>
> Theb. ii, 128.

---

* Go to the shades, ye cowards, all too few in number.

† Just as when a tigress, on hearing the cries of the huntsmen, has bristled up her dappled hide and shaken off the drowsiness of sleep,

Another simile may here be noticed, and for an opposite quality, that of tenderness. Hypsipyle, the ex-queen of Lemnos, who had become nurse in the family of Lycurgus and Eurydice, king and queen of Nemea, while she led the Argives to the water,* of which they stood so badly in need, left Opheltes, her infant charge, on the ground. In her absence the child was killed by a serpent. His mother, Eurydice, was frenzied with grief :—

Non secus ac primo fraudatum lacte juvencum,
Cui trepidæ vires, et solus ab ubere sanguis,
Seu fera, seu duras avexit pastor ad aras ;
Nunc vallem spoliata parens, nunc flumina questu,
Nunc armenta movet, vacuosque interrogat agros ;
Tunc piget ire domum, mæstoque novissima campo
Exit, et oppositas impasta avertitur herbas.†

Theb. vi, 186.

Capaneus

Capaneus, the giant, another of the seven heroes, is the object of some vigorous description on the part of the poet. He was a despiser of the gods. His valour and his sword were his deities :—

Virtus mihi numen, et ensis
Quem teneo.‡

Theb. iii, 615.

He upbraided Amphiaraus for his credulity, and to his end scoffed at oracles and divine portents. He was

just as she longs for war, and opens her jaws, and whets her talons, and anon rushes on the band, and bears off, to feed her blood-stained cubs, a man still breathing, even so the king, goaded by his passion, wastes his strength in imaginary fighting with his absent brother.

* The name of the fountain (or river) is Langia. Hypsipyle is with Dante 'she that shewed Langia' (*quella che mostrò Langia*, Purg. xxii, 112).

† Thus, when a young bull of unsteady limbs, whose only blood is his mother's milk, is torn from the teat and carried off, be it by wild beast, or by shepherd for the cruel altar, his bereaved dam stirs with her wailing now the vale, now the river, now the herds, and puts questions to the lonely fields, and loathes to go home, and is the last to leave the fatal plain, and, though famished, rejects the offered food.

(*Cf.* Lucret. ii, 355).

‡ Valour is my God, valour, and the sword I grasp.

smitten with a thunderbolt after scaling the ramparts of Thebes,* flouting and about to flout the thunderer.

Amphiaraus

Amphiaraus, the seer just mentioned, had refused to partake in the proposed war, foreseeing its fatal result, but the persuasion and reproaches of his comrades, the treachery of his wife Eriphyle, who coveted on any terms the possession of the bracelet of Harmonia, now owned by Argia, and the compulsion of heaven, forced him to yield. The earth opened and swallowed him up before the eyes of the Thebans (*agli occhi de' Teban*, Inf. xx, 32), after a wasting *aristeia* on his part, described by Statius with much animation, and some ridiculous traits.

Statius' characters have not much individuality. They somehow all get mixed in the rhapsodising.

The Hall of Sleep

In the tenth book there is a fine description of the Hall of Sleep, rich in allegorical imagery, and almost exhaling drowsy effluence :—

Ipse autem, vacuus curis, humentia subter
Antra, soporifero stipatus flore, tapetas
Incubat ; exhalant vestes, et corpore pigro
Strata calent, supraque torum niger efflat anhelo
Ore vapor ; manus hæc fusos a tempore lævo
Sustentat crines, hæc cornu oblita remisit.
Adsunt innumero circum vaga Somnia vultu,
Vera simul falsis, permixtaque tristia blandis,
Noctis opaca cohors, trabibusque, aut postibus hærent,
Aut tellure jacent. Tenuis, qui circuit aulam,
Invalidusque nitor, primosque hortantia somnos
Languida succiduis exspirant lumina flammis.†

Theb. x, 106.

---

* 'He that fell at Thebes down from the walls' (*quel che cadde a Tebe giù de' muri*), says Dante, Inf. xxv, 15.

† The god himself, free from care, reclines on a carpet in the dank cave, surrounded by drowsy flowers ; his garments give out perfume, and his lazy limbs warm his couch, above which rises, as he breathes, a black vapour ; one hand presses the scattered locks of his left temple, the other has carelessly let fall his horn. There flutter round him

One almost gets reconciled to Statius' exalted style, prone as he is to pass into the inflated and the ludicrous.

The poet's style and diction

The poet sounds his pompous notes to the revelation of much more than mere noise. He could coruscate to some purpose.

If the language has lost in real force since it was wielded by Virgil, it is, at any rate, to say nothing of its easy flow, always entertaining, not seldom graceful, and, on occasion, powerful. Statius was endowed with enough poetic diction and sentiment to set agoing half-a-dozen mere writers of lyrics, and, in speaking of Statius' faults, we must remember that they were the faults of his virtues. Statius was a highly-gifted poet, of brilliant imagination and genuine sentiment, who alone of his fellows was able to evoke from the lyre sounds that recalled the glories of the past.

One of the first things that attracts one's notice in reading the Thebaid is the surcharge of mythological allusion. Statius can call a man himself in ever so many different ways. It is not only an excessive use of ordinary names that is to be met with, but the frequent bestowal of *recherché* appellations. In fact, the nomenclature in general is so recondite as to lead to obscurity. One cannot recognise the object indicated under its mythological or geographical metamorphosis. No fact is allowed to stand barely, or only with that which strictly belongs to it ; there is always a bit of embroidery, always a long train of circumstance.

We have in this poet animation pushed into declamation, expression tormented into turgidity. The vocabulary is large, and the writer in full command of it. All the poets of this epoch are the slaves of words. They are whirled along by words ; what they write is not

dreams of countless aspect, true and false, cruel and kind commingled ; these, Night's sable attendants, cling to the beams, to the door-posts, or lie on the ground. A dim and feeble light fills the hall, and languid torches with failing flame, as they expire, counsel the first sleep.

informed with ideas, but is often merely highly-coloured word-play, dashed with sentiment, emotional, mythological, or pictorial. Lucan and Statius had more imagination and more distinction in style than the others. Lucan, at any rate, had genius. But both had the faults of their brother-poets. They dealt in gross exaggeration. Statius was a man of warm heart and tender feelings, but the choice of the same walk in poetry as that of predecessors or of a similar—and the matter to be poetised on was restricted not only by personal inclination, but by tradition and the poetical discernment of the time—a distinct dearth of ideas, and a very natural desire to strike out into some novelty, have forced him into many marked displays of exaggerated and pseudo-pathetic sentiment.

A simile from the eleventh book

Statius' diction is not only allusive and florid, not only overcrowded with words and inflated with big sentiment, but sown with similes, some of which are quite worthy of the masters of metaphoric language. I have quoted already two examples of the poet's similes. I shall now quote another, to be noted for its illustrative exactness. Not that complete parallelism in all details is necessary in an epical simile. Virgil and Homer, at least, often use similes which afford one common feature for comparison, after which the poet goes off at a tangent, and embellishes his similes without regard to discrepancies that may be noticed between the comparison and the thing compared. But to the simile. It is from the eleventh book. Eteocles has just furiously replied to Creon, who had taunted him for his supineness in accepting the challenge of Polynices. The king at last consents to walk the way along which he is being pushed, and swallows for the time being his resentment :—

> Ictus ut incerto pastoris vulnere serpens
> Erigitur gyro, longumque e corpore toto

> Virus in ora legit ; paullum si devius hostis
> Torsit iter, cecidere minæ, tumefactaque frustra
> Colla sedent, irasque sui bibit ipse veneni.*
>
> Theb. xi, 310.

Statius' workmanship

Statius was a born versifier. The numbers came tripping at his command. He wrote with more ease than Virgil. His art had in lavish measure every requisite that a poet-versifier needs, be it constantly or casually, except ideas. Such as he had were not those of a separate individuality, of a thinking unit, but were either borrowed or the common property of clever writers, or were, it may be, chafed into independent existence. Whatever capacity Statius had for the acquisition of ideas, or for that solitary communing and independence without which no high poetical work can be accomplished, must have deteriorated under the influence and exactions of the recitation-rooms. The atmosphere of such places was conducive to point-making, to mere sonorous phrasing, to disregard of personal intuitions, to neglect of breadth and the wooing of sustained inspiration, in fine, to the production of efforts in little. And it is in the execution of such miniature work that Statius excels. He can set down a description or hit off a situation most pleasingly, he has in his poem many snatches of true pathos, he can dress up a conceit in the daintiest of manners and with most polished phrase.

Statius was enslaved by traditionalism and fashion, he was depressingly overshadowed by predecessors whom he could not hope to excel or even equal.

A pleasing trait in the last few lines of the Thebaid is

* Just so a serpent, struck a wild blow by a shepherd, rises aloft above its coils, and gathers into its mouth from its whole body the diffused poison ; let, however, its adversary turn aside a little from the path, straightway its towering height is lowered, the neck vainly swollen contracts, and the reptile swallows its wrathful venom.

the poet's consciousness of personal fame, and modest and graceful acknowledgment of Virgil's superiority:—

His reverence for Virgil

Durabisne procul, dominoque legere superstes,
O mihi bissenos multum vigilata per annos
Thebai? jam certe præsens tibi fama benignum
Stravit iter, cœpitque novam monstrare futuris.
Jam te magnanimus dignatur noscere Cæsar,
Itala jam studio discit, memoratque juventus.
Vive, precor; nec tu divinam Æneida tenta,
Sed longe sequere, et vestigia semper adora.*

Theb. xii, 810.

Statius wrote two books of another epic poem called the Achilleid.† This was to enshrine all the *gesta* of Achilles except those mentioned by Homer. It is hard to see how this work, if it had

The Achilleid

* Thou wilt live far into the future, thou wilt survive thy lord, and be read, O Thebaid, over which for twice six years I have kept many a vigil? Already, indeed, in our day, Fame has graciously prepared a path for thee; already she begins to show thee all fresh to future times; already high-souled Cæsar deigns to make thy acquaintance; already the Italian youths eagerly learn and repeat thee. Live—such is my prayer: seek not to reach the glory of the divine Æneid, but follow it from afar, and worship alway its traces.

Compare what Dante makes Statius say of the Æneid:—

La qual mamma
Fummi, e fummi nutrice poetando;
Sanz' essa non fermai peso di dramma.*

Purg. xxi, 97.

Dante repays with interest the honour done to Virgil by Statius, when he permits him to be invited (*donnescamente*, 'as a gentle lady would') by Beatrice to drink after the poet of the river Eunoë.

† Dante makes him say:—

Cantai di Tebe, e poi del grande Achille;
Ma caddi in via con la seconda soma.†

Purg. xxi, 92.

---

* Which (the Æneid) was my mother, and was my nurse in poetising, without which I did not suspend a dram's weight.

† I sang of Thebes, and then of the great Achilles, but fell on the way with the second load.

been finished, would have added to the poet's reputation.

Such incident-picking, as the avowed purpose of the poem points to, could hardly have resulted in a good argument, or in even a passable unity. Now, the argument of the Thebaid, however prolix it may sometimes be, is intact, and its unity is unimpaired. Certain it is that in his second epic the poet, as regards workmanship, has lost none of his vigour, none of his art. The parts of Achilles' life described to us are his boyhood and early manhood under Chiron's guardianship, and his removal to and concealment in Scyros by his anxious mother. Statius still purveys the pictorial with pedantry and geography combined; he still supplies similes after requisite intervals, and he still pleases by the power of lukewarm intellectual effort rather than by the fiery flight of genius.

The scene of Achilles' discovery by Ulysses is finely managed, and has some most effective touches. Achilles shows to advantage in the fragment. At sight of the buckler and lance among Ulysses' wares, Achilles

> Infremuit, torsitque genas, et fronte relicta
> Surrexere comæ: nusquam mandata parentis,
> Nusquam occultus amor, totoque in pectore Troja est.*
> Achill. ii, 181.

Poor Deidameia got none of the gifts her youthful lover promised her when he set out for the war:—

> Irrita ventosæ rapiebant verba procellæ.†
> Achill. ii, 286.

Valerius Flaccus wrote the Argonautica, as we know

* Achilles uttered a wild cry, and rolled his eyes; his hair left his brow and stood erect; there is no place more for his mother's commands, no place more for his stolen love: Troy fills his whole heart.

† The wild winds bore away his useless words.

from the dedication, in the reign of the emperor Vespasian. Briefly, this is the argument:—Pelias, having usurped the throne of Æson, ruled in Iolcos. Jason the son of Æson and Alcimede, on growing to manhood, was an inconvenient presence at the court of Pelias, and was sent to fetch from Colchis the golden fleece that King Æetes, by murdering Phrixus, had possessed himself of. All the heroes of the age accompanied him. He took with him, as a hostage, Acastus the son of Pelias. The king in revenge plotted the death of Jason's parents, who, forewarned, committed suicide.

The Argonautica of Valerius Flaccus. Brief argument

Tiphys is the pilot of the Argo. The voyage is eventful. They dally some time at Lemnos detained by the Lemnian women. Hercules delivers the daughter of Laomedon. Cyzicus is accidentally slain. Hylas is lost and Hercules abandoned. Pollux kills Amycus in a boxing-match. Phineus is delivered from the harpies. The Cyanean Rocks are passed. Colchis is reached.

Medea assists Jason to accomplish his tasks, and flees with him. Absyrtus her brother, and Styrus her lover, pursue them. Styrus is drowned in a storm raised by Juno. The Argonauts blame Medea for their troubles. She complains to Jason, who had inwardly sided with his companions. Here the poem abruptly ends.

The Roman and Greek treatment of the theme

The epic treats of the same story that is treated of in the epic of the same name of Apollonius Rhodius. But there are distinct and considerable differences, both in the story and in the manner of telling it. There are much more life and picturesqueness in the Roman poet. There is a placid calm in the narrative of the Greek that forbids all excitement. One has, in reading the latter, rather the sensation of looking on a series of heroic pictures with appropriate delineation and appurtenance, than of realising in imagination, through the act of reading, the verity of the acts and scenes described. In the former state the eye is always alert enough to be conscious of the dead material, the visible unreality of the show; in the latter, it is in the power of a skilful writer to produce all but complete illusion. And Valerius Flaccus can produce a not ill-satisfying illusion.

Description in Valerius Flaccus

We have in the Argonautica taking bits of scenic description. The poet had a real feeling for natural beauty, and an ability to translate this feeling into words. The panorama of the shore on leaving Iolcos Colchiswards is pleasingly described, more so than in Apollonius. In the wake of the voyagers the ash-clad summits of Pelion first sink into the sea, while on the left the temple of Tisæan Diana still tops the waves; presently the isle of Sciathus disappears from view, and the promontory of Sepias flies to the horizon; now the Magnesian plain, with its grazing steeds, heaves in sight; away in the distance they seem to see the tomb of Dolops, and the river Amyrus winding into the sea. Here a breeze drives them towards land, but, rising to their oars, they just pass within hailing distance of Eurymenæ, and, under the impulsion of Auster, sail over the open sea by Pallene, where is the site of the Phlegræan plain, the battlefield of the gods and giants, lying on the left bow. This neighbourhood at once suggests to the poet an irrelevant reference to the interment of the giants, and the uprise of their mountainous *tumuli*:—

> Quos scopulis, trabibusque, parens miserata, jugisque
> Induit, et versos exstruxit in æthera montes.*
>
> Arg. ii, 19.

There are many not unpleasing descriptions, or notices, of places and natural scenery, strewn through the poem.

Just a little further on in the same book there occurs

* And them a pitying mother covered with cliffs, and beams, and hill-sides, and reared upwards into the sky the mound she had piled.

a noticeable description of the down-coming of night at sea, with its accompanying appearances, expressing admirably, I think, the vague obsession of fear that must sometimes have threatened to master the daring Argonauts :—

> Ipsa quies rerum, mundique silentia terrent,
> Astraque, et effusis stellatus crinibus æther.*
>
> Arg. ii, 41.

Other attractive, and sometimes felicitous descriptions of sunrise and sunset and concomitant events, either natural or mythological, are elsewhere to be found.

Battle-scenes

There are several battle-scenes in the Argonautica. That one in Book VI, which presents to us the combat of the Argonauts with the enemies of King Æetes is the most animated. First we are told of the allies that mustered to the help of Perses against his brother. The enumeration of the muster reads like a gazetteer of nations, every one with its little patch of description. The geography of the delineation is cumbersome and no detail is foreign to the poet's purpose, be it a trumpery bit of folk-lore, a tribal practice, or a climatic characteristic. The reader gets quite tired of the describing mania. The actual fighting is a bustling business ; it is of the single-combat, homeric type. But the thing is overdone ; duels crowd on one another in confuséd juxtaposition. Many redoubtable strokes and valorous onslaughts are mentioned, not without, now and then, a little virgilian phrasing and pathos

Virgilianisms

Thus Gesander, in his contest with Canthus, vaunts—the complete vaunt is too lengthy, I fear, for its general quality—his patriotism and the hardiness of his tribesmen :—

> Nunquam has hiemes, hæc saxa relinquam,
> Martis agros, ubi tam sævo duravimus amne

* The very stillness of nature awes them, and the silence of space, and the stars, and the sky all bespangled with comet-like lights.

Progeniem, natosque rudes, ubi copia leti
Tanta viris.*

Arg. vi, 335.

This language bears a strong resemblance to

Durum ab stirpe genus natos ad flumina primum
Deferimus, sævoque gelu duramus et undis.†

Æn. ix, 603.

And Tages, on whose outfit had been lavished the care of women, must die as doomed, in spite of his descent, and dearness to others :—

Tenuia non illum candentis carbasa lini,
Non auro depicta chlamys, non flava galeri
Cæsaries, pictoque juvant subtegmine bracæ.‡

Arg. vi, 225.

Colaxes, the son of Jove himself, must yield him to destiny, his father being unable to save him :—

Quin habeat sua quemque dies, cunctisque negabo,
Quæ mihi.§

Arg. vi, 628.

The haling of the dead Canthus is closely copied, even to the peculiar simile, from the Iliad (xvii, 389), where Patroclus' body is stretched, as is stretched, for a definite purpose, the oiled hide of a bull. Did it serve any purpose, I might further instance places where the poet copies Virgil, and translates, sometimes literally, Homer. In the above contest the Argonauts had need of all their strength and valour, if we are to believe the poet's iterations of the numberlessness of Perses' allies.

The poet's similes are often ornamental and traditional,

* I shall never leave this wintry clime, these rocks, the land of Mars, where in the cold stream we have hardened our children, our sturdy sons, where death presents so many fronts to men.

† We, a people of sturdy stock, carry our sons to the streams, as soon as we may, and harden them in the cold freezing water.

‡ His fine raiment of pure white linen avails him naught, nor his chlamys figured with gold, nor the tawny plume of his helmet, no, nor his trousers of brocaded stuff.

§ Nay, then (Jupiter speaks), let his own doomsday capture each, and I will refuse to all what I refuse to myself.

but sometimes not inapt. They are certainly numerous enough in some places. The metre is technically correct, and, what is more, conveys to the ear a good imitation of Virgil's rhythm, though it lacks the metrical thought, if such a description of mètre is permissible, that sounds in Virgil's verse. The expression is large, and displays decorative art enough, if it somewhat lack in smoothness.

Similes and metre

Deities interfere vigorously in the action of the poem, and this interference is often quite direct. It seems to me, however, that the Latin poet's deities retain more divinity than those of the Greek poet, who are often too diplomatic to be Olympian.

Points in a comparison of Valerius Flaccus and Apollonius Rhodius

The love of Medea for Jason is more rationally spoken of in Valerius Flaccus, and with more regard to woman's ways, than in Apollonius. In Apollonius it is all the doing of Cypris and her boy, while, in the Roman poet, although Medea is assisted into her passion by Juno, disguised as her sister Chalciope and aided by the borrowed necklace of Venus, which the maid unwittingly puts on, still in the Roman poem the passion is rather communicated by suggestion, being then almost free to run its natural course, than, as in the Greek poem, inflicted by divine act on a helpless victim. It is a pretty enough picture, that of the love-sick maid drinking in love as she gazes from the ramparts, whither she had been hurried, half-unwilling, by the disguised goddess, on the hero battling in her father's service.

The Argonautica, as an epic of adventure, is, as it seems to me, a much more successful production than the critics will allow, displaying considerable naturalness and story-telling power. The plot of the poem is not finished, but what of it there is displays more design than we find in the plot of Apollonius' poem, and, with the Roman poet, Jason better maintains his position as hero of the story.

Mr Morris's Jason

I like Mr Morris's account of the upgrowth of Medea's passion. It is so poetical and so human :—

> Therewith she made an end ; but while she spoke
> Came Love unseen, and cast his golden yoke
> About them both, and sweeter her voice grew,
> And softer ever, as betwixt them flew,
> With fluttering wings, the new-born strong desire ;
> And when her eyes met his grey eyes, on fire
> With that which burned her, then with sweet new shame
> Her fair face reddened, and there went and came
> Delicious tremors through her.
>
> Life and Death of Jason vii, 85.

This, if not so detailed and meltingly pretty, is more powerful than the corresponding passage of the Greek poet :—

> Τοῖος ἀπὸ ξανθοῖο καρήατος Αἰσονίδαο
> Στράπτεν Ἔρως ἡδεῖαν ἀπὸ φλόγα· τῆς δ' ἀμαρυγὰς
> Ὀφθαλμῶν ἥρπαζεν· ἰαίνετο δὲ φρένας εἴσω
> Τηκομένη, οἷόν τε περὶ ῥοδέῃσιν ἐέρση
> Τήκεται ἠῴοισιν ἰαινομένη φαέεσσιν.
> Ἄμφω δ' ἄλλοτε μέν τε κατ' οὔδεος ὄμματ' ἔρειδον
> Αἰδόμενοι, ὁτὲ δ' αὖτις ἐπὶ σφίσι βάλλον ὀπωπάς,
> Ἱμερόεν φαιδρῇσιν ὑπ' ὀφρύσι μειδιόωντες.*
>
> Arg. iii, 1016.

Apollonius, indeed, becomes animated and interesting when he treats of Medea. This theme imports stir into his placid pages and fills his blank vigour with the fulness of vitality. The whole story of Medea's passion is a most charming love-study, and when we consider that it

* In such wise did Eros dart a graceful brilliance from the head of fair-haired Áisonides, who drew on himself the lady's bright glances ; she dissolved into love as her heart within was warmed, just as the dew, warmed by the morning light, dissolveth round roses. Both now fixed modestly their eyes on the ground, now shot again glances at one another, smiling yearningly from under their bright eyebrows.

comes from the pen of an ancient, its force, passionateness, and psychology strike us as little less than wonderful. Virgil's love-story, which lends so much potency to his epic, owes much, were it only suggestion, to the Medea of Apollonius. And it owes more than suggestion, it owes details even.

We have travelled a long way since the days of Valerius Flaccus. Romance is a much greater fact now than it was then, when it was, so to speak, in its mere beginnings, and the copiousness and applicability of language for romantic purposes is beyond comparison greater now than then. And in romantic poetry of this sort how much effect is produced by dainty word-choice. Our modern poem of Jason, in virtue of its sensuous suggestiveness, its variety of colour, its life and movement, not to speak of its full expression of romantic wonder, leaves far behind the ancient poems on the same subject. And it, too, has its tinge of melancholy.

Silius Italicus: his Punica

Silius Italicus wrote in the time of Domitian an epic of seventeen books on the events of the Second Punic War, which he therefore styled Punica. In the active period of his life Silius had earned great professional reputation as an orator. He had also filled the various grades of office open to aspirants after official position under the empire. Altogether, a successful man: he had honoured, and profited by, his profession; he had served the state acceptably and been rewarded by the receipt of its highest dignities. He died of voluntary starvation, despairing of the cure of a tumour that caused him much painful discomfort.

He was a man of literary taste and capacity; he had always loved the literature of his country, and was, in particular, a pronounced devotee of Virgil. In the evening of his life, when he had received the foil of an honourably-earned leisure—he had become temporarily demoralised under Nero, it was said, but that was a demoralising period, as witness Lucan's lamentable lapse from manliness—he passed strikingly from an admirer into an imitator of Virgil, and proceeded to woo the Muses' help in the elaboration of an epic poem.

This poem is certainly one of the most fantastical examples of poetical epos. I do not at all think that it deserves the unmeasured contempt that some critics bestow on it. One feels a sort of yawning pleasure over its intermittent perusal. The poem ambles along with some pleasant insipidity of matter, and colourless correctness of metre. It is a farrago of historical fact, inconsequential incident, and descriptive detail. Occasionally, and at the regulation places, the poet lashes himself into excitement and passionate talk.

The theme of the poem and its treatment

The war from the siege of Saguntum to the battle of Zama is the theme of the Punica, and this war is supposed to be waged under the supervision, and, indeed, to have been caused by the instigation of the gods. Jupiter wished the Trojan-Romans to purge off their sloth by the necessity of facing dangers. The machinery of the Homeric and Virgilian epos is used to give an epical contour to a narrative of facts that, perhaps, could, owing to their nature and the circumstances of their occurrence, never have had anything but a purely historical value, that at any rate had been so appropriated and set forth by historians and made to assume such an aspect of material actuality and logical exactitude, that no epical ability, however great, supposing it to have been betrayed into a wrong choice of theme, could have produced aught but a whimsical medley of generals and soldiers masquerading as the pieces and pawns of the Olympian chessboard.

We have seen that Lucan tried to write an epic with

a historical basis, and although Lucan did not and could not succeed in writing a satisfactory epic under these conditions, he has yet given us a poem that is inspired by something like an epical afflatus, for in Lucan we have the young man eloquent, and eloquent unto the production of pleasure-giving, and, in its variety, fairly consistent poetry. Silius tried to turn into poetry the hard facts of bloody battles and strategic campaigning; he galvanised into quasi-poetical life, by the aid of the apparatus of the decadence, an incongruous whole that every now and then displays the laughable oddities that arise from the unholy alliance between historical verities and epic fable.

The reputation of Silius

The poet of the Punica had a considerable reputation among his contemporaries. We can imagine that Silius loved to be pointed at with the finger. He makes Hannibal say:—

> Quantum enim distant a morte silentia vitæ?*
>
> Pun. iii, 145.

Martial, in verses addressed to him, calls him the 'glory of the Castalian sisterhood' (*Castalidum decus sororum*); he makes many references to our poet (*perpetuus Silius*, he calls him), and felicitates himself on having him as one of his readers. Doubtless Martial had received many kindnesses at the hands of this amiable *littérateur* and patron of letters. It is a pity that none of Silius' orations have come down to us. Probably, too, he wrote many poems besides the Punica. Had these, and the orations, come down to us, we should then have better data for pronouncing on his ability. It will never do to gibbet a man because he has conspicuously failed to write an epic poem. Only, Pliny, who certainly knew his other work, says that he owed more to application than ability. Silius owned one of Cicero's villas. He had also

* How much does an obscure life differ from death?

purchased the property near Naples where Virgil is said to have been buried. Perhaps he imagined that he had thereby secured for himself the reversion of the poetical talent of the singer of the Æneid.

A reference to the fable of the poem

The facts of our epic poem are taken from Livy and Polybius. The poem, indeed, is an authority on the Punic wars, for comprehensiveness, not to speak of accuracy, is one of its virtues. The poet has filled some of the lacunæ left by preceding writers. The stop-gap excellence of this poetical historian is not likely to seduce many readers from the perusal of Livy's pictorial narrative. The siege of Saguntum is the real beginning of Silius' argument, but he preludes it with some account of the machinations of Juno, imitating Virgil both in arrangement of matter and in expression. Thereafter, the poet creeps on through all the events of the war, with embellishment, expansion, and description, to an account of the battle of Zama, where the reserved Scipio in the most apocryphal fashion is made to do the work of a sanguinary madman, and to finish off his action in the epic with a blatant challenge, which Hannibal eagerly accepts, only to find, Turnus-like, that Juno has cheated him with a phantom. Then, after an outburst of rhetorical imbecility, follows an abrupt suspension of Hannibal's activity in the poem—his subsequent fate is mentioned in the thirteenth book, as part of the Sibyl's revelation to Scipio—and the work ends. Perhaps the above references to the fable of the Punica, as a whole action, supply as much of notice as the importance of the poet warrants.

Hannibal and Scipio in the poem

Of this poet's characters the utmost that can be said is that the principal retain a certain historical verisimilitude; they are from an epical standpoint very unsatisfactory personages. Livy's description of Hannibal is, after making allowance for the historian's rhetoric and the mendacity of malevolent Roman gossip, the description of just such a person as we should expect a great military captain to be. Silius' Hannibal, besides being a monster of cruelty, is a man of bravado, a stilted theatrical person who delights to ride bareheaded under a thunderous sky, to back the fieriest possible steed, to deny himself, through sheer quixotry, the allaying of his natural thirst, and to swim his horse over barely fordable rivers.

Scipio the grave, self-contained Roman, the young man conscious of a mission, is similarly travestied.

The scenes between Hannibal and his wife Imilce are not badly conceived and wrought out, but marred as usual by exaggeration. Imilce is, after objurgation on her part, and consolatory suasion on the part of Hannibal, sent home, and bidden, in the event of Hannibal's death, make her boy swear, as his father had done before him, an oath of undying hostility to Rome.

Ennius and Archimedes

Silius introduces into his epic, with, at any rate, a feeling for historic effect, the name of Viriathus, and the persons of Ennius and Archimedes. The name of the Viriathus who led a contingent of Lusitanians to the help of Hannibal is used to point a reference to the disaster to the Roman arms that was to be caused by another Viriathus :—

Primo Viriathus in ævo,
Nomen Romanis factum mox nobile damnis.*

Pun. iii, 355.

Ennius is represented to us as a centurion fighting in the army of Torquatus in Sardinia, and as one who will be the first to sing in noble verse of the wars of Italy (*canet illustri primus bella Itala versu*). Of Archimedes

* Viriathus, in the flower of his age, a name soon made famous by Roman defeats.

we find repeated what Livy tells us of his accidental death :—

> Tu quoque, ductoris lacrimas memorande tulisti,
> Defensor patriæ, meditantem in pulvere formas,
> Nec turbatum animi, tanta feriente ruina.*
>
> Pun. xiv, 676.

Our poet, copying Virgil, makes Venus one of the active divinities of his epic. In her distress about the

Venus in the poem

Æneadæ she approaches Jupiter, who calms her, as in the Æneid, by a bit of prophecy. This prophecy begins in Virgil with *Parce metu* and in Silius with *Pelle metus*, but here the resemblance stops. Virgil's imaginative power of selection is not possessed by Silius, who makes Jupiter expound to Cytherea the motives of his action, and, after a mention of some facts of republican and imperial history, end in a long drawn-out panegyric of Domitian. One action of the same goddess in the epic is worth mentioning, as illustrative of some of the absurdities to be met with in this poet. The consul Scipio at the defeat of the Trebia is represented to us as exclaiming against the partiality of the river, whose sudden flood is said to have been due to the interference of Juno. The river-god, on his side, swells his waters menacingly in answer to Scipio's threat, and threatens to engulf the consul, whereat Venus ends the flood and the danger by copious casts of her husband's assuaging fire.

Silius finds a place in his poem for all the epic commonplaces. He has a hero's shield, a hero's dream, a hero's

Epic commonplaces

parting, heroic games, a vision of the underworld, and a catalogue of combatants. The last-mentioned is a tame, long-winded bit of composition, too geographical, too full of tribal customs and

* Thou, too, glorious defender of thy country, on whom the great ruin fell while quietly tracing figures in the sand, drew tears from the general.

paltry details. There is no simple description, say, of membership of a great gathering, no enumeration of nationalities, but a made-to-order deadly-dull bit of copyist work.

Hannibal's shield

Silius' grouping of the emblazonry on Hannibal's shield is a rambling juxtaposition of events of the past—some of them of the near past, of the all but present—not pressed into its service by the imagination, but inserted because jotted down as things to be included. The figuring on Æneas' shield is a historic mosaic of the future brightened by imagination. How apposite and emotionally satisfactory are many of the images—the glittering Gauls swarming up the capitol, Catiline clinging to and cowering on the rock, Cato legislating for the blest, and Cleopatra rattling her sistrum and relying on the aid of the dog-god Anubis. Hannibal, on donning the armour he had received as a present from the nations of the Ocean, indulges in some sanguinary twaddle about vengeance on the Roman senate. Virgil with true epic calm simply makes Æneas raise on his shoulders the figured shield that foreshadowed on its surface the glory and the destiny of Rome (*famamque et fata nepotum*).

Some incongruities

Scipio's vision of the underworld is one of the insupportably incongruous features of this epic of a historical war. Such also is Jupiter's direction of an arrow into Hannibal's body at the siege of Saguntum and Juno's extraction of the same, and Æolus' blinding of the Romans at Cannæ, at Juno's instance, by clouds of dust. Hannibal's dream is simply a versified account of the *Vastitas Italiæ* story in Livy.

Battle-pieces

Some of Silius' most vigorous writing is to be found in his battle-pieces. But the vigour has no sublimity with it, and vigour without sublimity, or at least intellectuality, produces a hammering monotony that is most tedious. The non-vigorous portions of the poem read like versified prose, with some mild-mannered purple colouring, and, in fact, the vigour, where present, is often forcibly generated—mere tea-cup tempestuousness, mill-pond commotion. There is really no imaginative play in Silius, only rhetoric, and indifferent at that.

Metre, etc.

The metre of the poem is of pale irreproachableness, of excremental whiteness. In epic metre metrical effect is not likely to be disassociated from inspiring sentiment, and though the poetry of the Punica has the genuine flow of the hexameter, it does not exhibit to the ear the musical syllabic units, or the congeries of word-harmonies heard in Virgil's poetry. The spaced-out glory of the Mantuan's beautiful lines has mind in it as well as metre. Silius, like the poets of the decadence, had some talent for description. His similes, though sometimes apt and illustrative, are yet as a rule of the ready-made foisted-in order.

CHAPTER II

THE ENGLISH EPIC

THE Beowulf, the oldest specimen of the English epos, and perhaps the most considerable monument of early Teutonic literature, has the following argument :—

The story of the Beowulf

Hrothgar, king of the Danes, of the royal line of Scyldings, built Heorot. This building was to be a place of entertainment for his thanes, and a state-hall for the distribution of rewards. Grendel, the march-stepper, heard the sounds of music that came from Heorot, and grudged the men their enjoyment of life. He burst into the hall, which was used as a sleeping-chamber, and carried off thirty thanes, repeating his raid after but one night's interval. The hall-banquets were abandoned and the building avoided. The monster terrorised the burg for twelve years.

Beowulf, the son of Ecgtheow, and liegeman and nephew of Hygelac, learned of the Danish distress, and sailed to Hrothgar's court to offer his services. These were accepted, for the need was dire, and Beowulf had ere now made a name for himself. The king entertained him in Heorot, and left him in charge of the building. At night Grendel came, and slew and devoured the sleeping Hondscio. He next tackled Beowulf, but met more than his match. He was outwrestled, and crushed, and had his arm wrenched from its socket. He fled howling across the moors to his haunt, bearing with him a mortal wound.

On the day after the exploit Hrothgar and Wealhtheow, his queen, entertain Beowulf. He receives gifts. Unferth, who had floutingly twitted him at the preliminary entertainment with defeat in the swimming match against Breca, is now silent and respectful. That night Grendel's mother, whose existence seems only to have been known of by report, comes to avenge her son, and carries off Æschere, the chief of the king's thanes, who had now re-occupied their hall. The hero desires to complete his task as deliverer, and is taken to the nickers' pool by the sea. He dives down into it, and, after much descending, reaches the bottom, where the wolfish mere-wife seizes and drags him into a cavern free from water. There, in the presence of the dead Grendel, a fight takes place and Beowulf is hard put to it. His sword makes no impression on the monster ; he flings it away and attempts to throw her, but is himself thrown, and almost stabbed through his byrnie. He manages to regain his feet, and discerns a sword in the cave, with which he kills his opponent. He rejoins his companions, taking with him Grendel's head, which he had cut off with the sword, and the sword-hilt, for the blade had melted through the effect of the hag's venom. Hrothgar praises and feasts the hero, who departs next morning for Hygelac's realm laden with gifts. Hygelac and his wife Hygd welcome him on his return. He receives estate, and position, and becomes the first thane of the realm.

Hygelac fell in the battle with the Hetware in West Friesland. Beowulf accompanied him, and avenged his death by the slaughter of many, killing Dæghrefn by the hug of his mighty arms. He was the only survivor on his side, and escaped capture by swimming. He acted as guardian of his uncle's child Heardred, and, on his being slain in battle, was chosen king, and reigned for fifty years. He met his death while trying to slay a fire-dragon that had frightened his subjects and devastated their property. His sword hit on bone and failed to wound the dragon, and it was only with Wiglaf's help that he was able to despatch the monster. He received in the fight a fatal hurt from its poisonous fangs. The ten accompanying thanes basely abstained from rendering assistance during the fight.

Beowulf was buried on Whalesness, as he himself had directed. His death cast a gloom over Gothland. The poet, by the mouth of one of his characters, grimly says that, as a result of the hero's removal, the time is approaching when 'the dark raven, in converse with the eagle, will boast of the feast he enjoyed in the company of the wolf.' The Beowulf, who fought by the side of the historic Chochilaicus, is himself historic, and was beyond doubt a warrior of exceptional worth.

The attractiveness of the poem

Apart from the charm of Beowulf's personality, the attractiveness of the poem rests on a certain multifariousness. It is the variety that pleases the discerning reader, the promise of fulness of fare in fact and character, the suggestions of legend and history, of turbulence in high places, of grandeur and royalty. There is an abundance of men and women in the poem, in real acting attitude, if not in activity. The style of the poet also counts for something in the pleasure produced, the strong style that carries us away, which may be to some extent the fashion of a school, or a national peculiarity, but at any rate comes naturally from our poet, and is really an effect due to the dignity of the thought and the simple power of the language that is its adornment. At times, indeed, as we approach the crises of the story, we feel an expectant hush in our minds.

Let it be that the scope of the poem is too narrow, though this statement needs qualification, that the range of poetic sympathy is not comprehensive enough, that the poetic power does not take us by storm, or surprise and win us into delight—defects which are due to the time, to its literary rudimentariness: still there is in the poem a proud and conscious pomp of style, a sense of story and an animation of endeavour that belong to epic work as such.

Our interest in the poem is quickened by the strong tragic cast that colours it. Arrogance (ὕβρις) is the sin that besets men of princely and noble estate when prosperous. Many such fall before this sin, most are broken by it, but Beowulf is not to be spoiled by success, or inflated by victory into neglect of duty and forgetfulness of destiny. He, the master of prowess and the favourite of fame, disowns arrogance and comports himself discreetly. The tolerant and unvexed melancholy of the poem's morality—the shadow projected by Wyrd—is taking. It is not contumacious striving that carries us happily whither we must go, but endurance, and sober and sturdy well-doing. Beowulf triumphed over arrogant inclining, and passed to the praise for which he had yearned.

The scenery

The nature of the poem is northern nature. She bears herself, on the whole, grimly. On land, she shows mist-covered moor, dark woods, mountain streams, and spirit-haunted background; on water, the tumbling sea, tossing ships, wind-swept headlands, and sea-pools of evil name. But she wears kindly aspects too. We have both aspects in this :—

Holm storme wēol,
Won with winde ; winter ȳthe beléac
Is-gebinde, oth thæt ōther cōm
Gēar in geardas, swā nū gyt dēth,
Thā the syngales sēle bewitiath

Wuldor-torhtan weder. Thā wæs winter scacen,
Fæger foldan bearm; fundode wrecca,
Gist of geardum.*

B. 1131.

And this has quite the joy of an epic morn :—

Gæst inne swæf,
Oth thæt hrefn blaca heofones wynne
Blīth-heort bodode.†

B. 1800.

The men of whom the following was written must have had a delight in the sea that was the reflex of their delight in their ship, must have felt the fascination of the element :—

Gewāt thā ofer wæg-holm winde gefȳsed
Flota fāmi-heals fugle gelīcost.‡

B. 217.

The royal township, stately enough to be called *hord-burh*, was belted about with lone land, and fen, and the sea.

The world of the poem

There was enough social life to produce private feuds and the need for strong government, enough wealth to necessitate the repelling of marauders, and enough oppression to require the redress of grievances. But adventure was the salt of the life of the men of these days. They were active; their needs were physical. Their preferred course of enjoyment was a sea voyage, a fight, and the mead cup. With these, and the sleep that fitted them for a renewal

* The sea heaved with storm, wrestled with wind; winter locked the waves in bonds of ice, till that another year came upon dwellings, as now it still doth, even the gloriously bright weather that always keeps to its season. Then was winter gone, the bosom of earth was fair; the wanderer made forth, the guest left dwellings.

† The guest slept within, till the black raven blithe-heartedly announced heaven's winsomeness.

‡ Then went over the billowy sea, sped by the wind, the foamy-necked ship, just like a bird.

of the triple course, they fleeted time pleasantly. Old age was not the crown of glory of life, but the quencher of real joy, and a time of sad reminiscence. It is said of Hrothgar :—

> Thæt wæs ān cyning
> Æghwæs orleahtre, oth thæt hine yldo benam
> Mægenes wynnum, sē the oft manegum scōd. *
> B. 1885.

The king was the rewarder of warrior-thanes, and the shepherd of his people. The men were wild in their fighting, and obstreperous in their joys. They meant to climb to glory by duty and daring, and their pleasures were the pauses between two actions. Their chief enjoyment was as aforesaid, but they took pleasure in decorated armour, or trophy, or heirloom, and their halls were adorned with barbaric tapestry and gold. Altogether, this life was not a bad one for the evolution of character and the teaching of aspiration.

The characters

We have a wonderful variety of characters in the Beowulf. There is certainly not much action for the display of personality, but the sketches of the actors in their recorded activity are distinctive and powerful. We have king Hrothgar of bygone might, now broken and didactic ; king Hygelac, warrior, conqueror, and defeated invader, a prominent figure in the history of his time ; loyal Wiglaf; and jeering, but not ungenerous Unferth. Outside of the main action appear vengeful Ingeld, and gloomy Heremod wandering, like Bellerophon, away from the haunts of men. We have these and other names of old renown. Among women there are the stately Wealhtheow, the young and wifely Hygd, and apart, in glimpse, moody Thrytho and golden Freawaru. Lastly, we have Beowulf, of strong gentleness and conquering gravity, of

* That was a king altogether blameless, till that age deprived him of joy in his strength, which hath often scathed many.

invincible manhood, physical and moral, the friend of men, the master, if also the servitor of Wyrd.

Beowulf

The poem has an opening that is not tame, or merely narrative. On the contrary, it is fine, mystic, just the sort of opening that a court-scop would favour as a means of glorifying the ancestry of kings, but the hero of the poem has no formal introduction. There is no special exordium for him. In the account of Hrothgar's trouble, it is simply said that Hygelac's thane, hearing thereof, set sail on a voyage of deliverance.

After the bit of old legend about Scyld, and Beowulf (Beowa), the first of the name, the principal character is abruptly introduced. In this legend is set down a genealogy for Hrothgar, and in it, also, is revealed to us the connection that had been established between the historical and the mythical Beowulf. Our Beowulf was a historical person. There is no doubt of that. He has too much sanity, too much life-like reality, to have been a myth or a mere poetic creation. His double of the poem has been made to appropriate the feats of a legendary king, but there is nothing impossible, still less absurd, in the things appropriated. For the existence of the monsters killed was an article of belief in the hero's days, and perhaps in the poet's. What more natural than that a hero of great strength should be thought capable of destroying everyday plagues. So that the story of the first English epic is not the strange story of a goblin-queller or serpent-slayer that has put on epic externals, but the intelligible account of an activity that was credible to its own age and to many subsequent ones. The tinge of the wonderful that we discern in the narration is the imaginative tinting that we give to matter of faith.

King Hrothgar had for twelve years suffered dire mischief by act of Grendel. His kingdom had been ravaged, his thanes murdered, and his glorious hall defiled. Gleemen had carried the news of Hrothgar's hurts and desperate needs to neighbouring courts. As a mere item in the detail we are informed of Beowulf's resolution. Its quickness is the earnest of the quick action of the poem. He heard, he pondered, he sailed. The perilous nature of the undertaking is hinted at. It was such an undertaking as no one cared to engage in, yet, with Beowulf as leader, fourteen chosen champions were willing to share its perils. The simplicity of the introduction is its most effective setting.

Our interest in Beowulf is not a little enhanced by the reception he meets with from the Danish coast-warden. Beowulf's features commanded attention, and produced confidence. His figure was of heroic mould. His war byrnie sat on him right royally, he was no lay figure in armour, but in port and in station a Goth of Goths.

The trait that most attracts our attention in the hero is his courtesy. Before leading the expedition against Grendel, his period of self-assertiveness had practically passed. He had just turned manhood, his strength was thrice the strength of ten. Once we see this quality of self-assertiveness prominently stirred into activity by Unferth's flouts. But the inevitable brag of northern heroes is not so marked in Beowulf, and what of it there is, is so dashed with courtly bearing and courteous speech, that it assumes the guise of lofty self-appreciation or mere poetic mannerism. Under ordinary conditions he can talk quite calmly and modestly. Witness the brief and purposeful statement to Wealhtheow of his resolve to conquer or die. The quest of honour and a sad sincerity modified and mellowed his braggadocio.

Daring is a characteristic of Beowulf. The man who dared the fight against Grendel, and who kept to his daring through all the preliminaries right into the wakeful watch for the monster, the hero of that stalwart struggle in Heorot, and of that deadly wrestling and that saving stroke in the eerie light of the submarine cave, the all-but-vanquished victor over the fire-spitting dragon, has, as regards daring, satisfied all requirements.

We cannot but admire Beowulf's loyalty. Its largeness is chivalrous, disciplined, prescient, and religious. At a time when few would have scrupled to use violence or even murder to gain a throne, he refused this dignity when it was freely offered, and elected to stand by his royal master's boyish son.

If one is inclined to compare Beowulf with other epic heroes, it is to be remembered that epics are properly comparable only in wholes, and that in placing one character beside another, it is not so much a question of character *versus* character, as of character with surroundings *versus* character with surroundings. In the Beowulf there is but one protagonist, if I may so speak, the poem being really a heroic biography with epic tone ; in the Iliad and other epics we have many active heroes on a big canvas, and consequently more material for defining a hero's functional and actual position in his epic. In comparing the Beowulf with the Iliad, we ought not, or ought not first, to compare character with character, say, Hygelac's thane with Peleus' son, but poem with poem. The legitimateness and accuracy of the former mode of comparison depend directly on the width and care with which the latter mode is pursued.

The poet's last reference to his hero is impressive. He is said to have been meek, kindly, and covetous of praise. The huge balefire on Hronesness long leaped and loudly crackled round the dead warrior ; the roving viking looked towards the mound on the headland, and, as he looked, remembered. This was all the immortality Beowulf himself dreamt of. But Wyrd had something greater in reserve. She found for him a *vates sacer*, whose last words are the hero's fittest eulogy.

The characterisation makes on us the same impression that the whole poem does, namely, that of power and ability to paint, strong in their presence, and, more so, in their potentiality. Many of the attachments of the story are undeveloped, and their presence in it at all proves the eye for effect the poet had, and proclaims his fine epic consciousness. Some of the episodes, if they had been wrought out, would have surpassed the main story in the virtue of sequence, and rivalled it in intensity. For example, we might have been told more of Ecgtheow, and more use might have been made of Ongentheow and Swedish relations generally. Much might have been made of Hygelac's expedition against the Hetware. The episode of Hnæf might have been more ordered, and that of Ingeld, son of Froda and husband of Freawaru, might have been expanded with effect. This extension of the reference of the poem would, I daresay, have meant the spoiling of the biographical story of the hero-deliverer.

The undeveloped reference of the poem

It is the biographical aspect of the Beowulf that gives the poem unity, the biographico-heroic, I might call it, which brings a man before us in prominent events, with retrospects, and only leaves him when he is dismissed into the unseen. The narrative heroic, the usual type, and the better, certainly, proceeds differently. It dismisses a man at the end of a transaction that may, or may not, coincide with the end of his life.

It is not my business, in writing of this poem, to deal with groups of lays or strata of story. I believe that the poet, poet-redactor we can call him, who gave shape and consistence to the whole, and it cannot be denied that one man's hand is visible throughout, is entitled to the credit of authorship. He has such credit as belongs to a constructive poet with certainly a modicum of the power and insight that

Its poetic author

enable a dramatist to compose, out of materials that lie to hand, a play showing originality of touch and plot-forming grasp of events, or that enable a cyclic poet of ability to invest with form, and meaning, and sequence, the legend he has under treatment.

Its antiqueness

The poem makes on one an impression of great antiqueness. Those who seek degrees of antiqueness will never, I think, reach a result that will affect our appreciation of the epic, or destroy our sense of its unity. The man or men who inserted the christian refrains, for I do not see that any christianiser altered the scope and purpose of the ancient poem, took advantage of its elegiac cast to make it more lesson-giving—I think it was always gnomic—than its great poetic shaper left it, who may have had a speaking acquaintance with Christianity, but only that, or he would have conserved less of its ancient spirit.

Paradise Lost: a literary epic

Paradise Lost belongs to the class of literary epics. The author of an epic of this class aims at interesting a reader with material of his own choosing. In doing this he is sure to have a manner proper to himself, but may also essay more or less the traditional epic manner. From him we shall have matter—that has been moulded and embellished to suit his fancy—presented in the fashion prescribed by his own literary individuality, and coloured, as indeed this individuality implies, by national modes of thinking. Personality, embellishing, and in some degree moulding, we find in Milton, but national colouring is from the nature of the subject absent.

In this class of subject we have to examine the suitability of the subject chosen. Does such and such a subject present facilities for epical treatment? Of course, to a large extent, this depends on the genius of the chooser. All the same, there are some themes that lend themselves more readily than others to such treatment. And, if we can with reason say that a given subject has, with a certain poet, in quite a wonderful way put on epical dimension, form, and beauty, what do we but nobly compliment the producer of such an unlooked-for result?

The difficulties of its subject

No one will care to deny that Milton has handled his chosen theme epically, and yet, were we for the moment to dismiss from our mind Milton's successful accomplishment of a hard task, could we, even in the case of a gifted poet, think of success as a thing likely to be again reached in such an undertaking? It may be said that the age of epic poets is past. But could any other dead poet of the epical past have secured success with such a subject? Milton had need of inventive skill to give epical largeness to his story. The full argument has inherent magnificence, but it needed opulent handling and much illustration to assume reality and grandeur as a narrative. It is all very well to say that the poet of Paradise Lost had the noblest of subjects, and that he has, in virtue of his choice, written the epic of humanity. Of course the theme had in it great possibilities, and we all believe this, now that Milton has evoked and realised them. But he had to overcome difficulties presented by the paucity of persons; he had to use the supernatural not merely as occasional machinery, but as a medium, as his very matter; he had, accepting the usual, in fact, the official statement of the subject of the poem, to convert dogmatic theology into entertaining epos.

The argument as usually received

The story, the fable of the poem, that which Milton proposed to sing of, is, according to the first line of the first book, the disobedience of man and its dire consequences, consequences that demand on the part of the poet a defence of the dealings of Eternal Justice. It is the story of the Fall, as told in Genesis and wrested by theology, that Milton ostensibly takes for his argument. He has added poetical expansion and embellishment. He found a background to the story, and an introduction to the poem in the tradition of the ruin of the rebel angels. He found, with others, a cause for the action of the serpent, and an explanation of its oversubtlety in the possession of the reptile by the greatest of the apostate angels.

Its unepical aspect

The argument as it stands in its sources has a quite unepical aspect. The theology that has gathered round the story of the Fall, and it is hardly bettered by Milton's systematisation, is scarcely the matter that a poet filled by the afflatus of the epic muse would instinctively choose for treatment in a poem. Nobody but a man self-conscious of power, prophetic of divine illumination, and with a high conception of the didactic functions of himself as poet, would have chosen this theme with its entanglements as the subject of an epic poem. There had been, it is true, a good deal of literary skirmishing about the theme or parts of it before and near Milton's day, the results of which he may have used in some way or other. For a time Milton had thought of a national subject, and had been much taken with the Arthurian legend, but, recognising either his own inability to create an epic out of these materials, or, and perhaps the puritan overpowered the poet, its unsuitability for his purpose, he at length chose the theme he has so adorned. It is worth while noticing that the poet who, in our day, has been fascinated by the epic potentialities of the same legend did not venture to call his poem on that subject an epic. There can be little doubt that Milton, at the period of his late choice, would have but indifferently succeeded in writing an Arthurian epic. I am not so sure, with all deference to those who appear to think otherwise, that the youthful Milton could not have given us an engaging and successful epic of Arthur.

Its theology

It is the narrow, the irrational character of the theology found in the epic that spoils it for literary treatment, since there is no reason why a theology that speaks of divine justice and mercy without expounding and without justification, if the term 'theology' has such application, should not have a literary and therefore narrative value. If we take the bare facts of the story and consider them detached from Milton's setting and embellishment we are struck by their poetical jejuneness. The relations in the poem between God and man are morally unsatisfactory, and, from a literary point of view, unlovely. In all except those wedded to authority in religious matters they excite a puzzled wonder passing into incredulity. Why should deity have put man on such a probation, and enjoined such an intellectual obedience? And why should disobedience to such an injunction be called sin? Surely not on account of the comminatory wording. There really is some moral force in Eve's justification of her impending action. Had Adam and Eve, before their fall, not the possession of that intellectual being and those thoughts that wander through eternity that Belial and the fallen angels retained after theirs? The poet and his contemporaries doubtless believed—certain doctrinal peculiarities of Milton excepted—the presentation of theology we meet with in the poem. This belief, if they took the poem to be a theological epic, removed many of the difficulties we feel, and prevented the uprise of sensations of incongruousness.

Nobody is troubled with doubts about the quality of the arguments of the other epics. Does any one ask why Achilles was angry, why Æneas sought out the ancient mother, why Godfrey went crusading, why Vasco da Gama sailed to India, why Roland flouted Ganelon, why Kriemhild nursed wrath against Hagen? No. And why? Because we have here either consistent incident, or historic fact, or sane legend. The inconsistent and the irrational are not fit subjects of literary art. In a poem written on epical lines, even theology of the highest order of sanity, if presented as doctrine, would have a marring effect.

After all, it is so set down in the sources, one may say, and Milton believed what he found in them, and there the matter ends. But the facts are not set down there as theology, and, in any case, if we are introduced into the region of omniscience and impeccability, we are naturally expectant of a surrounding rationally and righteously ordered. And I do not see how we can lose sight of the defects of a theological argument by reflection on the grand issues involved in the action and on the representative character of the actors engaged. "Before us," we are supposed to say, "is being unrolled the epic of humanity." This is magniloquent, but misleading. It is an attempt to transfer our admiration of the glorified argument of the poem to a strict theological aspect of the argument of the sources.

The quantity of the received argument

It is not only the quality of Milton's argument—in his own and the usual statement of it—that is defective from an epical point of view, but its quantity also is too meagre. The actors are few in number, and the direct action is too monotonous and occupies too short a time. In speaking of action I am thinking of the action of the Iliad and the Æneid, and certainly the so-called direct action in the Paradise Lost is poor in incident and colour when compared with what may be fairly called the direct action of these epics. We cannot, however, say that the direct action of modern epics like the Jerusalem Delivered and the Lusiads is particularly lengthy and varied, the one a short siege of Jerusalem, the other a voyage to India. The action in Milton's poem is too much concentrated, not that concentration in itself is necessarily faulty, but this concentration, it is said, is round two persons in an unchanging position. The action of the Odyssey is very much concentrated round one person, but what a variety of incident we have, what a movement, what a prodigality of personages.

The episodes of the Iliad and of the Æneid are connected with the action. Tasso's episodes are connected with the action, in the sense that they narrate incidents contemporaneous with the main incident, although they have an excrescent and manufactured character. The episodes in the Lusiads are neither contemporaneous in incident with the main action, such as it is, nor directly concerned with it. They have no connection with the actors even, but are bits of national pageantry that from excess of the historic imagination rise before the minds of the chief actors whenever possible listeners are present. The episodes of Paradise Lost belong to the past and the future of the direct action, that is, what is usually assumed to be such, and are deftly fitted in by the poet as completing parts of a story that, owing to dramatic narrowness, needs attachment to the past and the future to produce the sensation of continuity. No epic action, it is said, ever stood so much in need of the introduction of episodes as did that of our poem, and the cast and scope of the story is particularly favourable to their introduction. The argument of the epic has this peculiarity that, though the direct action covers very little time, the implied action, as it is called, began before Time began and only ends with the end of Time.

I cannot think that it will ever come to pass that we

shall be so unsympathetic towards Milton's poem as to be unable to adapt ourselves mentally to its theology, and thus to some extent to lose sensibility to its attractiveness. Pattison puts things much too strongly when he says that in two centuries, at the present rate of disappearance of dogmatic belief, 'the possibility of epic illusion will be lost to the whole scheme and economy of the poem.' Firstly, I believe and shall proceed to show that our admiration of the poem is almost independent of its theology, and secondly, though it were not, I think that the excellence of the poem, the enduring joy with which we are infused by contact with its beauties, will never permit such a result.

The attractiveness of Paradise Lost will endure in spite of its theology, is, in fact, independent of it

In the foregoing remarks I have put down the argument as usually received, as formulated in fact by Milton. I have patronised a usual line of criticism, justified by a literal acceptance of the poet's declaration, and always valid, in so far as it was unconsciously that the poet's didactic impulse was overruled by his epical sense, and in so far as the admixture of theology will always have a blurring effect on our conception of the story, whether we view it from the literary or the religious standpoint. The usual statement of the argument, if strictly interpreted, makes all those parts of the poem that do not immediately concern the erring pair to be episodic. The criticism that acquiesces in the statement, by its tenor, admits this. It evidently considers the extra matter partly as prologue to be accepted for its philosophy, partly as padding to be welcomed for its poetry. It is an alarming manufacture of the episodic that we witness, and it ought to make us look to our preliminaries. We may speak of direct action and implied action, of main action and subsidiary action, but

The usual statement of the argument makes too much of the poem episodic

implied or subsidiary action must practically mean episode, or we make an epic poem to have two actions, which is absurd.

According to the accepted definition of the argument the whole of the first and sixth books, more than three hundred lines of the second—in truth the whole of the second is more tied to diabolic than to human beings—and fifth, are episode. The energy of the angels and their leader is indeed the most impressive energy of the epic. The doings of Satan and his compeers are too important to be only auxiliar to the understanding of human disobedience. They, or their representative, partake in the commonly accepted action after a certain date as indispensable actors, but why has not their previous activity the same indispensability? The two activities are in sequence, indeed, in causal relation. If the action gather round our first parents, if they stand in it in a way as its centre, it is as Troy-town stood amid the surging tides of the immortal fray, as a prominent feature of the epic landscape, or, owing to the character of Milton's epic, as more, as the one human spot in the supernatural domain.

The ostensible and the real argument

There must be a synthesis that will reconcile and unify the ostensible and the real argument. The question is, Did Milton the poet confine himself to the argument set down by Milton the puritan? I say he did not. Do the major and minor, the direct and indirect, of the proem—I am referring to facts, as well as to characters, and mainly to facts—come out in the finished product with the same names? A short examination of the story will prove that they do not, and I think that unbiassed inspection, a little secular spirit, and an acquaintance with story-building, will discover the truth of this assertion.

There is a backbone of epic story in Milton's poem, and it can be made manifest. The poem is sometimes spoken of as if its manner, and not the story told, made it an epic. It is not the manner only and the grandness of subject that make it epical, but the quite discernible, though sometimes obscured, epic configuration of the argument.

There is one story, one action, in Paradise Lost, permitting of poetical or religious description

To my mind there runs through Paradise Lost one perceptible stream of story; there is in it an argument with a single action, of which the moments are —(*a*) Rebellion; (*b*) Defeat; (*c*) Rally; (*d*) Retaliation; (*e*) Success; (*f*) Final Discomfiture. If the action is to be described in such a way as to define to us the part played in it by human beings, then the three last heads may be said to be—(*d*) Temptation; (*e*) Fall; (*f*) Rescue. But these different namings are simply varieties, caprices of nomenclature, and do not in any way suggest that there are different actions, or that the unity of the one action is infringed, or imperilled. If our poem is looked at as a piece of literature, this, I feel sure, is the correct account of its matter. And this literary interpretation gives the poetical, the real subject, which is The Triumph of God over Satan. In this subject Man may be regarded as the means for the resistance of the angels, as the foil, one might almost say, to set off their activity.

The matter of Paradise Lost is, of course, religious matter, and a classification of its contents under this designation will number these aspects :—(*a*) Disobedience in heaven; (*b*) Punishment; (*c*) Disobedience on earth; (*d*) Woe and Death; (*e*) Salvation and Condemnation, the first for men (treated theologically), the second for angels. These aspects are the moments of the religious consciousness of the poet, which appears in the poem just as man's ordinary consciousness appears in ordinary written work, are these, rather than descriptions of an objective embodiment, and it is the nature of the subject that throws them into relief. They are parallel categories for the naming of matter, or, at best, labellings that tell the character of ingredients that are poetically treated and grouped. Of course Milton appears in the poem not only as an epical and religious poet, but also as an expounder of dogma, and it is this dogmatist, this mystagogue, who is responsible for the antinomy in the argument, and the obscuration of its epical quality. The religious subject of the poem is The Triumph of God over Disobedience. Man in the religious subject is the victim of archangelic malevolence, and has much attention paid to him, but so far as activity is concerned, the fallen angels in the person of Satan, their representative, count for more in it than he.

The real episodic portion of the argument

According to the above view of the fable, its episodic portions are not those that have to do with the rebel angels, but those that relate to Adam and Eve before they came into contact with Satan, and those that relate to the indoctrinating of Adam before and after the Fall. The last-mentioned portions and the theological portions are episodic on any view of the fable. It is somewhat difficult to distinguish between episode and direct action in the Paradise Lost, owing to the author's misapprehension as an individual, but not as a poet, of the really epical parts of his story.

Theological obscurations

The fable of Paradise Lost has a poetical and a religious side, and may be looked at from either. It was the exaggeration of a feature of the religious aspect of the argument, namely, the doctrinal notion that man's salvation within the limits of legality is the chief concern of Omniscience,—which must always be an obtrusive and unworkable ingredient in an epico-religious story, and I speak merely as a critic of story—and his high conception of his function as a teacher-poet that led Milton to conceive of his argument as man's disobedience, its cause and cure. A religious subject can be treated as story without having religion as dogma thrown into relief, which is so thrown into relief when a poet becomes expounder and apologist instead of narrator. There are two dislocating forces in the telling of the story of the epic, namely, dogmatic theology, and the theological aspect of the relations between God and man. The first is responsible for the theological interludes, the second for the too lengthy account of post-Adamic history, and the exposition of the facts of the Mosaic and Christian dispensations, as also for the title, which, however large and capturing as a designation, does not accurately describe the contents as epical matter.

The amplification of incident in the poem

In that part of his amplification which multiplies incident, Milton has been successful. Even the much discussed and somewhat rhyparographic allegory of Sin and Death presents aspects that forbid an unreserved condemnation of its introduction. The description of the skill in the pontifical art displayed by Sin and Death in the tenth book, where they are said to have bridged the tract of chaos between hell and earth, shows that Milton had carefully thought out the allegory, and meant it to be something more than a mere parabolic phantasy. He meant it as a serious, though figurative (in this case the only possible) account of the origin of evil. This evil, owing to its anteriority in time and the expansiveness of its nature, was the predisposing, if not the proximate cause of the fall of man, and therefore demanded attention in Milton's argument. It really is the moral side of that story of which the defeat and rout of the apostate angels is the physical side.

The Limbo of Vanities, the abode of those who have been duped by the dear delusions of earth, is a pure imaginative excess, a serio-comic and conscious extravaganza, full of Miltonic pomp, not germane to the subject, and foisted in for purposes of show.

Not so fanciful and unsuitable is the raising of Chaos into a kingdom and the enthronement of the Anarch old. For one thing, the vast spaces of the subcelestial region become hereby more real and more imaginatively striking than if they had been coldly denominated dimensionless, and the reader left to imagine immensity after his own fashion. Again, the peopling that vivifies Chaos, the ascription to it of a sensation of the thundering onset of Messiah's angels, and of a desire to regain the portion stolen from it by the creation of an ordered universe, such things as these bring into interrelation the various regions of space, and prevent Heaven, Hell, Chaos, and Earth from being thought of as so many isolated spots situated somewhere in infinitude. Earth groaned and trembled over our first parents' sin against heaven, and Chaos was in travail over the wild descent from heaven of the bands of the traitor angel.

The supplying and delineation of characters

The amplification that helps to multiply characters has not been so successful. It is not so easy a thing in the kind of action we find in Paradise Lost to exhibit variety in characterisation. The bad angels are the best-drawn characters in the poem, and this is the case because they are also the most active. Beings in motion are always more interesting than beings at rest. In fact, motion is the condition of variety. This is why the good angels are most interesting when they are stirred into activity by the activity of the rebellious angels. Milton's identification of the fallen angels with the heathen gods enables him to impart to them a distinct individuality. This individuality owes its distinctness to local colouring, and to the employment of legendary lore and biblical reminiscence. Besides, viciousness and variety have a strong bond of association. There is more room for versatility along the broad road of vicious meandering than on the narrow path of virtuous rectitude. Goodness in men is often, from the point of view of picturesqueness, uninteresting. And, if this is so in men, where it may be conjoined with a measure of activity, what must this quality appear in angels, whose modes of activity we cannot very well realise, far less depict? Contemplative and reverential beatitude has not, or, at all events, does not exhibit to our human sense, distinctive traits.

I cannot, however, say that I find the good angels so uninteresting as they are usually said to be. True, they are overshadowed by Paternal Deity and Filial Godhead, and their individuality is made blank, and, in a manner, effaced. Their condition is one of pure passiveness and obedient receptivity. They are all this, no doubt with reason, but, in virtue of being this, they differ much, and to their disadvantage, from the wicked angels. Still the functions and qualities of the prominent angels are striking enough to throw into relief a difference in character. We have Abdiel, the faithful among the faithless; Uriel, regent of the Sun; Raphael, the sociable spirit; Michael, prince of the celestial armies; and Gabriel, chief of the angelic guards—all definitely typical entities.

When Milton essayed the description of certain phases and actions of Godhead, the cast of the poem and the nature of his theology forced him to make Deity argumentative and assertive. A permitting and, at the same time, punishing Divine Power is bound to indulge in one-sided and apologetic ratiocination. An Almighty who at one time lays the reins on the neck, and at another draws them tight, and who does the one in order to have an occasion of doing the other, constitutes an antinomy that necessitates a little unravelling and justification on the part of that Almighty. Apart from any special theology, the character of Deity in the poem is godlike and ennobling, and his doings large and beneficent. The vicegerent son represents the terrible of his sire when he chariots and fulmines over the empyrean, and the tender when he descends to the garden and clothes human abasement in divine pity.

Milton chose his subject advisedly, and in spite of its difficulties. He has supplied such amplification as no one could have better supplied, and this amplification harmonises with the original matter by reason of correctness of choice and unity of treatment. No subject promised to Milton in such combination and such force, the true, the sublime, and the universal, no subject was so adapted to the purpose of a poet-prophet.

Milton's metre

One of the chief charms of Paradise Lost is to be found in its stately poetry. The metre of the poem has for its main characteristic an organ-toned sonority of plenary volume and haunting echo. This is to describe the metre to the outer ear, to the inner ear it sounds like sublimity set to music, to the music of the spheres. The verse makes an onward flow till all is submerged in harmony, then there is a momentary dipping-down of the front tide, and anon the refluence is checked by an advancing billow of noble sound that reharmonises and attunes all the wavy element. And this is not all. When one reads aloud Milton's typical harmonies and pauses at the stopping-places, what is a common experience? Why, the music continues. It sings on in the ears, it undulates harmoniously along the air, and dies away in a euthanasy of sound. Such is the power of Milton's poetry that by virtue of its lofty and capturing resonance we are lifted out of ourselves and rapt into a very heaven of harmony. We become for the moment potential poets. And the rhythm does not come in snatches of sound of comparatively brief duration, but it comes in masses, it flows in swells, it forms symphonies. Nor is the music of the verse wholly dependent on the matter, for Milton can touch with grandeur things that are common, he can charge with noble sound matter that, in other hands, would at best become a tinkling triviality. Some poets are said to have lisped in numbers, but Milton, a better endowment, thought in harmonies. Words that one would have thought untunable are by him made to trip along in melodious fellowship. Milton had 'learned the secret power of harmony.'

The tamer portions of the poem

I do not understand how some can say that smiles and yawns are the inevitable accompaniment of the perusal of certain portions of Paradise Lost. Why, the mere salt of Milton's style imparts to the tamer portion of his subject a savour that would even season twaddle, and no one, I think, has yet ventured so to describe any part of the poem. Can we conceive of any one who could invest with such tuneful dignity the prosy matter with which the poet had sometimes to deal?

Its allusiveness

A characteristic of Milton's style is its allusiveness. Much of the poem is in flower with the charm of literary reminiscence. The high art that enables a poet to import this charm to his matter is to be coveted. Literary power is the power to please, and he who can please not only by his own creation and its proper dress, but, over and above, by a suggestive diction that recalls to our minds the pleasures that are associated with books, times, and places, enhances in a singular way the effect of the result he specially aims at producing. And Milton, who, if anything, was an original genius, was none the less able to recreate by verbal imagery dead delights that are buried in the memory. Allusiveness has its dangers, and Milton has not always shunned the pedantic and the incongruous.

The reader of Paradise Lost is most impressed by those parts of the poem that describe the ruin and the deliberations of the fallen angels, the battle in the empyrean, the creation of the world, and the course and climax of the temptation.

The most impressive portion of the poem

It is in these that Milton displays conspicuously his imaginative constructiveness, his vigorous thought, his poetic vision, and his dramatic insight. The picture of the condition and actions of the arch-rebel and his following imprints itself indelibly on the memory. Satan sums up in himself the past, the present, and the future of the fallen powers. At one time he displays the less lovable qualities of dogged determination, and dominant egotism degenerating into blatant pride. At another his striking and all-powerful influence over his peers suggests previous manifestations of affectionate interest as well as superior mind. What lights and shadows his own energising presents—the light of his tears, of his semi-penitential sadness, of his half-instinctive and half-involuntary admiration of innocence; the shadow of his hopeless ruin, of his desperate denials of all virtuous influence, of his awful and inevitable access of criminality.

The description of the preliminaries, of the progress, and of the circumstances of the battle in the empyrean is worthy of the epic poet and his art. It is a narrative strong in its situations, in its actors, and in its acts. The flight to the North, the insinuating address of Satan, the at first pleading and then defiant defection of Abdiel, carry us on in expectant mood to the coming conflict. The battle-morn in colours of empyreal gold introduces us to the successive scenes of that momentous day—the massing of the mighty quadrate of celestial warriors, its swift and straight passage through space, the battailous aspect of the horizon bounded by the distant host of rebels, the initial encounter between Abdiel and Satan on the rough edge of battle, the fierce hosting of the adverse ranks, the homeric duels of the chief combatants, Satan ranging victorious through the ranks of the seraphim, and Michael brandishing his wide-wasting sword.

In the first day's strife Satan's pride was humbled by Michael's sharing blow, and his army taught meaner thoughts in their rout. Michael and his angels remained as masters on the foughten field. Milton's imagination rather runs riot in the description of the second day's fighting. The rebel artillery was silenced by the superimposition of the seated hills, and whole legions of rebels were buried under main promontories. On the third day Messiah militant drove his chariot across the empyrean, thundering amain, and the Satanic host, forgetting how to resist, were driven in bestial terror to the limits of heaven and shot over its crystal battlements, heaven ruining from heaven adown the deep descent of hell.

It is not surprising that there should be doubt as to Milton's conception of the part allotted to Satan in this epic of varied aspect and real duality of authorship. Milton would certainly never have advisedly chosen this being as the hero of the poem. To attribute such an intention to Milton is to falsify the whole history and theory of the poet's choice of a subject. I should not even care to say that he slipped unawares into such a frame of mind as would make him take this view of Satan. The term 'epic hero' means something more than a character of outstanding activity, and carries with it associations of straightforwardness, honour, and rectitude relative if not absolute.

Satan

In the theology of the poem—which is inconsistent, and reflects this defect on the presentation—the archfiend is at one time the goad, at another time the tool, and at another time the butt of the deity. His function in its epic action is an organic one. He is, in a measure, what Sainte Beuve would call the *cheville ouvrière* of the action, as Juno was of that of the Æneid, but he is also a doer of deeds, as well as the mainspring of the action and a marplot. The grandeur with which he is invested is due to, among other things, the working of the epical instinct of the poet. A prime character is a desideratum in an epic. The poet, knowing this, and conscious at the same time of the paucity of characters, of whom, too, some are too unsketchable, or too inactive in their parts, to be referred to continuously, concentrated his attention on Satan. We may be sure, too, that Milton discerned all the possibilities of characterisation in the case of this character, and it is just possible that the pity he felt for the estate of the ex-archangel dignified his conception of the same. To say, however, as has been said, that Milton's devil is in morality superior to his God seems to me sheer contradictoriness. It is true that Milton wrote as a poet, though he chose as a puritan, but not to the extent of mistaking villainy for virtue.

After all is said that can be said, and it is much, of Satan's part in the poem, we have to remember that in him Milton sketched a being whose rapid and self-inflicted moral declension is most marked. We feel that some excuse may possibly be made for his rebellion against the tyrannical nepotism of the father, and, even after the hideous ruin that overtook his daring defiance of Omnipotence, Satan is still a being to be respected. But all this grand assertiveness, prompted by a not altogether unjustifiable pride, declines upon an attack on the puny inhabitants of the newly created earth. True, the inmates of hell were not sure of the status and strength of the beings whom they deemed exposed to successful attack. They knew that they were to be little inferior to the angels. They did not know their numbers. Hearing, too, that they were to be highly favoured, they might easily have inferred that they would not be left to their own resources. To the end Satan was cautious, and even fearful, of a possible encounter with Adam, and this after he had learned the numbers of the human race and its vulnerability. This feeling, however, was probably produced by the debasing and enfeebling effects of evil.

The enterprise against man, then, could not have appeared devoid of danger, even to archangelic daring, and, indeed, hesitancy to undertake it was manifested by the Satanic peers; but Satan's part in the epic, and Milton's suggestive and powerful delineation of this, have so heightened expectation, that a feeling of wonder is provoked over the falling off between his words and his actions. The devil himself seems to have been half-conscious that he was pursuing an undignified course.

When Satan approached the actual inception of his task, he hesitated, and had to reinforce his purpose by high reasons of state and the promptings of private revenge. He was not conscience-smitten, for he parted with his conscience on Mount Niphates; but he experienced the compunctious visitings of a compassionate nature. The means taken to accomplish his end—the parting with the last remnant of nobility that the foul descent into the serpent involved—completes the obscuration of the glory of the ruined archangel. On his reappearance in the garden, after his expulsion by Gabriel, the devil has no compunctions, but is dominated by envy and spite. For a moment, and for the last time, the sight of Eve's attractive grace bereft him of hate, and staggered his hellish purpose.

How can Satan be the hero of the epic, a being whose deterioration is so swift and so progressively ugly all the poem through? When he raised himself from off the pool he was heroic, and possessed of a modicum of unselfishness. He wrestled through space on a voyage of discovery. He sought the New World. His purpose hardened as his knowledge of the World and Man became more definite, and it hardened in the direction of evil. The tempestuous struggle on Mount Niphates, induced by his solitary retrospect, was an important stage in Satan's moral declension. "Evil be thou my good," he said, and forthwith he was self-consecrated to obdurate impenitence. Dogged resistance and lofty opposition gave place to spiteful annoyance and contemptible trickery. The opponent of Deity—leaving out of view the necessities of the story—condescended to notice, and was base enough to inveigle, innocent frail man. His physical aspect took after his changing moral nature. The angel of the intrenched scars could don the aspect of an angel of light before Uriel. The angel of that sinful resolve on Mount Niphates, whatever of 'regal port, but faded splendour wan' his proper person might retain, could afterwards effect no higher metamorphosis than that which made him into a toad or a serpent. In his first speech in hell Satan wept over his comrades, but gradually came to think that they existed to do him reverence.

If Satan had been the hero of the poem, it would have ended with the tenth book. Those who make Messiah the hero have a strong case, if Paradise Regained be considered as the complement, or as in any way explanatory of Paradise Lost.

The quest after epic heroes is not always a successful one. For example, Who is the hero of the Nibelungenlied? Is it Siegfried or Hagen? Or is the chief character in this poem a woman, and is she Kriemhild? Can we definitely say who are the respective heroes of the Jerusalem Delivered and the Lusiads?

It is idle to call Paradise Regained an epic. It is obviously not an epic in the sense that the great epic poems of the world are such. The usual externals are absent. It has no action properly so called. Dialogue interspersed with description takes the place of action. There are, for the most part, only two persons placed before us. One baits a proposal with tempting allurements, the other rejects it in language that is now severely dignified, now expansively persuasive, now narrowly biblical, and now curtly denunciatory?

Paradise Regained: it is neither in matter nor in form an epic

There is no other sense in which the poem can be called epical. In form it is simply the denial with reasons annexed of certain requests. Such matter as it has is not set forth storywise, and on being looked into, is found to be mere projected reflexion. The objectivity is fictitious, but, accepted as objectivity and valued at its worth, it presents no full story of sequence and development. This is the argument:—Two persons meet, one in straits; an escape from the straits is offered and rejected. The persons disagree. The one tries to convince the other, but is refuted, which happens several times.

This is a meagre story, and it is, as regards narrative interest, thinly told. Such is what the epical quality of the matter of Paradise Regained comes to, when the poem is put forward as an epic and tested as this. An epic largeness of utterance, and a more than skilful accumulation of allusion, will not convert a duel between clever sophistry, and the pure vision of sinless simplicity into interesting and impersonal narrative of the epic order. The poem describes great issues, but so do many mystery-plays, and yet no one would ever dream of including these among epical products.

It is true that, considered as recording the last effort of Satan's struggle against the Almighty's purposes, the facts of the poem can find a place in an epic action, and form its closing moments. In no other way can the matter of Paradise Regained be made to put on epical quality. Its incidents, stripped of dramatic dress, arranged as narrative, and presented as vision, might conceivably have furnished a better ending to Paradise Lost than the historical, genealogical, theological narration of the twelfth book of that poem. One might, however, as well take the closing scenes of an epic action, say—Odyssey XXII, or Æneid XII, and, after extending the fighting over several days and propping it up with additional circumstance, and supplying a proem and ending, claim separate epic status for the enlargement, as call the dramatic setting and scenic enlargement—for the show of the specular mount imparts spaciousness—of the incidents of the Temptation an epic. Nay, the prior procedure would have the superior justification of being able to point to a narrative of real objectivity.

Its story might furnish a termination to an epic action

In Paradise Regained Milton has given scope and grandeur to the facts of the Temptation, he has adorned it with the glamour of that magnificent style of his, that is all. The original story has few incidents, and Milton could not invent incident without encroaching on ground he had already occupied. Besides, he severely repressed any surviving inclination to poetical dreaming, and set forth his facts in naked simplicity, using only such exhibition and embellishment as would best express and illustrate their intrinsic truth.

In spite of its shortness, there is more of the world as we know it in Paradise Regained than in the great epic.

The characters

As regards the supernatural characters, we are too conscious, I think, of set speech, in the portions of the dialogue delivered by the 'glorious eremite.' The language of an alleged sacred epic ought not to be so much a poetical paraphrase and adaptation of biblical phraseology, however finely the phraseology—its simplicity being only ennobled, not lost—is turned and adapted. The language of Paradise Lost is not biblical. Freshness of language, however, would have needed as a prerequisite fresh incident, and Milton meant to add not one jot or tittle to the biblical text. The Tempter, sophistical, and not that bold spirit who 'attempted the father's throne,' is not really so despicable as when he played the part of 'thief of paradise.' Then he was a betrayer, now he is a sophist. Then he attacked innocence, now he is matched by the divine instrument of his chastisement. A touch of pathos is not wanting in his delineation. Witness

> Though to that gentle brow
> Willingly I could fly.
>
> P. R. iii, 215.

Unless Milton meant this as a feature of the Tempter's wiles. I do not think so. It is somewhat akin to the

> Is there no place
> Left for repentance, none for pardon left?
>
> P. L. iv, 79.

of the Paradise Lost. The devil is made the mouthpiece of some of Milton's finest flights, and borrows, doubtless, a little dignity therefrom.

The Fourth Book

It is fine imaginative play, that of the fourth book, round the names, and all that these connote, of Rome and Athens. What a pen-portrait of Roman topography, pomp, and power! And Athens too. How the city stands out before us! What an evocation of clustering memories! What brilliant heraldic emblazonry!

The Faery Queen is the nearest approach in English

literature to the romantic epos on a large scale. Spenser is the representative of Ariosto in our literature. The two poets are, it is needless to say, separated by most pronounced differences. The most patent difference, involving most of the others, is one of character. Spenser was too serious a man and a poet to produce the matter of the Italian poem, which, however rich in imagination and delightful to read, may not incorrectly be described as mere literary fooling.

Spenser's Faery Queen

The romantic epos is a *genre* by itself, and not every specimen of it has a good or even plausible title to the name epic. On several grounds the Faery Queen cannot be included in the number of genuine epics. The poem has really no story, either in point of strong interest or pervading sequence. This is largely due to the character of the plot. A co-ordination of stories among themselves and a subordination to a main argument are not features likely to help to a narrative strong in situations and of marked development in the manner of the telling. These stories, we know, were not meant to be, as it were, simple beads on a straight wire, but were meant to form by pre-established arrangement the pattern of an argument. This pattern the poet did not exhibit in a completed poem, but only explained it to Raleigh in a prefatory epistle.

It is not only the character of the plot, but its matter, that is inimical to the success of the poem as a narrative. This has too much abstractness. Putting aside its gorgeous colouring and noble poetry, one feels in presence of its characters almost as one would feel in presence of the symbolical personages of a morality-play, half-humanised and not wholly comprehensible as agents. There is an air of unreality about Spenser's poem, and this no one but a fanatical Spenserian will deny. The allegory obtrudes itself to the detriment of the story.

In the first book, certainly, the story is strong enough to make us forget the allegory.

The Faery Queen has been called an allegorical epic. This is a contradiction in terms. Allegory is only a possible ornamentation of an epic poem, and not its natural and abiding dress. Our poem has an indefeasible claim to be considered one of the world's great literary products, but when status is claimed for it as a specimen of epic narrative, it must be judged according to the traditions and rules of such composition.

The poem is not merely an allegory but a didactic allegory. It has lessons to teach, an ethical end to accomplish, to wit, 'the fashioning a gentleman or noble person in virtuous or gentle discipline.' Now, the epic poet is no preacher. He has no rousing message for loiterers in virtue, no theorem in ethics to demonstrate, no vision of the beauty of holiness to set before his readers. This poet tells a story, a story such as his data permit, adorned by traits of humanity, and embellished by art and the thought of his own poetic soul. His characters have had pre-existence, they have had the objectivity of tradition or history. He cannot, then, remake these; any remaking that he engages in must be a process that is pursued on lines cognate to and consistent with tradition or history. To 'justify the ways of God to men' has a didactic ring about it, but the didactic element of Milton's argument is only a concomitant to the universal element. The didactics lie latent in Paradise Lost, and they only lie there at all because the religious and the didactic are supposed to be inseparable.

Ariosto's poem has far more variety than that of Spenser, who holds to his theme, while Ariosto roams, and has really no theme except the amusement of the reader, and variety is needed in the romantic epos, especially if it be of the type that lacks the concentration given by the presence of an overshadowing hero. Neither of the poems can boast of unity and continuity, but Ariosto's has more of these qualities than Spenser's. It has some share of finished-off roundness, and there are a few pivotal points in its narrative. The Italian was also a better story-teller and had more brilliance than the Englishman. He had no such serious strands in the fibre of his nature as had Spenser. He was a better story-teller, not merely by his variety, a variety that can hardly be staled, but by the possession of the worldly qualities of gayness, humour, and lightness. And over all there is the charm of chivalric romance with no ethical intention.

There is an air of reality about Ariosto's chivalry. Its members are human in their virtues, human in their frailties; they are not paragons, now militant, and now lapsing, but conceivable specimens of heroic humanity. Even the wonderful in the Orlando Furioso is so quasi-real as to find the reader in a state of preparedness, while that of the Faery Queen, if it be detachable from a real that exists in the poem, is sensibly factitious, unless to the initiated reader.

Our poem, then, cannot be classed as a specimen of the romantic epos. This species of epic poetry requires a capturing and fairly engrossing story, exhibiting progress and consummation of some sort, and a lightness of touch in the treatment of that story. The poet of the Faery Queen presents to us neither of these requirements. In fact, so far as literary qualities go, he has more affinity to the great epic poets than to the minor poets of the romantic epic. But his work is too stately and unbending to be compared to that of the former, and he really did not look at the life of the world, but at its idealised counterpart in a supramundane region of the imagination. It was a poem celebrating the praise of a full and religious manhood that Spenser wrote.

The poetry of the Faery Queen has got movement and flow. It reveals a rare feeling for beauty, actual and ideal, and a matchless skill in the expression thereof; it sings out a melody of voluptuous sweetness that only cloys as nature cloys, to be desired again and enjoyed anew after a short interval of disuse; but there are two prime defects that prevent it ranking as an epic, in any true sense of the term, and these may be correctly indicated by saying that it has no story and much ethics.

Southey's Roderick

Southey's narrative poem, Roderick, The Last of the Goths, may be brought forward as a specimen of the poet's putative epic handiwork. It is the story of the repentance and atonement of Roderick, the last of the Visigothic kings. Count Julian, a powerful Gothic baron, maddened by the wrong done to his daughter Florinda by the king, joined the Moors with his following. These, largely owing to this accession, were able to defeat the Goths in a great and decisive battle. Roderick disappeared from the field of battle, was thought dead, but, after ten years, convinced of his new mission, returned—his name was now Maccabee—in time to help in the rebellion against the Moors that resulted in the establishment of the kingship of Pelayo, a scion of the royal Gothic house, who had some family connection with the native Spanish race.

Roderick's retired and ascetic life had given him the aspect of an anchorite, and he remained unrecognised save by his mother and his dog Theron, until his purpose of self-effacing service to Spain had been nearly completed. In the battle against the Moors, where his valour was most helpful and contagious, he inadvertently shouted his war-cry, and was generally recognised and enthusiastically greeted, but, after the victory had been won, again disappeared.

M

The story is finely conceived, cleverly spaced, and adorned with much pictorial art. Some of the incidents are exceedingly pathetic. The scene in which Florinda, making the disguised and saint-like Roderick her confessor, incriminates herself and exculpates the king, has a pathos that tugs at the heart-strings.

It is, however, rather a story with a thesis, namely, the purification of the spirit by disaster, than a bit of narrative fitted to give the high pleasure of the animated story-telling called epos. It is a one character story, for, though there are other characters, as many as its limited action requires, and these well-marked, there is too little circumstantiality to give scope for and necessitate their portrayal. The area is too narrow and the action too confined. We have not the broad expanse of epic narrative with its scene-shifting, its variety of incident, and its bustling activity either in suspense or in realisation. There is too much concentration round one fast-approaching *dénouement,* to which the whole action hurriedly marches. The movement is too quick for epic.

The poem appeals to too few sympathies of the reader. An epic hero is a many-sided man, and commands not merely the pity, but the admiration of his observers. The Roderick is too abidingly sombre, and performs the end of tragedy rather than the end of epic. And the grounds for one's interest in the poem rest on too fanciful a basis.

It has too little real outwardness, for the outwardness that is found in it is only a medium for exhibiting the abounding inwardness of the principal character. One feels that the poet works strongly towards the effects of the poem, that these are emotional, in fact, full of tragic fervour, and that they do not occur naturally in an even-running story. I say this with reference to general epic characteristics, for, in its own manner, the story is naturally and facilely told.

The poem is a romantic tale with some strong situations and of great pathos, but not large enough, and, as a consequence, not sufficiently packed with action and actors to merit the name epic. It is too much shot through with the one predominant gloomy tint, and has got nothing like the appearance of the multi-coloured epic poem. Its ending, too, is peculiarly romantic.

As to Southey's other epics, it has to be said that, before a poet can write epic, he must choose a subject that has human interest and human probability, and that permits of an energising that is not foreign to heroic humanity. If a subject has romantic bearings and no human interest, an epic poem is an impossibility.

Joan of Arc displays the defects of historical epics. Besides, the story of the Maid presents too narrow a stage for epic treatment, and too little individual action and predominance to produce the illusion of the heroic.

Tennyson's Idylls of the King

The manner in which the Idylls of the King appeared argues the absence of the qualities that characterise an epic poem. Such a poem has a self-conscious continuity, a through and through treatment, and an artery of passed-on interest that postulate a simultaneous review of its parts as constituents of a completed whole, in other words, an appearance *en bloc*. Even the epic of growth, the epic of lays, had a kernel consisting of a whole formed of parts that had seen the world simultaneously. If one would shrink from calling each of the Idylls a miniature epic, how can the whole of them form an epic poem in any real sense of the term?

The aim of the so-called Tennysonian epic, namely, to 'shadow sense at war with soul,' is such as to justify a presumptive inference as to the non-epical character of the medium of such portraiture. It is not the function of the epopee to record the working-out of moral problems.

The characters of the poem appear in detachments that have no visible united action. We have a sort of solar system of greater and lesser lights, with concentric orbits of large or little compass that do not intersect or touch one another. The chord of connection of the parts has to be supplied in the main by the reader. It is a pattern-weaving business. The pattern can be woven after we have mastered its plan. The characters are certainly real and life-like. They are distinct enough, but the fact that the principal actors do not appear on the scene together and contribute each a different share in a common action lends itself to a certain sameness or monotony in the presentation. They are idealised, no doubt, but a certain amount of idealisation is permitted in an epic poem. It must be practised within certain limits, and, if there are no other violations of the epical rule of procedure, it will do small harm to the poem.

The unity of the Idylls of the King is subjective and intellectual, to be discerned by reflection. Essays in knight-errantry that are at the same time experiments in self-discipline have to be considered in themselves, and in their reference to the group. A dramatic poem has a unity that deploys itself in the plot, and is only fully realised and grasped after that is wrought out. The coherence of an epic poem is not the unity that belongs to the solution of a problem in ethics, but an all-pervading quality that environs us, that we do not seek for, because it is in the atmosphere of the poem.

The aspect of our poem that best confers on it the title to the name epic is that which leads us to call it the story of the life and death of king Arthur. The poem gives the reader the story of king Arthur, if we supply the gaps. He must string the beads, he must piece out the plan. No doubt its parts are speakingly present, they lie before us dovetailed and waiting to be joined, but it is we who effect the junction, and not the poet. An epic poem should secrete, as it were, its own unity, and its poet should supply any linking the story needs.

The epical quality of the Idylls of the King is to be found in its manner—and the adjective marks out only one quality of the exquisite magnificence of this manner—for barring the fact that it is a narrative poem I see in it no other prescriptive epical characteristics. One may, I think, without being called a stickler for conventional and dispensable requisites in this sort of poetry, say that the matter of the poem has neither the arrangement nor the interrelation of the epic poem. The poem is not an epic poem, and Tennyson did not call it such.

Morris's Jason

Such a poem as Mr Morris's Life and Death of Jason is too exclusively romantic to be included, as it is by some, among epics. In it one breathes the very air of romance, and to me its languorous verse sounds like the very dirge of the old epic manner. It has the beauty, the sadness, and the mystery of romanticism. Its ending is romantic, for Jason 'died strangely,' and the story, which commemorates the different stations in a drifting series of adventures, could not have been treated so finely, as it has been, unless from the point of view of romance. Its adventure, its ornament, and its poetisation are more prominent than any character-drawing of individuals.

There really is no pivot in the story of the poem, no centripetal trend of action, no emphatic though long-deferred home-coming to unify and crown a pilgrimage of adventure. The movement is not to a terminus, but shifts from point to point with no causal nexus or progressive realisation. If a poem has the epic manner and the epic machinery, one is almost constrained to call it an epic for form's sake, in spite of deficiencies in the fable. In this case the appellation conveys no compliment. But the Jason needs no commendation beyond the recognition of the thing that it is, namely, a romantic poem of rare sensuous and pensive beauty.

The romantic elements are the strength of the poem. Its progress is not epical, and it has not much of a consummation of any sort. There are present much elaboration and decorative detail. The manner of the telling is too ornate and has too little projecting power to be that of an epic poem. The poem has the scope and breadth of an epic, and it is not an isolated event that it treats romantically, but a considerable grouping of incident. There is a temptation to enrol anything big in the way of narrative and of high literary quality as a claimant for epical honours. Perhaps the epic manner is now outworn, and we slow to admit the fact.

CHAPTER III

THE FRENCH EPIC

CHARLES, King of the Franks, by invitation of a Saracen prince in straits, or for conquest, had made an inroad into Spain and had besieged Spanish towns. Pampeluna he had captured, but before Saragossa he had been foiled. By pact, or by policy, he began a homeward march into France. The main body of the army reached French soil in safety, but the rearguard was attacked by Basques, and massacred in the mountain-passes.

Song of Roland. The historical in the poem

On this occasion was slain, among other prominent warriors, Roland, warden of the marches of Brittany—*Hruodlandus Britannici limitis præfectus*, to quote the words of Eginhard. This is what history has veritably transmitted to us regarding the hero of a thousand tales. This is the historical seed that has so grown, that has so flowered, that has shot up into so many and such rare corymbs, the kernel of fact behind the idealisations of legend, the expansions of story-tellers, and the embellishments of poetic and pious imaginations.

The colouring and amplification of the historical facts

In the Song of Roland the real facts are coloured, added to, and perverted. Not by border tribesmen, it was argued, could such a defeat have been inflicted on the monarch that played the greatest part in early mediæval Christendom. Never would this puissant prince have allowed a defeat of such magnitude to pass by unavenged, and almost unnoticed. It was impossible that soldiers officered by peers of the great Karl should have been hurled down a mountain side, huddled into a narrow space, and massacred to a man. And so a passing foray was converted into a miniature crusade, and the obscure Basques gave place to the mighty Moslems. It would not have suited the poet's plan to have tampered with the tradition of the defeat. He turned the tradition to account. With him the defeat is a defeat only in name. The dying Roland is left in possession of the field.

It was a worse than Pyrrhic victory that the Moslems gained. It was gained by traitor's aid and at awful cost. The emperor's retaliation was terrible. Recalled by the belated blast of Roland's horn—

> Cumpainz Rollanz, l'olifant kar sunez ;
> Si l'orrat Carles, fera l'ost returner —*
> (So vainly advised Olivier) C. de R. 1059.

he rudely routed the troops of Marsil the Moslem king, annihilated the army of his ally, the Emir of Babylon, seized Saragossa, sacked its shrines, forced thousands to abjure their faith, and led Queen Bramimonde into captivity.

The details of the story as magnified, idealised, and embellished by the poet, form a subject worthy of epic song. We have a great theme—the patriotic fight for national honour against fearful odds ; they are worthy foemen—Karl's soldiers and the Saracen paynims. Symmetrical, too, is the action, granting that, in comparison with the action of certain other epics, it is narrow and bald. The poet has been able by setting and circumstance to make his catastrophe epically attrac-

* Comrade Roland, come, sound your horn ; (thus) Charles will hear it, he will make the host return.

tive and satisfying. The nature of this catastrophe perhaps required a sequel containing poetic justice. At any rate one has been supplied.

The poet of the Chanson created out of his materials a noble argument, and he has treated this argument not unworthily. He has power, he has fire, he has pathos, he can enlist the sympathies, fire the feelings, and pierce the hearts of his readers.

The animation of the poet. His battle-pictures

He excels in descriptions of fighting. He paints combats most realistically, and in so doing, displays much epical verisimilitude, in spite of features, which, even from an epical standpoint, are decided exaggerations. Our poet has all a warrior's joy in battle. His verse grows warm over the straight spear-thrust, the strong sword-stab, and the slashing sword-stroke. His heroes inflict fearful wounds; they hack, cut, and strike with elemental vigour; the might of their sword-arm is something titanic. By sheer strength, and weight of vertical down-stroke, Roland could on occasion cut horse and rider in two, beginning from the rider's helmet downwards through the horse's chine, as easily as we can slice a lemon. His battle is a scene of feverish animation. Duel follows duel in rapid succession. Homer devotes a rhapsody to each *aristeia*; in this poem we have several *aristeiai* to less than the space of one rhapsody. It may be thought that, even for a fighting canto, the fighting business is too obtrusive. But no. The circumstances are such that much fighting is a necessity, and the poet has known by bits of character drawing, by picturesque detail, by temporary shifting of scene, and by an occasional brooding note of woe, to forestall tedium. What with smashing of helmets, shattering of shields, and resounding blows on hauberk, metallic thuds on mail, and ringing cries of *Montjoie*, we may form to ourselves a highly coloured sound-picture of the mellay. Olivier cried out :—

> Gente est nostre bataille.*
>
> C. de R. 1274.

It is natural that savagery should have some place in such fighting. We have not, as in Homer, minute anatomical details of the wounding, but precise mention is certainly made of its gruesome effects. The combatants were truculent and their deeds cruel. They dashed out eyes, they spilt brains. There never was such fighting, there never were such fighters, except, perhaps, in that wild *schlachtgetümmel* of blows and blood in Etzel's hall.

His tenderness and patriotism

Were the poet's claim on our appreciation confined to the skilful word-painting of single combats, we should pay him but qualified homage. But he is more than a poet of fighting. He is as tender, chivalrous, and true as his own Roland. From his pages breathes the very spirit of refined and chivalrous patriotism. His patriotism shines through the patriotism of his characters. France is for him '*dulce France*,' '*tere majur*,' and he every now and then invokes for her heaven's protection. He is the poet of feudal loyalty. Over and over again phrases inculcating on vassals the performance of duty are met with. There is not a base thought in the whole poem. Faith, valour, and brotherliness are the virtues the poet presents to us.

Roland's qualities

Roland is one of the most taking characters that epic poet has ever drawn. Of open and smiling countenance and of stout port—

> Cors ad gaillart, le vis cler et riant—†
>
> C. de R. 1159.

---

* A fine battle is ours.

† He has a powerful frame, an open and smiling countenance.

he is the pride and sunshine of his men. His fame as a doughty and dauntless warrior, as Charlemagne's right hand, was world-wide, and at Roncesvalles he did not belie his reputation. There, as nowhere else, were conspicuous the resistless dash of his onset, and the keen and massive vigour of his blows. The paladins are all, as regards these qualities, made more or less in the same mould (I by no means speak of a sameness that surfeits), they are all accessible to attacks of the battle frenzy—with more or less of Gallic swashbucklerism—and their swords are always swift to deal death. But Roland, pre-eminent as he is in physical qualities, is no less so in the softer qualities of the heart. His love to Olivier, a love passing the love of women, his brotherliness to his comrades-in-arms, his tenderness to the Frankish soldiers, not to speak of his devotion to Charlemagne, make a Bellona's bridegroom into something like the mirror of chivalry. That dogged obstinacy which prevented him winding his horn, which the poet as craftsman has known how to utilise, but which, as man, he, by the mouth of Olivier, censures in the line—

> Kar vasselage par sens nen est folie—*
>
> C. de R. 1724.

is redeemed by the inspiriting daring with which, as heir of his family's honour, and peer of the puissant Karl, he prolonged the struggle till family and personal pride yielded to the compassion felt for his comrades fordone with fighting and wounds.

Olivier's death

There are few more melting episodes than that which tells of the passage of Roland on his horse Veillantif to the succour of Olivier hard pressed and mortally wounded. Roland, with friendly haste, rides to the relief of his comrade, but Olivier,

* Assuredly courage with reason is not folly.

blinded by his own blood, taking him for a paynim, strikes at him with Halteclere, and hits his helm. There follows a surprised and sorrowful query on the part of Roland, and the quavering reply of one who is too near death to do more than plead his blindness, mention the name of God, and ask to be forgiven. Then, says the poet, they bent lovingly towards one another, embraced, and parted. Almost immediately Olivier died, praying God to bless Roland, above all others. Roland, with the weeping outburst—

> Ne m'fesis mal, ne jo ne l'te forsfis—*
>
> C. de R. 2029.

swooned on his charger, but mastered his swoon, and pressed to another part of the battle-field to assist the last remnant of his army.

To my mind this is one of the most piercingly pathetic incidents in literature. It almost excels in pathos—and this is saying much—the bitter entreaty of Priam in the tent of Achilles, the death of Clorinda by the weapon and in the embrace of Tancredi, and the forced and fatal fight of Margrave Rüdiger against the friends of his own escorting in that dread hall of Hunland.

The last scene of an *aristeia* that is only measured by the length of the poem makes the moribund Roland, on the flight of the Saracens at the sound of the clarions of the approaching Charlemagne, cross the Spanish border, and, in token of victory, possess himself of a mound containing four flights of marble steps with a tree on either side. A mortal faintness, the herald of coming death, caused him to sink on the sward at the base of the mound. There, a Saracen who had feigned death, watching his opportunity, attempted to wrest from Roland his sword Durendal, but, in the attempt, roused Roland, who,

Roland's death

* Thou hast not done me ill, nor I, have I done thee wrong in aught.

summoning all his strength for a last effort, brained him with his ivory horn. The action of the Saracen caused Roland to take means to prevent any possible abstraction of his good sword. He approached the mound, and smote the weapon strongly ten times on a brown rock, then on the marble steps, and again on the mound. He rasped and partially damaged, but neither broke, nor even notched the sword, which, on the cessation of the smiting, always regained its former shape and elasticity. Foiled by the temper of the blade, and already in the grip of death, he fell on the sward, his sword and horn beneath him, and his face towards Spain.

Before passing from earth, this christian fighter of a genuine fight, thought at once resignedly and wistfully of France, and friends, and Charlemagne, and the busy battling of his past life, and, as the last act of one, who, though a hero, was oppressed by a sense of failure, raised his glove aloft to heaven as a sign of penitence. God, by his messenger Gabriel, received and removed the offering. After the count's death his soul, under convoy of two angels, was taken to paradise :—

> L'anme de l'Cunte portent en pareïs.*
>
> C. de R. 2396.

It is not difficult for us, who, though reading the poem under many obvious disadvantages of time, nationality, and fellow-feeling, are yet touched to the quick by its perusal, to understand the power of the jongleur who with its story could draw tears down the cheeks of his hearers and send them sobbing home. If, and the purport of tradition does not forbid the possibility, it was snatches from this poem that Taillefer sang to the embattled soldiers of the Norman foreigner, then the victors of Senlac fought under most favourable auspices.

* They carry the soul of the Count to paradise.

Roland was in a sense responsible for the disaster at Roncesvalles. It was he, who, by treating his step-father Ganelon floutingly, had engendered in his heart the thought of treason. In particular, by mischievously, or, it may be, without conscious motive (though he laughed at the peer's quandary), counselling the employment of Ganelon on an important and risky embassy to Marsil at Saragossa, he turned Ganelon's fugitive thoughts into steady resolve. But Ganelon—*li fels, li parjurez*—is no ordinary traitor. He is never disloyal in thought to Charlemagne, he even acknowledges the brilliance and superiority of Roland. He seems to have taken the initial and irrevocable step, while smarting under the sting of wounded personal vanity. True, after the first traitorous step, he is rapidly besmirched with all the foulness of treason and ends by swallowing bribes rich in number and variety.

Ganelon

We must needs accord to Roland the same prerogative of untarnishable manliness that we accord to Achilles. If Achilles in wrath is never less than demigod obscured, so Roland in flouting mood can never have been less than hero at play.

Next to Roland, Olivier and Turpin are the prominent characters. Olivier has a position subordinate to that of Roland, and is the meeker of the two. He is modelled on the same lines as Roland, fights equally well, but has not his fiery personal pride, or fierce pertinacity. He plays Patroclus to Roland's Achilles. Turpin, warrior priest and prelate militant, is as pugnacious as any of the peers. His religious creed has two aspects, a negative and a positive, the negative refusing paradise to the poltroon, the positive enjoining penance by action of one's sword on the persons of the enemy. In his exhortations to the soldiers he has the advantage of his brother peers. He can kindle valour, not by example only, but also by his

Olivier and Turpin

benison, and by the promise of bliss and communion with the saints :—

> Mais d'une chose vus sui jo bien guarant :
> Seinz Pareïs vus iert abandunant ;
> As Innocenz vus en serez seant.*
>
> C. de R. 1479.

Very fine is that scene in the Chanson, where Roland, himself wounded to death, collected the bodies of the dead paladins, and laid them at the feet of the battered bishop for benediction. And that benediction, how terse it reads :—

> Tutes vos anmes ait Deus li glorius ;
> En pareïs les metet en seintes flurs ;
> La meie mort me rent si anguissus :
> Ja ne verrai le riche Empereür.† C. de R. 2196.

Roland and Turpin were sole survivors, and of these, Turpin was the first to die, while vainly attempting to bring a draught of water to Roland, who had swooned on seeing the line of dead peers and among them the body of Olivier.

Charlemagne

Charlemagne's part in the poem is somewhat ornamental, and quite paternal. He is biddable, irascible and somewhat exacting. He has reached the Nestor stage—*Carles li vielz, à la barbe flurie*—both in age and action. Nestor, however, was not so emotional. Charlemagne, in trouble, weeps, and tears his hair and beard. The Franks of the poem are given to these manifestations. They are an emotional race ; they swoon in groups of a hundred thousand.

The spirit of the poem

Everywhere in the poem we have manifested burning scorn for cowardice, and chivalrous contempt for dastardy. The poet's patriotism and sense of the tearful in human things are im-

* But for one thing I am indeed warranty to you : "To you Holy Paradise will be free, you will sit beside the Saints."

† May the God of glory take all your souls ; may He place them as holy flowers in paradise ; my death makes me so full of anguish ; never shall I see the glorious Emperor.

pressive and omnipresent. He has even enough manliness and generosity to do justice by Saracen courage, never suffering, it is true, the prowess of paladin to pale before the heroism of paynim. Roland's, or Olivier's, or Turpin's wearied virtue is mightier far than the vigilant valour of any paynim peer whatsoever.

The overdone might of Karl's paladins is due, partly to national vanity, partly to epic conventionalities, partly, also, it is the reflex of fanatical religious fervour, which required Christian barons to be as superior to Moslem champions, as Christ was superior to Mahound.

Its place among epics

France has reason to be proud of her epic. If any one has a desire to read something of virginal freshness, to drink for a season of the *integri fontes* of the nobly simple and the intensely human, to such a one I commend a perusal of the Chanson de Roland. As a whole, it is indeed vastly inferior to the great epics of the world. These have accustomed us to noble rhythm—to the organ-toned sonority of Milton, to the languishing cadence of Tasso, to the stately harmony of Virgil, or to the many-voiced music of Homer. The metre of the Chanson—ten-syllabled line, written in leashes or stanzas, with assonant rhyme of the last accented vowel—has in it nothing of this soul-satisfying rhythm. Its diction, too, is naive and without figure. But if the poet has not the *os magna sonaturum* he has certainly something of *ingenium* and *mens divinior*.

We have it on the authority of Voltaire, that the France he knew was not capable of producing an epic. Certainly his banal and bastard performance does not supply the imagined want. The Henriade proves, if proof were necessary, that not even a superlatively clever man can write an epic poem. Luckily for France, her epic was produced in a far-away pre-Voltairian time, when this assumed incapacity of the brilliant Gallic genius was not yet discernible, for the Song of Roland has much of the matter and store of the spirit of genuine epic.

The Henriade. Its argument

The argument of the Henriade is taken from history, and many of us have made a pleasant acquaintance with it in Dumas. It records directly, or by episode, the struggles between Catholics and Protestants, the efforts of the party of the Duke of Guise to displace Henry III, the murder of the latter, and the progress of Henry of Navarre to the throne.

The documentary heroic

An epic poet does well to go far back in time for his subject. Not every person whom we call a national hero can be an epic hero. The evidence about him may be too documentary, a fatal check to imaginative handling in an objective poem. It is very difficult to invest historic personages with the epic illusion, unless they can be surrounded with the halo of legend, or, at anyrate, hallowed by the consecration of the past.

There must be some adaptability in the matter and manner of epic

It is plain that if epic poetry, with a fairly modern subject, is to continue to be written, it must be because the application and operation of its characteristic machinery can be modified. Subjects belonging to times of old-fashioned superstitions and beliefs are pretty well exhausted, and poets impelled to write by an epical afflatus, will perforce have to choose their subjects from an epoch less credulous of the supernatural. But it is not merely the conditions of their subject that will be less favourable to the employment of the supernatural. The minds of readers are, perhaps, now less tolerant, in all subjects, save those of great remoteness, of the presence of divine agencies, even though these have the sanction of belief. They would like the epic modernised. The hypothetical epic poet is not, therefore, as it seems to me, gravelled for lack of matter, or hopelessly hampered by the disparagement of the old mode. He must indeed choose his subject well, must choose one that has a pull on our feelings of veneration. He has the romantic to fall back on, and this, employed in due measure, ought to be a powerful coadjutor to him in his efforts to adapt and temper the miraculous. Good poetry with the essentials of the epic manner, will, I take it, most readily reconcile us to the absence of what may be called the idiosyncrasies of the epic poet, the *eidola* of his craft.

Voltaire's elaborate epic exterior

Instead of suiting his epic to its surroundings and writing a historico-heroic poem, which might have approximated to an epic, Voltaire tried to be epical to his finger-tips. He imported all the epical machinery. Lucan's method of writing an historic epic was better than Voltaire's. He discarded all the apparatus of divine intervention, retaining only a pale substitute—witchcraft. With all his faults he produced a great poem. Voltaire travestied the epic manner, stole epic machines, and produced merely a *tour-de-force* in verse. He did not succeed in the task he imposed on himself, nor would he have succeeded had he been less anxious to have the externals of epic poetry. Apart from the difficulties of the subject he chose, and the bad instrument he had in the conventional metre—I should think it an extremely difficult task to attain to epic dignity with French alexandrines, or the English heroic couplet, for that terrible tinkle-tinkle at the end of each pair of lines is dragging and likely to be tawdry—there were other obstacles to success. Voltaire was essentially an unpoetical spirit, and his enthusiasm over this poem was volitional, and not of the temperament. He had some intuition of the heroic in action, but none of the heroic in sentiment.

With Camoens, the historic epic meant an epic of the whole history of Portugal, and unity was secured by personifying Portugal, as it were, in the person of Vasco da Gama. He thus avoided in his poem the pettiness that attends an attempt to write an epic on the events of a short stretch of time. Camoens had also the wit to choose for his epic an excellent framework, namely, the Portuguese discovery of India, and he had a poetical talent that enabled him to write with dignity and embellish with effect. And this, though he recorded events that were much less distant from his time than were those of the Henriade from Voltaire's.

Camoens and his historical subject

Two main reasons for Voltaire's failure to write an epic were his natural unsuitability for the task imposed, and the lavish use he made of epical machines. His subject, moreover, had more than its share of the drawbacks of historical subjects. Parts of the story are earthy, and even squalid. Henry IV was a politician rather than a hero, a man of practical instincts rather than a man all soul, and with no faults but those of human nature. An epic hero is not a balancer in religion. He is religious, very much as he is brave, because it is his nature to be so. If he belong to an old-time period he will have more or less the religion of his fellows, sublimated by a consciousness of the religious quality of activity on behalf of his nation,* and a conviction of the transitoriness of passing human life ; if he belong to a more modern period he must still have a consciousness of the nobility of action, and an intuition of the brevity of life, but, in addition, he must have intellectual steadiness and tenacity of belief.

Reasons for Voltaire's failure. Henri Quatre

Henry of Navarre made merchandise of his belief, he temporised with occasion to secure a stable throne, he sank manliness under policy. It is true that the perfidy

* Hector says :—

Εἷς οἰωνὸς ἄριστος, ἀμύνεσθαι περὶ πάτρης. Il. xii., 243.

There is but one excellent omen, to fight for one's country.

of his act may be qualified by describing it as high policy, and lofty patriotism, and he certainly spiced his great betrayal with justice and legal guarantees. In any case, his were not the surroundings to produce an epic hero, and we can hardly say that Henry was brilliantly superior to his surroundings. These were too unheroic to permit of the growth of a heroism deserving commemoration in a national epic.

Some facts illustrating the argument of the Henriade will better than anything else give an idea of Voltaire's handling of the story:—The King of Navarre is sent by Henry III, whose ally he had become, to the Court of Queen Elizabeth to ask for help. There he narrates to the Queen the story of events that had lately transpired in France. This story extends over two books, the second and third; Voltaire evidently had in mind Virgil's arrangement of his matter. Æneas begins his story in the second Æneid, and continues it over the third, and Voltaire makes his hero do likewise. Queen Elizabeth is Voltaire's Dido. Just as Æneas saw Tartarus and passed into Elysium, so Henry must be passed into the afterworld. In a trance he is rapt from earth, and under the guidance of St. Louis visits heaven and hell. In heaven he sees the Deity on His throne; in hell he sees various abstract and mythological figures, and Jacques Clément; in the Abodes of Innocence he saw Charlemagne, Clovis, Jeanne d'Arc, and Bayard. If Milton makes God talk like a school divine, Voltaire makes him talk, well, like Voltaire sermonising, surely a greater error.

Specimens of the argument

Anchises, in the sixth Æneid, reviewed before Æneas the historic pageantry of the kings and heroes that were to be—Romulus, Camillus, the Decii, Augustus and Marcellus. So St. Louis showed to Henry of Navarre, in the Palace of the Fates, Richelieu, Mazarin, Louis XIV, Louis XV, and Philippe d'Orléans. Contrast Augustus with Louis XIV. Virgil's vision of the future is full of pathos, and variety, and crowning dignity, Voltaire's of vanity, tameness, and anti-climax. Perhaps, however, Louis XIV was as great a man as Augustus, and perhaps the latter, as the prophesied one, appeared as ridiculous to unemotional Romans as Louis XIV does to us. Do antiquity and the poet make all the difference?

After the vision the King of Navarre had a face as radiant as was that of the law-giver of the Jews when he descended from the Mount of Law. Fancy the Béarnais with the aureole of Moses.

Angels watched the issue of the single combat between D'Aumale and Turenne. That a man with Voltaire's keen sense of the ridiculous did not see the queer bathos and the mirth-moving situations of his epic shows how much he was engrossed in playing the part of an epic poet.

St. Louis prayed the Most High to convert Henry of Navarre to the Catholic faith, and his prayer was answered. What a ridiculous trait in a poem of such pretentions! To make the Almighty a sectary! John Milton narrowed his Deity's dignity, but not to this extent. He saw him through his own individuality, but did not quite attribute partisanship to him.

Henry has, like Rinaldo, to undergo eclipse through the obscuration caused by an Armida, in the shape of Gabrielle D'Estrées. Why does Rinaldo in the toils of Armida cut a tolerable figure, and Henry the Great, enthralled by Gabrielle, cut a ridiculous one? The reason is to be found in the nature of Tasso's subject, in the romantic accessories of his poem, and in the high poetic art of the poet.

CHAPTER IV

THE GERMAN EPIC

I SHALL begin my notice of the Nibelungenlied with a short argument:—There lived at Worms in Burgundy, Queen Ute, widow of King Dankrat. The three young kings, her sons, were called Gunther, Gernot, and Giselher. There was one daughter, Kriemhild. The principal vassals of the royal house were Hagen of Tronje, his brother Dankwart, Ortwein, Eckewart, Gere, and Volker. One night Kriemhild dreamt a dream of a pet falcon torn to death by two eagles. Her mother, to the professed distaste of the daughter, identified the falcon with her future husband.

The Nibelungenlied. Its argument

Siegfried, the son of Siegmund, King of the Netherlands, and of his Queen Siegelind, came from Xanten to Worms, to woo the far-famed beauty, Kriemhild. Siegfried's fame had ere now filled the world. Hagen recognised Siegfried, and told Gunther how, by the aid of his good sword, Balmung, he had got possession of the hoard of the Nibelungs, how he had conquered the dwarf Alberich, winning by this conquest the *tarnkappe*, or cloak of darkness, and made himself guardian of the hoard. He told him also, how a bath in the blood of a dragon he had slain had made the hero invulnerable.

Siegfried blustered a bit in Burgundy, but was won over to help in resisting the invasion of the Saxons.

These were defeated, mainly through his instrumentality, and after the campaign Kriemhild and he met, and loved. Siegfried next went with Gunther to Island to help him to gain Brunhild to wife. A successful suitor had to conquer this marriageable amazon in three feats. Gunther, with the invisible help of Siegfried, clad in the *tarnkappe*, managed to do this. Siegfried was in Gunther's train, and appeared to Brunhild to be his inferior, his man. On the return to Worms, Gunther was married to Brunhild, and Siegfried to Kriemhild. Kriemhild received as bridegroom's gift, or *morgengabe*, the Nibelung treasure. Brunhild disliked this marriage of her husband's sister to a vassal, and asked an explanation from Gunther, who put her off. Siegfried's aid had again to be utilised before the sulky Brunhild would loosen her zone. Siegfried presented to his wife the ring and belt he had stolen from Brunhild. The latter was permanently embittered against her sister-in-law and brother-in-law, and never surmounted her bitterness.

On Siegfried and Kriemhild visiting Worms some years later, the two wives had quarrels, which reached a climax, when Brunhild insisted on her right to precede Kriemhild in entering church. Kriemhild refused to give way, and told the real story of Brunhild's subjugation to wifehood. Brunhild lamented, and complained to her lord. Hagen advised the death of Siegfried. This was accomplished on a hunting expedition by treachery. Hagen had previously, counterfeiting concern for her husband, wormed from Kriemhild the secret of Siegfried's invulnerability. He was invulnerable, save in one spot, where a leaf had fallen as he took the blood-bath.

Kriemhild lived for some time in sorrow at Worms. She was asked in marriage by Etzel, king of the Huns, who had lost his wife Hecla. His envoy, Rüdiger, persuaded Kriemhild to accept the offer, but first had to swear an oath to assist her in making return for ills done. Kriemhild then became Etzel's wife, and bore him a son, Ortlieb. After seven years she invited Gunther and his following to Hunland, meaning to exact vengeance for her wrongs. The Burgundians, fate-impelled, went to Etzelburg. Omens alarmed them on the way, but the sweep of doom was too compelling. Young Giselher was betrothed to Rüdiger's daughter in Bechlaren, but this promise of sunlight was never fulfilled.

At Etzel's court Kriemhild incites the leading Huns to kill her guests. The hall where they had banqueted is attacked and defended, is half burnt, and still defended. Many noble Huns are slain, and countless inferior men. Rüdiger, as liegeman of Etzel, has to fight against his own guests, and is slain. Finally, after all Dietrich of Bern's followers, the last troop launched against the Nibelungs, as they are now called since they got the treasure, have been slain, except Hildebrand, the Burgundians are reduced to two fighting men, Gunther and Hagen. These are taken prisoners. Hagen refuses to tell where he hid the Nibelung treasure, so long as Gunther, to whom he had sworn an oath of secrecy, is in life. When his master's head is shown him he declines to make the promised disclosure. Kriemhild kills him with Balmung, the sword of Siegfried, which had come into her possession after Hagen's capture, and is herself slain by Hildebrand, angry at the death of such a famous warrior by a woman's hand.

Metre

The lines, when given fully, have in the first half three iambs and an unaccented syllable, followed by three iambs in the second half. The fourth line of the verse has often four iambs in its second half. The lines rhyme in pairs. Suppression of unaccented syllables is common enough.

The poem begins well. The writer attunes modestly his first lines to the high theme he is to sing of, thus avoiding the inopportune and inflated opening of the *scriptor cyclicus* of Horace, and proving himself no mean judge of propriety in matters of his craft. He next passes to the mention of Kriemhild, and therein does well, for she is the be-all and the end-all of the poem. Her revenge is the pivot of the whole of the second part of the poem, and, in the first part, she it is, and not Siegfried, that primarily claims our attention. Siegfried's story is told only in terms of his relations to her. This would hardly have been done, had the first part been an arrangement of Siegfried lays. On this supposition we should have been told more about the hero's youth, and his pre-Burgundian period generally.

Prominence of Kriemhild

It was mainly as a wooer that Siegfried came to Worms; the fight that he fought for Gunther against the Saxons was motived by a desire to gain Kriemhild's hand; and he accompanied the king to Isenstein on the understanding that marriage with his sister was to be the price of co-operation. It is fitting, then, that the early mention of Kriemhild's bodeful dream should push her into the foreground of the action. It was the fell hatred between her and another woman that wrought all the woe of the story.

The meeting between Siegfried and Kriemhild

The winning of Kriemhild is the subject of the beginning of the epic. It is a taking tale, strongly coloured with the sentiment of the period. Siegfried spent a considerable time at the court of Gunther without seeing the object of his affection. Curiosity, the forerunner of love, had prompted her, on her side, to steal some furtive glances at the hero as he jousted in the court below. It was after the successful termination of the campaign against the Saxons that the lovers first met. The meeting was formally arranged by Gunther. In it his sister was to thank Siegfried for his services. Siegfried blushingly received the maid's thanks, their eyes met in fond glances, and the poet, speaking in proper person, naively suggests that if their hands did not caress one another, it was a sort of treason that two loving hearts (*zwei minne gerndiu herze*) ought not to have been guilty of.

It is an agreeable picture of pretty tenderness, and truthful and winning artlessness. Minnesong and truth are here in accord. The facts themselves have immortal youth, and the manner of the proceeding is of a fashion that dies not. Siegfried now reached something like the zenith of pleasure :—

> Bî der sumerzîte und gên des meijen tagen
> dorft er niht mêre in sîme herze tragen
> sô vil hôher fröude, sô er dâ gewan,
> dô im diu gie an hende, die er ze trûte gerte hân.*
>
> N. 301.

The relations between Siegfried and his wife were always tender. Before he went to the fatal hunt, he kissed, says the poet, his sweet wife on the mouth (*sîne triutinne kust er an den munt*).

Over against Kriemhild the poet has set Hagen, a strong character, stronger in action than Kriemhild.

Kriemhild and Hagen

Each character is in a way the foil of the other. Hagen got Kriemhild's treasure stolen from her and sunk it in the Rhine. The old tradition of the sinking of the hoard in the Rhine is utilised by the poet in an artistic way. By this outrage, ascribed as it is to Hagen, Kriemhild's hatred of the murderer is deepened and quickened, and the way paved for the acceptance of Etzel's offer of marriage. Her

* In summer-time, and during the approach of May, never more could he bear in his heart so much of lofty joy, as then he won, when she whom he desired to have for his love went by his side (hand).

desire for revenge, and a conjoint helplessness to procure any gratification of the desire, caused her in the end, after reflection, to exchange her honourable widowhood for a heathenish husband. But the Etzel's wife of the second part of the poem really accomplished the long premeditated purposes of Siegfried's widow. Her first public act at Etzel's court had for its object the realisation of her dark purpose. The journey of the Burgundians to Etzelburg is always represented in the poem as a journey to doom, and as the preliminary to an awful consummation. Siegfried's death is not regarded as a mere isolated occurrence containing its own finality, but as an event fruitful in results and demanding expiation.

The manner of the narrative

The narrative of the Nibelungenlied flows on evenly and loquaciously. A theme is chosen for each *aventiure*, and it is ridden to death with a garrulity that knows no limit. The poet has a perfect flux of words. He abounds in small talk, and weaves and weaves with spider-like facility. He ambles along with many trumpery ups and downs and store of over-emphasis. He has a deal of jongleurs' gag, and indulges in much repetition, and not always the tenfold repetition that is sure to please. He is always describing some nonpareil of bravery or power, some *ne plus ultra* of grandeur. The great non-suchness of all he cites is insisted on with somewhat nauseous iteration. For tinselly grandiosity commend me to the writer of the Nibelungenlied. Descriptions of vestments, of largess, of jousts, of courtly magnificence, and of flaunting wealth are part of his ordinary stock in trade. In fact, the constant occurrence of these is an argument for the unifying touch of a single hand.

These remarks are more particularly applicable to the first part of the poem. There is a stronger drift of events in the last part, and a more straightforward action. Events are not very many in the first portion of the epic ;

there is a fair amount of scene-shifting, but the action is action in a circle. This, in the absence of strong countervailing attractions of manner and story-telling capacity, is apt to beget tedium, and the story of our poem at times becomes distinctly tedious. Now, I do not think that any one would say of the story of the Odyssey, zigzag though the plot in a measure is, that it produces tedium. The prancing metre of the German epic beguiles one, however, and conveys the sensation of forwardness. The metre has a good swing in it, certainly, but in time there grows a commonness in this that jars on the reader's ear. High tragedy in a lilting metre has the charm of novelty about it, but the lack of nobility in an epical measure is a fatal defect, and in the long run is sure to make itself felt to the ear and mind of the reader.

An amount of tedium in the poem

There is undoubtedly an aspect of the poem that will lead us to call it a glib chronicle with much repetition and no little shallowness. What is it, then, that lends lustre to the Nibelungenlied, and gives it a respectable place among the big books of the world? What is it that ensures to it its enduring attractiveness? It is very deficient in noble rhythm, in variety that is not staled, in epic plot, pure and simple. Well, it has volume, and grandeur, and ringing pathos, and heroic humanity. There is, in the story, a strong tragic undercurrent, whose attractive force bears us on ; there are pointed references to impending doom that, though they pall, still compel our attention ; the poet has a tender grace in narration, and a kindly humanity of sentiment ; he has a strong belief in the worth and tragic significance of his story ; we are dazzled by the hurry, the fire, the battling, and the bravado of the fighting cantos ; we have anticipations of a quick and awful ending, which are continually deferred, and again excited, and at last we face a full and fatal end with an unexpected,

But enduring attractiveness

but just rebound. Verily, the Nibelungenlied is a complete and satisfying tragedy of strong situations, and he who dispenses with the reading of it, dispenses therewith to his own great loss.

The characters of the poem

Those are fine characters, too, in this poem, firmly and takingly drawn—Siegfried, Rüdiger, Volker, etc. They wooed honour as one would woo a bride ; they reverenced women. What a pleasing character is Siegfried, a man whom it was impossible to hate, a knight as good as he was bold (*an allen dingen ein ritter küene unde guot*). The reader plains with the poet over his violent death :—

Erblichen was sîn varwe ; er mohte niht gestên.
sînes lîbes sterke muoste gar zergên,
wand er des todes zeichen in liehter varwe truoc. *
N. 1016, 1-3

Dô viel in die bluomen der Kriemhilde man ;
daz bluot von sîner wunden sach man vaste gân. †
N. 1017, 1-2.

The literary presentation

The literary presentation of the Nibelungenlied exhibits less decorative detail and more restraint than the specimens of courtly narrative poetry. There exists no desire for trivialities, and there is an obvious avoidance of vulgar comedy. The motives and feelings of the actors are pointedly and powerfully treated after the fashion of the old lyric poetry.‡

* All pallid was his colour ; he could not stand. His body's strength was forcibly fordone, for in his pale hue he wore the mark of death.

† Then fell among the flowers the spouse of Kriemhild ; down from his wounds one saw the blood run wildly.

‡ In Austria, while chivalrous lyric was coming to maturity, there appeared, c. 1160, as we are given to understand by a notice in an old writer, an epic poem celebrating the heroism of Rüdiger, margrave of Bechlaren, and Dietrich of Bern. Some considerable time thereafter, there appeared, probably in the same district, the Nibelungenlied, as we now have it, a poetic narrative of considerable length, meant to

In the poem we have exemplified the guiding idea of the heroic saga, the idea of loyalty, in the shape of spousal troth kept beyond the grave, of mutual faith between vassal and lord passionately maintained till death. We have depicted the ancient hero with his joyous defiance of death, his unyielding bravery, his antique style of fighting with spear and sword. With these ancient ingredients there intermingle certain modern elements. The heroes step on the stage in knightly trappings, with a knightly air, and fight with a semblance of knightly style. The narrative has minnesong aspects.* It has

The root-idea exemplified in the poem

be recited. In it there is used the metrical form popularised by Kurenberg. The fact that this metre, adapted rather for singing than for another purpose, is used in a poem meant for recitation, makes it probable that the metre, as is the case with the matter, was taken from the older poetry of the school, which is likely to have been of the epico-lyrical species. The Nibelungenlied, now that it had assumed the proportions of a large and complete work, and was meant to be read aloud in courtly circles, was not left to the uncertainties of oral tradition, but written down. It is not probable that the basal epic hero-songs had been committed to writing. These lays had none of the characteristics of minstrel poetry of the lower sort, but exhibited many of the qualities of Old Austrian lyric poetry. They had its ideas and its manner of expression. They had its union of popular and knightly elements, for in Austria the perfecting of the popular chivalrous minnesong went hand in hand with that of the popular chivalrous hero-song. (The remarks in this and the succeeding note are put together out of Paul's Grundriss. The same great work has helped me in other parts of this chapter.)

* For a considerable period the French epic did not find an entrance into Austria. It was national poetry, in addition, of course, to religious, that was cultivated in this country. By the side of the development of epic hero-song, there took place a parallel development of chivalrous lyric poetry on a popular basis. There had existed in Germany, from time immemorial, a non-epic folk-song. We have proofs of the existence of laudatory, satirical, and abusive poems, also of improvisations of sundry sorts; there passed between lovers love-greetings and love-messages in verse; dance songs were sung, welcoming the fair summer-time, and not excluding an erotic element. The above poetry was naturally written in very simple metre.

Out of this species of verse, as the 12th century wore on, there was developed a distinct type of lyrical love poetry, whose aim it was to give poetical expression to the feelings of a person in love, and this, in words adapted, in independence of the special occasion, to gratify the common descriptions of courtly feasts and the preliminaries of such, of magnificent clothing, of jousts, and of embassies and journeys from court to court that interrupt, overlay, and obscure the old saga-story. These are copyings of the courtly manner to be met with in all modernised folk-epic.

Kriemhild's blood-guiltiness

Kriemhild tried to sacrifice Hagen alone, but her project miscarried. She could not isolate the vassal. She was thereupon driven into a war of extermination against her own kindred, a war in which numberless innocent persons perished before she had handed over to her the guilty parties. After her vengeance had been exacted, she, who had incurred blood-guiltiness in order to avenge blood-guiltiness, had to atone for her criminality. Even Siegfried had incurred some show of guilt. He had twice deceived Brunhild, in the courting, and on the nuptial night, and, by the thoughtless delivery to Kriemhild of the proofs of the former lady's abasement, he had added to this guilt.

The unity of the poem

It is not worth my while to record the come and go of the various swings of the pendulum in favour of, or against the theory of separate lays. So far as my own reading of the poem goes, I find it difficult to believe in the absolute separateness, or autonomy, if I máy so express it, of the putative lays. There is to be met with in the poem not only unity in

taste for poetry, and awake kindred feelings in a total stranger. This poetry was, in fact, the beginning of Minnesong.

In Austria there were many points of contact between epic and lyric in their further development. The same contact took place in other countries than Austria, but had a different significance. In those countries both epic and lyric were modelled on French exemplars. The epic of this country was not for a long time, save indirectly, exposed to French epic influence, not till a type of court-epic, with modern tone certainly, but of natural stamp and sympathies, had established itself. The lyric was early enough subjected to French influence. Marks of contact between the natural minnesong and a minnesong with romance affinities are traceable in some early lays. The latter type of minnesong was probably transplanted to the Vienna Court, where it flourished and received willing patronage, by Reinmar von Hagenau before 1190.

the loose sense in which the term is sometimes used, but unity pronounced and prepense.

It is not possible to settle the wording of original component parts of the poem. The question does not admit of solution. We have no data for inference. It is a matter of subjectivity. Different answers, more or less, will be given, according as one is of a conservative or cavilling spirit. Instead of trying to solve the insoluble, it would be far better to try to gain an historically accurate conception of what has been handed down to us.

Its ending

The poem ends with the second last rather than with the last verse. Its logical ending is like its logical beginning, for the epic expoundeth

Wie liebe mit leide ze jungest lônen kan. *

N. 17, 3.

Pain treads on the heels of pleasure. If proof is wished for, think on Kriemhild passioning for the death of her lord.

I shall condense my account of the northern version, and limit it pretty much to the story of the characters that appear in the Nibelungenlied.

Northern version of the Nibelung story

Sigmund, son of Volsung, drew out of the Branstock (the oak trunk that stood in the Volsung hall), when no other could, the sword that Odin had thrust therein. He was not for that reason the favourite of the god, for in a big and stiff battle Odin opposed to his sword-stroke a bill, against which the sword broke. In this battle Sigmund was fatally wounded. To him there was born a posthumous child, Sigurd (Siegfried). It was Regin the smith who played the part of Chiron to the youthful Achilles. For him he made a sword out of the two shards of his father's blade, with which the youthful hero did rare deeds at the head of an army that he had led against the slayers of his father. After avenging his father he slew the drake Fafnir, and possessed himself of its hoard, which had once belonged to the dwarf

* How love (joy) at last may requite us with sorrow.

Andvari. Fafnir had aforetime been a man, the brother of Regin, but, after his father Hreidmar had obtained as atonement from the three gods who had brought about the death of Otter the wealth and ring of Andvari, he, pregnant with cupidity, made away with his father, flouted his brother's claim, and appropriated the treasure. By force of wickedness, and avaricious brooding over the gold, he was metamorphosed into a serpent, and crawled about on Gnitaheath.

After slaying Fafnir, Sigurd, on the advice of Regin, who occupied himself with the drinking of its blood, proceeded to roast the worm's heart, and in the process sampled, cook-wise, the quality of the product. Scarcely had the dragon's blood touched his tongue than his range of hearing was enlarged, and he understood the twittering of birds. Obeying the admonitions of the birds, he slew Regin and ate of the heart. Sigurd was now master of the dragon's hoard.

Thereafter he went to the flame-girt castle on the fell, and woke Brunhild the shield-may. Her conduct in a certain battle had displeased Odin, who pricked her with the sleep-thorn, and condemned her to the loss of her maiden independence. Brunhild resolved that she would only forfeit this to the bravest of the brave, and the god seems to have concurred. After she had imparted to Sigurd some sage love advice, they plighted troth, and parted. He afterwards met her at Hlymdale, where she was so far gone in domesticity that she was embroidering in gold his great deeds. Here he renewed his troth to her, with much affectionate accompaniment, but Brunhild, in spite of her passion for Sigurd, was in a retrospective and regretful mood, and gloomily spoke out her knowledge of the future. Sigurd calmed her with protestation and gave her Andvari's ring.

Sigurd now finds his way south to the Rhine to the Court of Giuki. To this king there are three sons, Gunnar, Hogni, and Guttorm, and a daughter, Gudrun. She is the Kriemhild of the northern story, a name, oddly enough, borne by her mother, Giuki's wife, who is called Ute in the southern story. Here Giuki's wife, a match-making mother skilled in magic, discerning the advantage of having for a son-in-law the valorous and wealthy Sigurd, gives him to drink a potion that brings forgetfulness of Brunhild. She then throws the young people together, and Sigurd, snared, marries Gudrun, and, to make her his equal, gives her to eat of the serpent's heart.

Gudrun had had some inkling of the events that were to befall her, for she had dreamt strange things, to wit, that a fair hawk of golden feathers had lit on her wrist, that a hart of golden coat had become hers, been slain by Brunhild, and been replaced by a wolf-cub, which bespattered her with the blood of her kindred. She had consulted Brunhild and been advised of the future.

Gudrun's mother at once used Sigurd to effect her own ends. By his aid she married Gunnar to Brunhild. Gunnar was unable to accomplish his own destiny. The task assigned to a successful wooer was to ride through the fence of flame that surrounded Brunhild's castle. Sigurd, assuming the form of Gunnar, rode his horse Grani (a present from Odin in the days of the hero's pupilage) at the fire, passed through it, and claimed the reward. Brunhild gave him Andvari's ring, and received another in return. She seems to have been a little perplexed by the Sigurd-Gunnar manifestation, but the conditions of her capture had been fulfilled, and what could she do but submit to become the wife of Gunnar.

Brunhild clung to the belief that she was the wife of the best man in the world. She salved her lost maidenhood thereby. She still believed in the peerlessness of Sigurd, but regard for accomplished fact, her sense of dignity, and perhaps her doubt of the reality of her position, drove her to self-assertion. She insisted on bathing higher up the stream than Gudrun, and, when called to account, justified her conduct by affirming her superior wifely status. Gudrun, who is more assertive and more forward than her double in the Nibelungenlied, and this not so much out of enthusiasm in her lord's defence as in virtue of her own nature, retorted in wrathful terms, and laid bare the truth.

All Brunhild's dormant passion for her first love, her troth-plight, awoke after this revelation, and she refused to be pacified. The wifehood that alone made her lot tolerable was no longer hers. Her false lover had not only broken his vow but had assisted to palm off on her a debased wifehood. Love, pride, and regret buffeted her about. Sigurd, the effect of whose potion had worn off at Gunnar's marriage feast, visited the storm-spent queen to console and make amends.

It is a fine part of the story, that in which Brunhild, refusing to be reconciled to life with Gunnar, denounces, in hating-loving terms, Sigurd and his apologies, and at the same time rejects all guilty compounding of her wretchedness. She reproachfully reminds him of their early love, and of their troth on the mountain, and, when he offers to divorce Gudrun and marry her, she proclaims the impossibility of accommodation, and magnificently faces the situation, saying, "Thee I cannot have, nor will I have another." Her only way out of the deadlock is death.

Gunnar is driven by Brunhild to compass the slaying of Sigurd. His own craving after Sigurd's wealth counts for something in the resolution he takes. Hogni protests, but at length acquiesces. Guttorm slays Sigurd in his bed, but is himself slain. Brunhild, on hearing Gudrun lament, laughs one eldritch laugh, but after that her countenance is overspread with wanness. She stabs herself. The body of Sigurd is burnt on the bale, and Brunhild with him. Grani wailed his lord's death, as the horses Xanthus and Balios did theirs.

Gudrun spent seven seasons in sorrow, but, in the end, her mother overcame by the potion of forgetfulness her repugnance to her kindred, and forced her to marry Atli (in the saga the brother of Brunhild). The latter, coveting the gold of the Nibelungs, invited them to his court. Gudrun warned them of their danger by runes sent with the messengers. Her purpose was detected, and the runes falsified. Gunnar and Hogni, in spite of omens, set out for Atli's land. They are treacherously dealt with, and required to surrender the gold that now belongs of right to Gudrun. They refuse, and in the fight that ensues, Gunnar and Hogni alone survive of their company. Gudrun fought by the side of her brothers. These are separated and bound. Gunnar declines to tell anything of the treasure, until Hogni's heart is brought to him. He then refuses to speak further, and is thrown into the worm-close, where he dies.

This is the northern version of the events of the Nibelungenlied, and may be read in the Volsung Saga and certain northern lays. It is a taking tale of noble simplicity and great power. It is all naturalness and has no padding. It has certainly a national manner of thought, viz., the contiguity of the marvellous and the human. It tells of bright things and of dark things, of manly courtesy, of manly employment, of lealty, of old-time wonders, of magic, and of treachery; it tells of healthful and joyous activity, and of the complexity and cross-purpose play of life; it tells of open and honest manhood building the fabric of its own good fortune, and of a mysterious and malignant fate that refuses to ratify its own seeming promises.

A fine character is that of Sigurd. He loved his friends and bettered their lot at the expense of his enemies. With all his affluence of manly beauty and fearlessness of spirit, he had a touch of the common human in him.

The Nibelung Saga is said to have travelled to Scandinavia towards the close of the sixth century. The northern version has an air of greater primitiveness, and, presumably, no doubt with alterations and additions, has retained many of the main features of the original story.

The fight in Etzel's hall

The fighting cantos of the last part of the poem present a picture of sober realism to be contrasted with the processional pageantry, and the endless descriptions of gorgeous vestments and courtly magnificence of much of the first part. The finger-posts to doom that accompany the reader on his journey now lead him to the very hall of destiny. The Nibelungs are in the mills of fate, and most heroically do they take the grinding.

Such fighting — a defensive-offensive struggle for a day and more against fearful odds. And such fighters—men animated by berserker rage and the grim resolution of heroic despair. The fighting in this part of the Nibelungenlied is wilder, more indiscriminate, and more ferocious than that usually met with in epics. This is due, to a large extent, to the circumstances of the case. The combat takes place in a comparatively narrow space, in Etzel's hall, and the Burgundians are not fighting under fair conditions, and for the glory that success in a cause brings, but have been trapped, and are struggling for dear life. But one might speak of the fighting of the poem as a whole, and with right say that it is not so punctilious, not so sane as that of the Iliad. There are single combats in the Nibelungenlied, as well as in the Iliad, but there is not so much of the ordered duel about them.

Its wildness

The warriors of our poem, as befits the circumstances, display more bustle and dash in the fight than is usual in poems of this class. They are, however, not only human animals, standing at bay, but warriors born. Hagen is determination incarnate—not flinty-hearted by any means—and of the type of man that revenges an insult where given,

The behaviour of the warriors

> If it were in the court of heaven.

Dietrich, it is true, is a very self-possessed warrior, but he does not belong to the injured side, and only intervenes at the close, is in at the death, as it were.

Such men as the Burgundians driven into a blind alley, and embittered by traitorous treatment, and the prospect of a hopeless struggle, were likely to sell their lives dearly. And they did not belie their nature and reputation. They engaged in a battle royal, girding at their adversaries with jibes and despiteful shouts. They let out at them wildly and savagely. They danced across the hall, pinking and slashing *à outrance*.

In the Iliad it is the effect of sword- and spear-play on the person that is specially noted. Our combat in the hall is very prolific in armour-effects. Helmets are smashed, shields are banged and shattered, swords clang and clash, sparks are struck from hauberks and shields, armour is shattered and the shivers sent flying. As a result of all this tumultuous beating, blood flows profusely; the men, the armour, the floor are quite incarnadined. What a diabolic din there must have been in that banqueting-hall, noise as from a score of smithies. There is one armour effect recorded in Homer. When a hero falls down in death it is often said that his armour rattled over him. This is fine. It is effective. And it is natural. It sounds like a requiem.

Armour-effects in the fight

There are lulls in the fighting. But soon the hurly-burly of blows begins again. Passion mounts. The warriors combat as if in deadly feud, where one has to fight to the bitter end. They hurtle about over the hall in impetuous battle-frenzy, daring and truculent, the sons of the furies proving their sonship. Kriemhild, unforgetting and unforgiving, urges on the assailants. In the hall, Volker, the fiddler-fighter, grimly combines his two functions of warrior and gleeman, and strikes out melody from his opponent's helmets and hauberks with his sword-fiddlebow. As the encircling sweep of the narrative increases, so do its picturesqueness and pathos.

Ebb and flow in the fighting

It was a slaughter grim and great that took place that midsummer day in the hall at Etzelburg. Many thousands were slain. But it is not mere description of the sound and fury of battle that this poet presents to us. He presents these to us in an attractive wording. His language is inspiriting, and rings out the sound of doughty strokes, and reflects the animation of fast and furious fighting. The mellay is not a simple thrust-and-cut multiplication of slaughter, but has knightly aspects and traits. Iring, as he springs forward to face Hagen, says :—

Its verbal descriptions and knightly aspects

Ich hân ûf êre lâzen nu lange mîniu dinc,
und hân in volkes stürmen des besten vil getân. *

N. 2102, 2-3.

Wolfhart, dying, puts these words among others in the mouth of his uncle, the probable reporter of his death :—

Vor eines küneges handen lig ich hie hêrlîchen tôt. †

N. 2381, 4.

Sometimes the narrative passes into elegy :—

Sîn varwe was erblichen ; des tôdes zeichen truoc
Îrinc der vil küene : daz was in leit genuoc.
Genesen niht enmohte der Hâwartes man. ‡

N. 2143, 1-3.

There are pathetic incidents enough. Such are Rüdiger's present of a shield to Hagen, just before commencing to fight, the same prince's intercession for his daughter with his son-in-law that was to be, both men being doomed, the lament over the dead Gernot and Rüdiger, etc. After reading of the fight we are constrained to say "The pity of it." We seem to see

Pathetic side of the fighting

* For long I have made my conduct repose on honour, and have done a deal of bravery in national fights.

† At a king's hands I lie here in glorious death.

‡ His colour turned pale. Iring the greatly bold bore death's imprint. That was sorrow enough to them. In nowise might Hawart's man recover.

manliness and misfortune walking hand in hand the downward slope to death. Death is a felt presence :—

> Der tôt der suochte sêre dâ sîn gesinde was.*
>
> N. 2302, 3.

In these fighting cantos we feel strongly the contrast between the metre and the matter. It is as if a deemster were to give to his doom the form and the cast of a dance-lyric.

Siegfried

There is a superior attractiveness about the character of Siegfried. To put this attractiveness broadly, it is like that which attaches itself to some strong and chivalrous hero of romance.

He was of fair, vigorous, and courteous manhood. If Prometheus had had to make a man on his model, he would have taken equal parts of a Hercules and an Apollo, and distributed among these the parts of a Bayard, dashing the whole with some of the characteristics of a roving seeker after conquest and adventure. In the Nibelungenlied, perhaps his affability and renown, apart from actual recorded achievements, are most emphasised ; in the Volsung Saga, with the same reservation, his beauty and fearlessness. A man endowed with the triad of beauty, courage, and amiability, is irresistible, either in life or romance.

To the glory of the dragon-killer Siegfried added the grace of the expert in all knightly practices. Not only was he of amiable manners, but he was free from every taint of baseness, the mirror of honour undimmed by a single whiff of the breath of suspicion. There were bonds between him and the world of magic and mystery, and he at his own pleasure disposed of some of the forces of elfland. He bore a charmed and fateful life, a life that was of moment to men, and regulated by unseen powers. Add to these attractions the fact that he is the hero of a

* Death, he sought sorely where his retinue was.

tender love-tale, the impassioned, but patient and modest suitor of the beauteous and coy Kriemhild, and we have an assemblage of attractions concentrated in one individual that ought to deify him to our imaginations. We quite lose the ruffling champion on a pilgrimage of adventure in the many-sided dragon-queller, fairy prince, courtly knight, and redoubtable warrior.

There is another fact that imparts a pathetic interest to Siegfried's story, and that is, his undeserved death for another's fault, and at the hands of those whom he had benefited, on whom he had laid unforgettable obligations.

Kriemhild

Kriemhild is the heroine of the story in a sense in which Siegfried cannot be said to be its hero. The story begins and ends with her; she is the connecting link between the two parts, being the good genius of the first, and the evil genius of the second part. Her love, her sorrow, and her revenge may be said to be the three aspects of the story. These aspects, it is true, might be given otherwise as the advent, the assertion, and the *aristeia* of Hagen. The argument is a fabric with three façades.

The Nibelungenlied is a love story. The dawning of the passion that was to enthrall Kriemhild, by which she was to become enfeoffed to vengeance, and almost unsexed, is well described. Her feelings pass from maidenly modesty, sex-antagonism, and coy aloofness, into feminine curiosity, sex-affinity, and womanly passion.

The relations between Kriemhild and Brunhild are explicit enough, and present no complexity requiring analysis. Brunhild is haughty and ambitious, and seems to value her husband's rank and position rather than her own wifehood. Not so does Kriemhild. In praising her husband she says that among men he is like the sun among the stars. Brunhild coldly and tamely, if proudly, says that hers is the first of kings. Kriemhild praises her husband with more animation, more floweriness, than

Brunhild. She loves and admires him more than the other does hers. Kriemhild was before marriage meek, but marriage rapidly ripened her. The defence of her husband's honour sharpened her tongue ; she completely out-talked and flattened her adversary. The latter scratched the seeming meek dove, and found a veritable termagant. The weapons Kriemhild used were scarcely legitimate, but Brunhild was insufferable. She persisted in asserting Siegfried's vassalage. Kriemhild deprecated bitter words, but was forced to lift the glove thrown down to her.

Brunhild's perturbation is not accounted for by her jealousy over her husband's position and her anxiety to conserve it. It is doubtless a survival from the older version of the story, in which the early relations between her and Siegfried are set down as very intimate.

Hagen

In Hagen we have depicted a personage who from being, one might say, the villain of the piece, passes into its hero. His character is drawn in rather black colours in the first part of the poem. He appears to us fanatically, nay, offensively, loyal to his lady and her lord. His behaviour to Kriemhild is ruthlessly cruel. She had had some regard for him, for she wished him to go with her to Netherland. This Hagen had refused to do, sourly maintaining that it was his duty and the duty of his family to serve the royal princes of the Burgundian house. When Siegfried went on the fatal hunt, she even confided him to Hagen's care, intrusting the latter with the secret of her husband's invulnerability. Perhaps Hagen secretly hated Siegfried, being jealous of his fame, and afterwards instinctively reciprocated the feeling the widowed and betrayed lady bore him.

I daresay the duty of Hagen the vassal to his liege-lord explains everything. Anyhow, if he is the most brilliant, he is at the same time the most sinister embodiment of the loyalty due by a vassal to his lord. It is to be surmised that in those workings on the old plot that have given us our Nibelungenlied there has been effected for artistic purposes a considerable colouring of the aspect of the seamy side of Hagen's virtues. Hogni in the Volsung Saga is no such uncompromising character as is Hagen. He even dissuades Gunnar from murdering Sigurd.

It is after the resolve has been taken to visit Hunland that Hagen steps into pleasing prominence. He did not counsel this journey, being suspicious of Kriemhild's proffered entertainment, but willingly acquiesced in the decision of his superiors, partly for duty's sake, partly as a protestation against the taunting remarks of Gernot and Giselher. After this, neither omens, nor prophecies, nor demonstrations of doom can deter, or even daunt him. He is impervious to fear, and a stranger to superstition. His stubbornness reaches the pitch of sublimity. He yields not to man, nor to fate. He was not, however, unimpressionable. The gift of a shield from Rüdiger, at a critical moment of the fight in the hall, drew tears down his cheeks. He wept over the deaths of Rüdiger and Gernot. The fate of Volker affected him deeply. Human magnanimity and human fragility moved him to tears. He died heroically, conserving to the end his loyalty to his master and his master's interests. He had proved himself faithful, pushing his faith even into the employment of craft and treachery against the common enemy. Hildebrand saved such a man from the reproach of having died unavenged at the hands of a woman, for,

> "Wâfen," sprach der fürste, "wie ist nu tôt gelegen
> von eines wîbes handen der aller beste degen,
> der ie kom ze sturme oder ie schilt getruoc!
> swie vînt aber ich im waere, ez ist mir leide genuoc." *
>
> N., 2454.

* "Alack," said the prince, "that there should now lie, slain by the hands of a woman, the very best of all thanes that ever came to battle, or ever bore a shield. However much I was his enemy, I have sorrow enough."

The task that Klopstock set himself did not contain the elements of success. No one could have made a satisfactory and entertaining story of activity and accomplishment out of the materials that our poet was pleased to incorporate into his poem. It is not only that invention is to a large extent shackled by the character of the story, but that there is no adequate basis on which to exercise it. Satisfaction, from the point of view of heroic narrative, can only be got out of a story of broad human aspects, or capable of much humanisation. Secular activity, such as is shown by men, or such as is so in virtue of its quality, is essential to the success of the epic tale. Now the chief person in the story is, in many ways, an exponent of passivity, and where the poet introduces masterfulness—one should rather say, employs masterful agents—he does so by the introduction of unepical force. Fervid assertions on the part of the poet, or of a cloud of witnesses, of the hero's uniqueness, are not an allowable substitute for activity.

The Messiah. The quality of Klopstock's matter

Klopstock recounts the usual facts about the Messiah with some notable additions and adaptations, but he confines his narrative to the last few weeks of his hero's life, thus missing the only opportunity his matter afforded him of executing something in epic. He might have told the whole story of Jesus' life, the story of the man who died for an idea; he might have developed and respectfully augmented his human activity; he might have included as actors, or, at all events, as remotely connected with the action, the great personages of the land. The biblical narrative affords matter and justification for this handling. But the divine side of the story would have needed careful management, and could only have been referred to allusively, and this would not have suited the poet, who, as a devout and militant christian, a poet-

His handling of the matter

missionary I might call him, had beliefs and meant to assert their validity.

The poet has not then made the most of his topic, for, by treating only the climax of the story, he has cut himself off from the possibility of having a properly built climax in his own version of the events, and has been forced to replace incident by monologues, rhapsodical matter, and general pietistic detail. I daresay the epic he would thus have produced would have been a pale, if not tame one, and it would have been difficult to refrain from sermonising in it. One would have been strongly tempted to bring into it sidelight effects, and these would have led the introducer into rhapsody, just where similar manœuvres have led Klopstock.

Many actors are introduced for the manufacture of circumstance, which in this poem means the record of emotions, or what, for the lack of a better name, we must call spectacular effect. Some cantos are positively crammed with actors, or rather, individuals under notice, for nobody acts much in the poem, who come up, each one, for brief mention. It has been made a subject of reproach to Milton that he gave Adam too little to do. Klopstock has atoned for the neglect. He has given plenty of work to Adam and to Eve.

A specimen

The method and materials of a canto might be thus described :—A series of tableaux is chosen. The feelings of the various personages are thought out, either to be described by the poet, or spoken by their possessor. The result then runs out and we have impassioned apostrophes, lyrical emotion done into words, snatches of narrative, soliloquies, and speeches, lachrymose or noisy, as the case may be.

This author is particularly fond of the trope apostrophe. Everything is apostrophised—heaven and earth, natural objects, the past, the future. The interlocutors do not speak to a definite point, but in the air. They do not so much address as apostrophise, if one may so speak, one another.

Klopstock's matter is mainly an analysis of the subjectivity of the actors, and that subjectivity consists of exaggerated emotion. The tumultuous imaginings of the poet are often hysterical in manner, and vary between highly-wrought religious exaltation and the merest maundering. Wickedness is blackened, and goodness glorified, and both made grotesque. Sometimes the poem reads like a tale told by one half-frenzied, we are so much troubled by the hyperecstatic religious fervour of some of the characters, and the wild mental dervishry of others. It cannot be that this tortured record of subjectivity, whipped into self-consciousness and translated into speech, is epic narrative proper, which flows on broadly and calmly, with now and then a natural access of rapidity, but with never a trace of such tempestuous and frothy activity. The fact is that, so long as the objective tack of epos is kept to, there is no danger of this storm and stress of words.

The poet analyses the subjectivity of the actors

If one reads the poem with conscious reference to the metre, its effect is more pleasing than on another method. Such a reading sheds a sort of blandness over its emotional tirades, and tempers its vehemence with a show of stateliness. Klopstock seems to seek verse effects, and to make them, not by disposition of the strict metrical feet, nor by any exact trick of metre, but by the employment of rhythmical verbal feet of one or more words. The verse, then, is only verse by convention with an artistic adaptation of accents. I am not a competent judge of the qualities of German hexameter. I can recite the Messiah, but have often to stop and scan my line before I can resume recitation. Klopstock does not tie himself down to the classical pauses.

The metre of the poem

Perhaps a brief account of the argument of one book will help to an understanding of the poet's manner. I choose for this purpose the ninth :—Eloah (the most excellent of the angels and messenger of the Almighty) returns from the throne of God to the cross, and relates what he has seen to the patriarchs, who, as the previous book tells us, had been summoned thither. (Jesus had been nailed to the cross in the previous canto, and remains thereon for three cantos.) Peter wanders about the neighbourhood of the cross, a prey to his own sorrowful reflections. He is consoled by his guardian angel and ventures within sight of the Crucified. Abraham, Isaac, and Moses converse together. Abraham prays to the Messiah. The souls of pious heathens are brought to the cross. The Redeemer addresses Mary and John, who stand at the foot of the cross. The earthquake begins again, and its shocks reach even to a subterranean cavern of Olivet where Abbadona is hiding his sorrow. He comes to Calvary, and, donning the aspect of an angel of light, approaches the cross, and puts a question to Abdiel regarding the sufferer. Abdiel simply pronounces the word Abbadona, whereat the fallen angel takes to flight. Lastly, Obaddon, the angel of death, brings the soul of Judas to the cross, takes him to view heaven, and then casts him into torment.

The argument of one book

Let us now give some attention to the characters of the Messias. Abbadona is one of the most pleasing characters in the poem. It is true that his portraiture exhibits the vices of the poet's manner. His soliloquies are incoherent and tediously plaintive; he raves in one strain, and harks back on his raving. With all its faults the characterisation of Abbadona is a fine study in pathos, reaching its climax, I think, in the scene round the cross above mentioned. Abbadona had been the friend of Abdiel, but had lacked his sturdy faith. He had hesitated and

The characters. Abbadona

been lost, but was swiftly repentant. He proved his repentance by his opposition to Satan in council. With tearful and yearning interest he followed the Messiah's sufferings, and was at length admitted to pardon. The relations between Abdiel and Abbadona were no doubt suggested by those between Satan and Beelzebub in Paradise Lost.

Philo

Philo is one of the most distasteful characters ever presented to a reader. The poet represents him as the leader of the persecution of Jesus by the Pharisees. His truculence and inveterate hostility to the Messiah are painfully horrible, *e.g.*, he thus addresses the accused, at the trial :—

> Der soll so leise nicht schlafen !
> Lieg' dann bei den Erwürgten, die Gott verworfen hat ! Schlaf' dort,
> Dort den eisernen Schlaf, dort, wo die kommende Sonne
> Und der wandelnde Mond den Dampf der Verwesungen auftrinkt,
> Bis der Tod reift, und von Gebeinen Golgatha weiss wird ! *
> M. vi, 286.

I think that Klopstock must have meant to describe in him the sinner against the Holy Ghost. His every act is detestable and reeking with hatred. His traits are too strongly drawn, and his faults too darkly inked in, to be those of a mere self-righteous Pharisee. The contrast between the calm of the Messiah, and the hate and frenzy of Philo and Caiaphas, described in the same place, strikes the reader curiously :—

> Alle Hoheit, sogar die Hoheit des sterblichen Weisen
> Leget 'er ab und war nur ruhig, als säh 'er den Abfall
> Einer Quelle vor sich.† M. vi, 227.

---

* Thou shalt not sleep so lightly (as those thou hast raised). Lie down then beside the slaughtered whom God has cursed. Sleep the iron sleep of death there, there where the advancing sun and the wandering moon drink up the fumes of corruption, till death mellows all and Golgotha is white with bones.

† All loftiness he laid aside, even the loftiness of the mortal sage, and showed only the calm of him that gazeth on the fall of some trickling stream.

Philo committed tragic suicide when he learned of the empty tomb. He is a man of impossible actions and motives. Caiaphas is another exaggerated character. He is too vengeful, too much so for the testimony of holy writ, and too much for poetic dignity.

Our author's theory of Judas' conduct deserves attention. He regards him as a sort of deluded visionary trying to force on a day that was to give him temporal magnificence. Our taste, I take it, will not approve of the epic device by which Satan appears to Judas as the spirit of his dead father, and from the vantage ground of that form successfully tempts him to sin. The manner in which Iscariot is made to play his part in the epic, and the punishment meted out to him, are not quite consistent with the above apologetic theory. The facts, however, of the biblical narrative had to be taken into account. There is a piled-up horror about the account of Judas' suicide that is most repulsive, when it is not half-comic. After death the poor wretch's disembodied spirit is quite gratuitously haled to the cross to receive an object lesson on the redemption of all men but himself; wafted to a spot whence he could discern heaven, that he might call to remembrance the happy things, the saintship that had been missed; and then formally plunged into hell with the loss of salvation dinned into his ears.

Judas

Satan, in Klopstock, is rather a squalid spirit, and so are his compeers, with the exception of Abbadona. They have no nobility about them, not even nobility on the wane. There is more of the heavy devil and trickster in them than of the ruined seraph. The plans they form have some affinities to those in Paradise Lost, and, indeed, there is many an echo of Milton in the poem, but Milton watered, enfeebled, and perverted. Klopstock is as like Milton as a well-meaning, ranting evangelist of passable parts is like an archangel,

Satan

and the brilliance of their respective poems, when compared, is as that of the steady, all-illumining sun to that of a gusty, garish light.

Portia

Portia, the wife of Pilate, takes a more than woman's interest in Jesus. She discerns his majesty through his meekness, is strangely troubled, and driven to reflection. Mary visits her to intercede for her son, when Portia relates a dream she had had overnight. In it Socrates had appeared, and had imparted to her partly instruction, partly revelation, but had left a weight of mystery. Portia is a good conception, only it has not the realisation it might have had, and its working out is disfigured by the too sinking pathos and religionism of the author.

Similes

The poem has some noticeable attempts in the way of simile-making. Of the similes in the Messiad, those that bring nature before us are the best. Nature similes are usually old, but they are none the less inevitable on that account, and may now and again be invested with fresh beauty. I shall cite one or two. The first is an old and well-worn simile, but pleasingly turned nevertheless. The words are Eve's and spoken over the martyrs that are to be :—

> Ach wie in Sturm gebrochen die Purpurblume dahinsinkt,
> Also werden von euch die Geliebteren vor der Erwürger
> Schwerte sinken und, wenn sie sinken, dem Tode noch lächeln.*
>
> M. viii, 471.

The second is a well-known mode of comparison for persuasive speech :—

> Wie vom Hermon der Tau, wenn der Morgen erwacht ist,

---

* Alas, just as the purple flower, broken in a gale, droopeth away, so will the dearest among you sink under the murderers' sword, and, while sinking, aye smile on death.

Träufelt und wie wohlriechende Lüfte vom Oelbaum fliessen,
Also fliesst von Philippus' Munde die liebliche Rede.*
M. iii, 209.

The third is unusual and likens Mary to the Mount of Transfiguration :—

Wie vor allen Bergen Judäas Tabor hervorragt,
Er der Zeuge der Herrlichkeit Jesus'—
. . . .
Also war unter den heiligen Frauen die hohe Maria.†
M. iv, 713.

The fourth is said of Gabriel on his passage to the abode of the guardian angels in the centre of the earth :—

Wie zu der Zeit, wenn der Winter belebt, ein heiliger Festtag
Ueber beschneiten Gebirgen nach trüben Tagen hervorgeht ;
Wolken und Nacht entfliehen vor ihm, die beeisten Gefilde,
Hohe durchsichtige Wälder entnebeln ihr Antlitz und glänzen :
So ging Gabriel jetzt auf den mitternächtlichen Bergen.‡
M. i, 603.

Sometimes the simile is expanded for beauty's sake merely, and not for illustration, as in the above, and in the following simile, said of the descent of Satan upon Judas :—

Also nahet die Pest in mitternächtlicher Stunde
Schlummerden Städten. Es liegt auf ihren verbreiteten Flügeln
An den Mauern der Tod und haucht verderbende Dünste.
Jetzo liegen die Städte noch ruhig ; bei nächtlicher Lampe
Wacht noch der Weise ; noch unterreden sich edlere Freunde,

---

* As at morn's awakening, the dew trickleth from Hermon, and as odorous breaths are wafted from the olive, even so sweet speech cometh from the lips of Philips.

† Just as above all the hills of Judah Tabor riseth up, Tabor, the witness of Jesus' glory, even so stood out Mary, betwixt the holy women.

‡ As in keen wintertime, a holy festive day-dawn passeth forth over snowclad hills after days of gloom, and clouds and night fly before it, and icy plains and lofty re-appearing woods show their bright faces through the mist, even so now passed Gabriel over the darksome hills.

Bei unentheiligtem Wein, in dem Schatten duftender Lauben,
Von der Seele, der Freundschaft, und ihrer unsterblichen Dauer ;
Aber bald wird der furchtbare Tod—*

M. iii, 539.

The last one I shall quote is noticeable rather for novelty than merit. The person compared is Matthew, whom the poet represents to have been brought up luxuriously, and to have lived for this world, before his abnegation of self :—

So entreisst sich ein Held der Könige weichlichen Töchtern ;
Ruft ihn der Tod für das Vaterland.†

M. iii, 281.

There is a large variety of similes in the Messiad, but some are prosy, some even tame.

Poetical fervour

The poetical skill and force of some of the verses in the poem claim a little attention. I shall quote a finely imaginative passage with just a trace of incoherence in it. It is said of Christ in Gethsemane :—

Hätt' ich die Hoheit
Eines Propheten, zu fassen die ewige Seele des Menschen
Und mit gewaltigem Arm sie fortzureissen ; und hätt 'ich
Eines Seraphs erhabene Stimme, mit welcher er Gott singt ;
Tönete mir von dem Munde die schreckenvolle Posaune,
Die auf Sina erklang, dass unter ihr bebte des Bergs Fuss ;
Sprächen der Cherubim Donner aus mir, Gedanken zu sagen,
Deren Hoheit selbst der Posaune Ton nicht erreichte ;

---

* Thus the pestilence, at midnight, draweth nigh slumbering cities. Death, hiding in its outspread wings, hovereth near their walls, and breatheth forth deadly vapours. All is yet peace in the cities ; over his midnight lamp the student still poreth ; friendship, noble and pure, beneath odorous bowers, still discourseth, over unmisused wine, of the undying soul, and of unending amity; but soon will dread death—

† Thus a hero teareth himself from the dainty daughters of kings, when death calleth him to die for his fatherland.

Dennoch ersänk 'ich, du Gottversöhner! dein Leiden zu singen,
Als mit dem Tode du rangst, als unerbittlich dein Gott war.*

M. v, 348.

Here is a fine idyllic picture of family life on the Star of Innocence :—

An der Rechten des Liebenden stand die Mutter der Menschen,
Seiner Kinder, so schön, als ob der bildende Schöpfer
Ihres Mannes Umarmungen jetzt die Unsterbliche brächte;
Unter ihren blühenden Töchtern der Männinnen schönste.
An der linken Seite stand ihm sein erstgeborner,
Würdiger Sohn, nach dem Bilde des Vaters voll himmlischer Unschuld.
Ausgebreitet zu seinen Füssen, auf lachenden Hügeln,
Leichtumkränzet mit Blumen ihr Haar, das lockichter wurde,
Und mit klopfendem Herzen des Vaters Tugend zu folgen,
Sassen die jüngsten Enkel.†

M. v, 162.

It can hardly be said that Klopstock has neglected the main story for episodes, for he scarcely exhibits any such thing as a main story, presenting merely a loose arrangement of scenes. There is less and less story in the epic as it proceeds; we simply meet with accretions. It was not wrestling with the difficulties of a subject, though these exist plentifully, that drove our poet into the subjective method of treatment. More could have been made of the subject, and the work of the

The poet has not epic force

* Had I a prophet's grandeur to capture the immortal soul of man, and with mighty power bear it with me; had I a seraph's lofty voice, with which he singeth God; did there thunder from my mouth the awful trumpet that sounded on Sinai, so that the base of the mount did quake beneath it; did the thunder of the cherubim speak from my lips, and proclaim thoughts whose height not even the trumpet's note hath ever reached, still should I fail, Divine Redeemer, to sing Thy sorrow, when Thou didst wrestle with death, when Thy God turned His face from Thee.

† On her husband's right stood the mother of men, her children, as fair as if creating God had but now led her immortality to her husband's embrace, fairest of the group of women, and that, standing among her youthful daughters. On his left side stood his first-born, a dutiful son, the image of his father, full of heavenly innocence. Scattered around him on the smiling knolls, their ringleted hair lightly crowned with flowers, sat the youngest grandchildren, with hearts eager to copy their father's virtue.

poet reveals plainly enough his incapacity for the virile handling of any epical theme. He has no characterisation properly so called. The harangues and soliloquies he imposes on his principal actors are unsatisfactory as revelations of character, and the pen-portraits of minor actors are pictures of shadowy figures with thin rims of framework. His best qualities, pathos and benignity, are comparatively cheap, and a faculty for projecting and describing emotion is not the highest possession of the mind.

He has general literary power and the gift of language

No one can deny Klopstock the possession of considerable literary power. He had the gift of copious expression, and a strong sense of colour in language, which often, however, led him into a rant of figurative and flowery expression. He must have had a fine eye for the loveliness of the outside world, for his language is often finely suggestive of natural beauties.

We do come across bits of simple and subdued narrative, sometimes powerful, sometimes degenerating into commonness, but the reader is never very far from a rapture, and the gossiping chronicle of moralities, apart from action, becomes wearisome. Speaking, then, of the poem as a whole, one is constrained to say that the matter is diffuse and inappropriate, and that the movement is the uninteresting movement of mediocrity.

CHAPTER V

THE ITALIAN EPIC

The Jerusalem Delivered. The first crusade as a subject for an epic

THE first crusade for many reasons was a good subject for an epic. Such a subject appealed to the imaginations and sympathies of the men of Tasso's time, and still appeals to ours. It was a case of Europe *versus* Asia, of Christ against Mahound. Its religious aspect lent it the validity and compulsion of a national subject. Italians could have a fellow-feeling in regard to it, and so, for that matter, such was the scope of its appeal, could men of other nationalities. The holders of the Holy Sepulchre became an object of dislike to Christians at an early period, and they were in especial abhorrence in the poet's days. The motives and object of the crusaders were of the most hallowed imaginable. For themselves, and by proxy, they were to prove the gratitude of Christians to their crucified Saviour by freeing his place of sepulture from the desecration that its possession by unbelievers was held to imply. They were to restore to Christianity the outward memento of the life and death of its founder, to be a quickener of its faith, and a guarantee of the solidity of the same. The taking of the holy city was to be at once an assertion of the superiority of Christ's people and knights to heathen miscreants, and its possession a symbol of the coming predominance of the cross in the world, a symbol, if not an anticipation of the second advent. All the fervour, all the gratitude, all the ambition of Christendom, as Christendom, was outpoured in the crusades. The singer of the first crusade had then a subject, than which, for modernity, resonance, and enchaining attractiveness, a better could not well be found.

The subject suited Tasso

The subject suited Tasso. It gave him the serious stand he required to assume before he could invest himself with the gravity, or take up the purposeful attitude of the epic poet. Sonnets, a pastoral, even the authorship of a Rinaldo do not always neighbour the qualities that make such a poet. The momentum that impels to the writing of epic poetry is an inward-outward one, and its elements may be present in very unequal quantities. John Milton's poetic preluding did not, it is true, necessarily argue the poet of Paradise Lost. But Milton was a more serious, more self-contained, and stronger man altogether than Tasso. One can regard him as an epic poet by heavenly compulsion, but Tasso was the favoured and flattering poet of a court, and an epic subject, before it had any likelihood of being well-treated, had to touch him on his serious side. This the Gerusalemme Liberata did, for Tasso was a religious man, and had been brought up pietistically. His subsequent madness was due in a certain degree to religious mania, and, to disarm clerical opposition, he invented an allegorical interpretation for the matter of his poem. It was religious enthusiasm that reinforced Tasso's patriotic promptings, and stood to him in the place of a passion for the heroic.

Its potentialities

The cause of the crusaders was such as evoked and demanded heroic action. As soon as a soldier assumed the badge of the cross he became theoretically a Christian hero. The vows of a knight, by his participation in the expedition, became still more binding and consecrating. Heroism gilded with sanctity, humanity glorified by heroism and with all alloy of selfishness removed, furnished to the enthusiastic and mounting imagination of our poet a theme of no ordinary promise. The illusion of the heroic was three parts already there. The great powers of the poet were set free to adorn the noble action. He was at full liberty to study romantic embellishments, and to indulge his forte for the tender and the elegiac. He could undistractedly add to the lessons he had received from the epic schooling of Virgil and Homer the teachings of his own doctrine of the mixture of the antique and romantic.

The strong individuality in the crusading army

The crusading army was composed of semi-independent detachments mustered and led by men of exalted position and knightly sentiments. Each one would have chafed at the undue repression of his personal activity and forwardness, and, indeed, war had not yet by any means ceased to be the fights of paladins against paladins. These facts help to explain the prominent individuality to be found in Tasso's epic. His actors in many regards bear a resemblance to the homeric *βασιλεῖς*. The quality of his matter and his mixing of two poetical modes, the classical and the romantic, enabled him to write for us a stirring and many-featured poem. Rinaldo, Tancredi, Goffredo, Raimondo, Argante, Solimano, Clorinda, Armida, and Erminia are characters that impress us markedly and variously. Strong individuality and variety of it there certainly is in the Jerusalem Delivered, and, if its presence in these two aspects of strength and variety does not impress us as the same quality with the same aspects does in Homer, it is because of the factitiousness of the modern epic.

Homer was, as has been said, nature, and the naturalness of the acting and surroundings in his world augments the impression made by pure strength. The amount of feigning and man-making in modern work is bound to abstract from distinctness, for art is not as versatile as nature, is baffled, and repeats. Homer certainly repeats, but he repeats automatically, and quietly, and not under effort and with circumstance, and amid the repetition there is always some bit of nature to hold by.

The argument

Tasso begins the poem with the despatch of the angel Gabriel to Tortosa, a town near Antioch, where the crusaders were wintering, to urge Godfrey to call a meeting of the chiefs and exhort them to resume the march to Jerusalem. Godfrey obeys, and is chosen to lead the army.

Aladino, the king of Jerusalem, hears with dismay of the approach of the crusaders. Acting on the advice of the wizard Ismeno, he causes an image of the Virgin to be removed from the Christian temple and placed in the king's mosque. It is asserted by Ismeno that the purloined statue will be a palladium for the city. The image is stolen from the mosque overnight, and the king's rage thereat leads him to proclaim a massacre of Christians. Sofronia, to save her fellow-believers, takes upon herself the guilt of the act, and is condemned to be burned alive. Olindo, an ardent but unrecognised lover, denies her part in the deed, and declares that he alone is the guilty person. The king orders them both to be burned, and burned they would have been, had not Clorinda, who was coming to offer her services to Aladino, at this juncture appeared on the scene. She orders them to be set free, and persuades the king to ratify her act.

The Christian army on its march to the holy city arrives at Emmaus. There it is met by two envoys from the king of Egypt. Alethes, one of these, a man of a smooth tongue, fruitlessly tries to persuade Godfrey to stay his hand, and rest content with what had been won.

Argante, the other of the envoys, a man of war, does not return to Egypt with Alethes, but makes his way to Jerusalem to help the defenders. The army advances to Jerusalem, which is beheld with rapture. A sally is made from the city by Clorinda, and Tancredi is detached to drive back her following. The Christian host is now quite visible from the walls, and Erminia, a fugitive princess, daughter of Cassano the late king of Antioch, like another Helen from another Troy, shows and names to Aladino the different leaders of the crusading army. Meantime Tancredi dishelms Clorinda, and recognises her as the maid whom he had seen by the fountain, and whose beauty had haunted him ever since. The pagans are being driven back to the city, when Argante, with a force posted for that purpose, rushes to their help. Dudone, leader of the *avventurieri*, reinforces Tancredi, and repels the pagans, but is himself slain.

The devils meet in conclave, and on the advice of Pluto, a scowling and recalcitrant spirit, resolve to offer active opposition to the Christians. Idraote, king of Damascus, a famous sorcerer, at the instigation of the infernals, sends his niece Armida, the pearl of the orient, and a sorceress as well, among the western soldiers to work them confusion and ill. She feigns herself to have been dispossessed of the kingdom of Damascus by an intriguing uncle, and asks Godfrey to reinstate her by granting the service of ten of his bravest knights. He refuses to entertain her request, so long as his great task is unaccomplished, but, on the intercession of his brother Eustace, agrees to let her have ten of the *avventurieri*, the choice of whom he delegates to Dudone's successor. Armida remains some time in the camp, and ensnares in her toils many of the more youthful and impressionable knights. Eustace, deeply smitten, and anxious to be one of the ten, approaches Rinaldo, and offers to help him to obtain Dudone's post, if he will promise to choose him for one of Armida's attendant knights. Gernando, the Norwegian prince, who desires to succeed Dudone, resents Rinaldo's pretensions, and, misled by ambition, tries to belittle his reputation. A quarrel is the result, in which Gernando is killed, and Rinaldo has to flee from the camp.

Armida's ten are chosen by lot, and depart with their enslaver. Others secretly follow her, and the army is enfeebled by the withdrawal of so many knights. They are brought to her castle on the Dead Sea, regaled for some time, and then changed into fishes. The witch lifts the enchantment, and promises them her goodwill, if they become pagans, and agree to kill Godfrey. This, all, save Rambaldo, refuse to do, and, after a short imprisonment, are sent disarmed and in chains to the king of Egypt.

Of their number is Tancredi, who had been decoyed to Armida's castle. He had accepted Argante's challenge to single combat issued to the Christian leaders. After a severe, but indecisive contest, the two were separated, to meet again after six days. Meanwhile Erminia, whose heart had been won by Tancredi's princely demeanour towards her after the capture of Antioch, determined to leave the city and nurse the wounded chief. For this purpose she donned Clorinda's armour, and passed outside the city walls, accompanied by her squire and maid. Her squire was sent to apprise Tancredi of the approach of a lady to the Christian camp. Between the despatch and the return of the messenger the two women fell in with some soldiers of the crusading army posted there to intercept a convoy that was being brought to Jerusalem. They took to hurried flight. Tancredi, impatient of the non-arrival of the lady, whom he deemed to be Clorinda, rose from his couch, put on some armour, and rode out in search of her. It was while following her traces that he was lured to Armida's castle, and while imprudently pursuing the renegade Rambaldo, whom he had defeated, into it, that he was entrapped and imprisoned.

During Tancredi's absence, Godfrey, in default of another champion, desires to fight with Argante, but is dissuaded by Raimondo, who takes up the challenge, and is much helped by an intervening, but invisible angel. While the fight is in progress, an archer shoots an arrow at Raimondo and wounds him, thus breaking the truce. Godfrey, irritated at this, and alarmed for the safety of his champion, attacks the pagans and drives them back, but the infernals raise a storm which blows right in the faces of the Christians, and Clorinda, taking advantage of this, charges her enemies and drives them back to their camp.

News is brought to the Christians that Sveno, the only son of the king of Denmark, while leading a large body of warriors to join the crusade, had been surprised on the borders of Palestine by Solimano, and slain. It is Carlo who brings the news, and he carries also with him the sword of his master to be delivered, so Heaven ordained, to the chosen avenger, to Rinaldo. The Christians are further discouraged by the arrival of a party of foragers with armour recognised to be Rinaldo's, which they declare to have been taken from a body they had found in a little inclosed plain not far from Gaza. It was Armida who had thrust a corse into the suit of armour discarded by Rinaldo, when he assumed a pagan disguise, and put it in the way of straggling parties from the army of the crusaders. The soldiers, from the nature of the report, are made to suspect treachery, and under the leadership of Argillano break out into open mutiny.

Solimano, who slew Sveno, had been the sultan of Nicea, but had been defeated and made a wanderer by the crusaders. He had entered the service of the king of Egypt, who had employed him to gain over the Arabs. He secured their adherence, and with their enlisted bands performed many services. He was mindful of his former high estate, and purposed a deed that should bring him both vengeance and distinction. With one in this mood the fury Alecto had an easy task, when she incited him to a night attack on Godfrey's camp. The attack is delivered, and at the same time a sally, headed by Argante and Clorinda, is made from the city. The Christians are hard pressed. Argillano, the mutineer, escapes from confinement, and redeems his fault by brave deeds, but is killed by Solimano. Matters are looking very serious for the crusaders, when a company of fifty knights joins them, and turns the fortunes of the day. These are the knights whom Armida beguiled, and sent as captives to the king of Egypt at Gaza, and whom Rinaldo has just set free, after killing their convoy.

Solimano's blow had missed, and its despondent author prepares to seek the army of the king of Egypt, when Ismeno follows him, comforts him, and brings him back to the city in a magic car. The presence of the fiery Nicene infuses new vigour into the defence. On the other side Godfrey prepares his first assault. The assault is successful, to the extent that a breach is made in the wall, but the crusading chief, who had undertaken the fatigues and performed the task of a common soldier, is wounded and has to retire from the field. Solimano and Argante make a partially successful attempt to destroy the siege-engines, but are driven back by Tancredi. Godfrey, his wounds miraculously healed, returns to the fight, and continues it vigorously till nightfall.

Next day Clorinda, anxious to emulate the daring of Solimano and Argante, determined to sally out at night and destroy the huge tower of the besiegers. Her attendant, the eunuch Arsete, endeavours to dissuade her, and to strengthen his efforts, tells her that she is the child of Christian parents, her father being Senapo, king of Ethiopia. She had, he told Clorinda, been removed by him from Ethiopia by her mother's orders. This same mother had directed her to be baptised as a Christian, but this he, Arsete, being a bigoted Mahometan, had neglected to do. His mistress, though strangely affected by the tale, for it threw light on a disquieting dream she had had some time before, refuses to abandon her purpose. She and Argante, for he had insisted on accompanying her, leave the town walls, and fire and burn the tower. They had not done this undiscovered, but had to fight for the accomplishment of their purpose. Their task done, they retire to the town, pursued, and Clorinda, through indiscreet attention to a soldier who had wounded her, is shut out of the city. Tancredi overtakes her, as she hurries round the ramparts seeking another entrance, and, not discerning her person, or her sex, provokes her to battle. They fight violently. In truth, the poet's account of the contest displays a good deal of exaggeration. Clorinda is overcome. Tancredi's grief at the discovery of the identity of his opponent is unbounded. She asks him to perform the rite of baptism on her before she dies, and this he does with the water of a brook, using his helmet as a font.

Ismeno, to prevent the Christians from constructing new machines, lays the wood from which they obtained materials under an enchantment, and no one could break this enchantment, not even Tancredi, for, just as he was crowning his success by cutting down an enchanted tree, the dead Clorinda spoke from it and reproached him with wounding her afresh.

Godfrey, obedient to a vision, accedes to Guelfo's request for the recall of Rinaldo. Carlo, the friend of Sveno, and Ubaldo are sent to fetch the hero back. They set out for Ascalon, where, on arriving, they see a reverend old man walking on the waters of a river.

He entertains them, shows them wonders, and tells them what has befallen Rinaldo, and where he at present is. This hero, after he had freed the knights who were on their road to Egypt, became a special object of resentment to Armida. She dogged his footsteps, and, when in his wandering he had reached the river Orontes, arranged an enchantment, and by means of a lovely island, and a lovely singing naiad, bewitched the young warrior into sleep. He was now in her power, but the love she felt, as she gazed on the sleeping Apollo, drove out of her all desire for vengeance. The enamoured witch then conveyed him by magic art to an islet of the Isles of Fortune. The two warriors are instructed by the old man how to reach this place and pass through its enchantments. They take ship and are steered to the isles by a divinely-sent maid. On reaching their destination they penetrate to Armida's bower, and, taking advantage of her temporary absence, press to Rinaldo's side and show him his reflection in the diamond shield that the old man had provided them with. Rinaldo is amazed and conscience-stricken at his effeminate reflection in the truth-revealing shield, and follows the knights to the shore. He disregards all the entreaties of Armida, who follows him imploringly, and with his two companions sails to Palestine, where he receives from the aforesaid old man a suit of armour and an emblazoned shield, and from Carlo the sword of Sveno.

Armida, after her desertion by Rinaldo, dispels and destroys, with the aid of three hundred demons, her enchanted palace, and speeds through the air to her castle on the Dead Sea. There she decides to join the king of Egypt and second his efforts against the Christians. This monarch was mustering an army at Gaza, with which to raise the siege of Jerusalem. Too old himself for war, he hands over the command of his army to Emireno, an Armenian, and an apostate. Armida arrives among the Egyptians, and, in the course of a speech, offers to marry him who kills Rinaldo.

On his return to the camp Rinaldo enters the enchanted wood, and, undeterred by prodigies, cuts down a tree, by which act the enchantment is broken. Godfrey is now able to construct his warlike machines, and the siege is pressed on with great vigour. One day, during these preparations, a dove pursued by a hawk drops into Godfrey's bosom. She is the bearer of a note from the Egyptian captain to Aladino bidding him hold out for a few days longer. An immediate assault is decided on, and in this assault the city is taken. Ismeno, the wizard, is slain on the walls in the exercise of his incantations. Tancredi and Argante meet in the assault, and retire to fight out their quarrel, and in the duel Argante is slain. Solimano and Aladino, seeing the city taken, retire to the Tower of David.

Vafrino, Tancredi's squire, who had been sent as a spy into the Egyptian army, returns and gives Godfrey valuable information. He brings with him Erminia. She had found refuge and a welcome in a shepherd's hut after her flight from the Christian outposts. Wandering from her place of shelter she was made prisoner by a band of marauders, and taken to Gaza, where she received the protection of Armida. There she heard of a plot against Godfrey's life, to be put into execution by a few knights armed in the Frankish manner, and discovered it to Vafrino.

The Egyptian army is defeated, and many of its leaders slain. Rinaldo performs prodigies of valour. Solimano and Aladino rush out from the tower to join the Egyptians. The former escapes, the latter is slain in the effort to escape. Gildippe, the Christian amazon, and Odoardo, her husband, are slain by Solimano, who in his turn is slain by Rinaldo. Armida, seeing that the day is lost, retires from the battle and prepares to commit suicide. Rinaldo comes up with her, speaks to her tenderly, and wooes her from paganism. She consents to become a Christian.

Tasso's characters

Tasso's characters are distinctly drawn. In the drawing he observes impartiality, and does not unduly exalt the Christians to the disadvantage of the Saracens. Of course he had to be guided by the necessities of the story, and could not escape the predilections of creed and race. In epic, as in other storytelling, some persons have got to be inferior to others, and the vanquished serve in some degree as a foil to the victors. Tasso, as a European and Christian poet, and as the chooser of a subject that presented popular heroes to be eulogised, was constrained to depreciate the Saracens by comparison. There is, everything considered, a discernible belittling of the male pagans. The part he plays, and his circumstances, make Aladino rather a poor specimen of kinghood. But Solimano and Argante, who fill great parts, and are personally commanding men, might touch the heroic at more points. The pagan women have almost all the field to themselves, and they are not belittled. Sofronia and Gildippe are the only women on the Christian side.

Impartiality in the character-drawing of epic

Milton is impartial. Indeed, he is usually alleged to have made a wrong distribution of glory. Homer invests with glory Hector and others on the Trojan side. His combatants, however, are worshippers of the same gods, and this means the absence of what has sometimes been a considerable incentive to partiality. Ariosto is very impartial, though he celebrates combatants of different creeds. Ruggiero and Marphisa, it is true, two of his principal pagan characters, are of Christian stock. The idea of a false and a true religion has a perverting effect on a poet as a drawer of character.

Clorinda is a fine creation, but she does not fascinate

Q

us as does Camilla. There is something unconventional, something aerial, about the latter. And yet Clorinda is no vulgar amazon. She has enough of bravery, dash, and general derring-do, but many other more amiable virtues as well. She is just and magnanimous to Olindo and Sofronia. One of the best uses of the episode in which these appear is to serve to introduce to us the person of Clorinda. It was a happy stroke of art on Tasso's part to make it the setting for the introduction of Clorinda, and this value of the episode outweighs any biographical value it may have. She lives on sisterly terms with Erminia, the lioness with the hind. Still there is a mannishness with Clorinda that we do not find with Camilla. Tasso had not had Virgil's dream of fair militant girlhood, and the exigences of the story, that is, the more civilised character of the fighting, and a narrative more in leash, darken the poetic tracings. We feel Clorinda to be older than Camilla, and are conscious of a hardening, a coarsening of character. This consciousness only manifests itself in us relatively to Camilla, for, with this one exception, Clorinda is the most fascinating of the warrior-maids of epic. She is superior to Marphisa and Bradamante. Brunhild is a battle-fay, hardly a *bellatrix*, and as such not eligible for comparison with the *bellatrices*, but taken as a character at her worth she has not the charm and place in the Nibelungenlied that Clorinda has in the Gerusalemme Liberata. I had forgotten Quintus Smyrnæus and his Penthesilea. I am not sure that Clorinda's part is better drawn than that of Penthesilea, over whose sunny hair and fair goddess' face Achilles wept with a grief that effaced his grief for Patroclus.

Clorinda

Clorinda and Camilla are both devoted to the cult of darts and virginity, but Clorinda is sicklied over with the reflection of Tancredi's hopeless love, while Camilla, though desired afar off by

Clorinda and Camilla

mothers, and dreamed of by youth, retains a brightness undimmed by the shadow of anything common. She represents the imagined and the ideal of Virgil's thoughts, and he does not weaken the force of her intangibility by overdrawing her, or by particularising too much. She appears among the mustering bands, she passes out of sight, she essays the encounter with the Tuscan cavalry, she fights, she dies. These verbs express the brevity of Camilla's action in Virgil's epic. There is nothing repellent about Camilla. She is a *bellatrix*, it is true, and does her share of fighting and fuming, but never loses her fine aroma of graceful girlhood. There is an indefinable attractiveness about her, due to her upbringing, her youth, her wonder-rousing passage, the grace of her rapidity, and an I know not what of elemental and feminine mixing with manly virtues. She leads the Volscian cavalcade, and her presence enriches its glitter with the soft light of early morn, or the fresh brightness of springtide.

Warrior-maids have often to die out of their poems

Armida and Erminia are susceptible of domestication. Clorinda and Camilla are not (or, owing to their character and place in the story, epic can take no cognisance of such a contingency), and must die out of their poems. Tradition and art deal hardly with many warrior-maids. A domesticated Clorinda is an impossibility, a domesticated Camilla a sacrilege. Bradamante's domestication is possible and heralded, but she is a virago as well as a *bellatrix*, and one is sceptical about her wifely success. Bellona wived is not likely to develop into the matron that was potential in Nausicaa, or, indeed, into any lovable type. Brunhild becomes a wife, and an unlovely one, but she has been part of the supernatural machinery of the poem, and may not die, but be transformed, and her epic is one of mystery and old-time wonders.

Erminia is the most womanly of Tasso's heroines, and, therefore, the most enduringly attractive. We put off and put on an Armida according to the mood of the moment, or according to natural temperament, but an Erminia, though she may not in a trice, and with the strong grip of nature's omnipotence, capture the senses and desires of beholders, has a saner, more far-reaching, and more abiding charm. Even Clorinda, whose battling and pathetic surroundings engross our attention, as we read the epic, hardly leaves in the memory the lasting imprint that Erminia leaves. The pleasure that a character like Erminia gives us is at will largely recoverable from the memory without a reperusal of the poem. Of the three female types presented by Tasso—the woman, the witch, and the warrior-maid—the woman wins preference.

Erminia: her enduring attractiveness

Erminia had a woman's feelings towards her generous captor, but she was as sensitive to honour as a king's daughter ought to be. Racked between contending desires, she abjured the king's daughter for the maid unfettered by conventionality, and free to follow the lodestar of love. On such a character, and such a situation, Tasso could spend himself finely. He could fancy and express the woman's feelings, and sound the elegiac and idyllic note of the circumstances. He passed into exaggeration, it is true, when Erminia is made to wish she had been Clorinda, that she might mayhap have conquered her lover, and kept him in love's bondage, or else met pleasing death at his hands.

Erminia is the heroine of a pleasing pastoral. As the argument has said, she passed out of Jerusalem in the armour of Clorinda, meaning to enter the Christian lines and nurse Tancredi.

Erminia's flight from the city

It is an enchanting picture that Erminia makes as she desecrates her dainty neck and golden hair with the steel helmet, and, taking in her delicate hand the weighty shield, apes a martial gait, all in the presence of little Love, who smiles, as he smiled when he engowned the sturdy Hercules. In the interval between the despatch of the messenger to Tancredi and her startled flight, she nurses her impatience and speaks out her thoughts to the inviting neighbourhood :—

> Era la notte, e il suo stellato velo
> Chiaro spiegava e senza nube alcuna ;
> E già spargea rai luminosi e gelo
> Di vive perle la sorgente luna.
> L' innamorata donna iva col cielo
> Le sue fiamme sfogando ad una ad una ;
> E secretarj del suo amore antico
> Fea i muti campi e quel silenzio amico.*
>
> G. L. vi, 103.

Tasso's translation of feeling into sound

It is a fine conceit, that of this stanza, Petrarcan in quality, and the words of the octave hang together in musical concord and contrast like pearls of similar and dissimilar lustre. Thought exhaling into melody, no mere forcible or painted indication of sentiment, but a transmigration, a translation of feeling into sound that recalls, suggests, and immortalises mental fantasy—this is the forte of Tasso.

Erminia's life with the shepherd

Erminia had not gone far when the lonely night and feminine tremors affrighted her. Scared by the encounter of an outpost of the crusading army she fled incontinently, and continued her flight till she reached the waters of Jordan. There, with sorrow for food and tears for drink, she slept till she was waked by the birds singing to the dawn, and

* Night reigned, and, clear and cloudless, outspread her star-bespangled veil. Ere now the rising moon was strewing bright rays and frostwork of living pearls. The burning maid, like the heaven, shot forth, one by one, her beams of light, and made the dumb fields and that friendly stillness confidants of her enduring love.

the murmur of the river and trees, and the wind frolicking with the waves and flowers. A rare old shepherd, once the gardener of a Memphian king, received her into his hut, and family of three boys, and for a while she led the silvan life of the place, a life that in this time of war was protected by heaven or spared by the lightning that strikes lofty summits but spares the lowly plain. She carved her plaints on the rind of beeches and laurels, partly because she wished to have the tearful luxury of reading her own story, and partly because she, always expectant of some recognition or lament on the part of Tancredi, hoped he might some day read her carvings and pity her.

The story of Tancredi and Erminia unfinished

The story of the relations between Tancredi and Erminia is unfinished. It is broken off abruptly, and this could not be otherwise, for the natural ending of the poem does not establish or necessitate a closer approximation between these persons, and an epic is not a novel, which favours an epilogue, and a general finger-pointing to the road taken by individuals in an aftertime. Such a thing is sometimes managed in epic by a vision of the future, when the importance or solemnity of the information requires it.

Armida: her palace

Armida's palace is a place of pleasance. On the panels of the gates of the principal entrance are carved examples of the worship of women, viz., the obscuration of Alcides, and the unmanning of Antony. All sensuous delights are here. It incloses what is at once an Alcinous' garden, a grove of song-birds, and a paradise of all-pervading love. All nature speaks affection and throbs with sympathy. Art has proclaimed and proved herself nature's twin. The rescuing knights are not acclimatised, but it is only by steadfastly hardening their souls to the winsomeness of everything. They had passed with somewhat quivering resolution through the seductions of the precincts of the palace, and doubly victorious now, victorious over the impulse to commit sin, and the inclination to condone it, they are in a mood and of a force to rouse the hero out of his enchanted love-languor.

Her delineation is the love-song of a youthful poet

In Armida the poet sings of love, such love as youthful poets feel, the love that is passion and that is youth, the love that is self-centred and that is pagan, the love that is a cult, and that can draw on enchantment for surroundings and solitude. The woman who has first felt and then inspired the love is fair, and passing fair, Cupid's bait, and Nature's magnet, one to shake the saintship of an anchorite. Spenser's Acrasia is a vulgar person compared to Armida, a sort of wanton vampire. The other of the enamoured pair of the garden is not benumbed and bedrugged by pleasure as is Acrasia's victim, but conscious, actively fond, and with some relics of male dominance. His badge of servitude is a mirror. In this Armida beholds herself, while he glasses himself in her eyes.

Armida in her abandonment

Armida in her abandonment is moving, but hysterical. Her appeal has not and could not have the validity and dignity of Dido's, for Armida in her capacity of enchantress had been the betrayer, and, as a specimen of sex, she is, alongside of the woman Dido, a plaything for a sunshiny day. The reproach of the parentage of icy Caucasus and of the nursing of the Hyrcanian tiger falls upon our ears with a conventional and stagey ring, but it is impossible not to sympathise with the wail of the witch metamorphosed into the woman and now in abandonment more than ever conscious of womanhood, and with her prodigality of humble supplication. Tasso must have had a mist of tears in his eyes when he wrote these pathetic stanzas. Æneas' tardy piety and lame excuse of predestination are perhaps on a par with Rinaldo's admonitory ethics and crocodile consolation, but a Dido who threats and hides her heart-sickness by retiral gives a stronger picture than an Armida who threats and faints in the presence of her fleeing lover. Spenser, I have said, owes a debt to Tasso, and Tasso has profited by the poem of his predecessor Camoens. He had read and admired the poem of the Portuguese, and scrupled not to receive hints and to borrow incidents from it for use in the allied parts of his own poem.

Armida's part in the poem. Her conversion

Armida serves a triple purpose in the poem. She is an agent in its supernatural action, an instrument in delaying the story proper of the poem, and in eking out the historical matter, and a peg on which to hang romance and a love-story. The Armida episode lends itself very well to allegorical interpretation, and, were not allegory pronounced to be a later refuge and subterfuge of the poet, I should be disposed to say that here it is in operation. But it is so easy with a little straining to apply allegory, as witness the general applicability of the solar myth theory.

There seems to me a considerable amount of bathos in Armida's conversion, and I cannot quite follow the transcendental meaning that is sometimes read into it. Not so with that of Clorinda, for she had been born of Christian parents, and there is a sort of poetic justice in her return to their religion.

Camoens perhaps warmer than Tasso

I think that Camoens in his description in the Isle of Loves canto is decidedly more sultry than Tasso. The latter has more verbal decoration, but I cannot say that Camoens is his inferior in fervour. Tasso has plenty of fervour, but it is dying fervour rather. Camoens' fervour is more thrilling, more hortatory, I might call it. It seems often to exhort us to self-experience. He does not describe a love-lorn maid like Armida, and, if he had, he would not have spun out the account as Tasso has done.

The descriptive erotic of Spenser and Tasso

Spenser is, in his description of the Bower of Bliss, so far as exuberance goes, much warmer than Tasso. He has more painting, but less feeling. He is pictorial and has more luscious growth of words, but not the same speaking voice, I might say, ring of sincerity. There is intense feeling in Tasso's lyric snatches, the poet is the man's interpreter, indeed, the man and the poet speak together. Tasso speaks as one who feels the force of his own pagan outbursts, as one whose bosom swells with the tumultuous tides of youth. The elegiac cast adds to and vouches for his sincerity. A certain similarity to this in Spenser is not elegy but didactics. Tasso lives into his description more than Spenser, for the latter is copying the former and colouring his copy. There is a perfume of personality about the descriptive erotic of Tasso that is not discernible in that of Spenser.

Sincerity in amatory poetry

Amatory poetry, even that concerning the poet himself, is not always serious. Horace is a cold poet, he is outside the feelings he describes. Not so Catullus and Propertius. They are inside the flame they describe, and one can read in the description their own mirrored hearts. Spenser is, in the erotic work of the canto, considered a decorative poet, a careful and nice observer and embellisher, but without introspection. Tasso is not so superabundant as Spenser, but he has the note of verity, he speaks from the heart outward. I do not mean that he displays the passionate sincerity that belongs only to the love-song with the personal element in it, but that he displays something different from the orgastic dilettanteism of Spenser.

Spenser describes bodily beauty like the critic of a work of art, with an eye both for effect and detail, and with a critic's fulness and personal coolness, which, judging from the warmth of the language employed, from its tropical suggestiveness, must be due to the second-handness of the material, to a copyist's leisure for embellishment. At the same time only voluptuous sensibility, let it be, as, from its roaming and studied behaviour, I fancy it is, under a strong volitional curb, could have reproduced and extended the passionate picturing of the Armida cantos. Tasso essays description, but, before getting very far, stayed by excess of animation, and impatient of verbal painting, he halts a while, closes his eyes, and, falling back on his faculty of song to expound the sensuous invitingness of the situation, bursts into a poetical similitude takingly appropriate, or sings a song of the senses of dulcet or dulcet-bitter quality. These songs of the senses are most captivating. For example, one of the *donzellette garrule e lascive* of Armida's haunt says to Ubaldo and Carlo :—

Spenser's method in description. Tasso's

> Questo è il porto del mondo, e qui il restoro
> Delle sue noje, e quel piacer si sente,
> Che già sentì ne'secoli dell'oro
> L'antica e senza fren libera gente.*
>
> G. L. xv, 63.

The siren by the waters of the Orontes thus appeals to Rinaldo as a youth among youths :—

> O giovinetti, mentre aprile e maggio
> Vi ammantan di fiorite e verdi spoglie,
> Di gloria o di virtu fallace raggio
> La tenerella mente ah non v'invoglie!
> Solo chi segue ciò che piace è saggio,
> E in sua stagion degli anni il frutto coglie.

* This is the haven of the world, here is comfort for all its troubles, here is felt that pleasure, which erewhile, in the ages of gold, the antique and perfectly free people felt.

Questo grida natura. Or dunque voi
Indurerete l'alma ai detti suoi? *

G. L. xiv, 62.

Folli, perchè gettate il caro dono,
Che breve è sì, di vostra età novella?
Nomi, e senza soggetto idoli sono
Ciò che pregio e valore il mondo appella.
La fama che invaghisce a un dolce suono
Voi superbi mortali, e par sì bella,
È un' eco, un sogno, anzi del sogno un'ombra,
Che ad ogni vento si dilegua e sgombra.†

G. L. xiv, 63.

The wondrous bird with its lay of human voice lulls Rinaldo in his dream of easy deliciousness :—

The rose blooms, opens, languishes, and is no longer the desired of maids and lovers, and,

Così trapassa al trapassar di un giorno
Della vita mortale il fiore e il verde;
Nè perchè faccia indietro april ritorno,
Si rinfiora ella mai, nè si rinverde.
Cogliam la rosa in sul mattino adorno
Di questo dì, che tosto il seren perde:
Cogliam di amor la rosa: amiamo or, quando
Esser si puote riamato amando.‡

G. L. xvi, 15.

---

* O youths, while April and May clothe you with garlands and greenery, let not glory's or virtue's false ray excite your youngling mind. Only he who follows what is pleasing, is wise, who gathers the fruit of the years in its season. This nature cries. And will ye now harden your soul against her words.

† Fools, why throw away the rich gift, so short time offered of your early years. Names and shows without substance are the things that the world calls esteem and valour. Fame, which with its sweet sound beguiles you proud mortals and seems so fair, is but an echo, a dream, nay, the dream's mere shadow, which at every breath of wind melts away and disappears.

‡ Thus passeth in the passing of a day the flower and leafage of mortal life, nor, though April returneth back, doth life ever again put on flower or leafage. Let us gather the rose on this day's gay morn, for soon it loseth its brightness; let us gather the rose of love, let us love now, when loving, we may be loved again.

Compare Spenser :—

> So passeth in the passing of a day,
> Of mortall life, the leafe, the bud, the flowere : etc.
>
> F. Q. ii, 12, 75.

Argante

Argante is made too noisy and brawny and self-assertive. He is almost as truculent as a homeric hero, or as Goliath of Gath. His enemies are food for his sword, stepping-stones to his exaltation. His fighting is his all, but, let us remember, it is patriotic fighting. Even Clorinda seems to have left his rugged nature untouched by any feeling, save that which was due to a comrade in arms. She exercises no softening influence on him, although his regret for her death is perhaps more poignant owing to the fact that she is a woman. His manly reserve, his engrossing patriotism certainly lend him distinction, when set beside the instability of many of Godfrey's knights, the somewhat moping bravery of Tancredi, and the transfigurations of that half-youngling half-titan, Rinaldo. The finest thing said about Argante is said in Canto XIX, just before that duel in which Tancredi, though fighting like a nimble craft with a towering three-decker, finally prevailed over his enemy by his superior swordsmanship. Argante looks moody, and to Tancredi's twitting inquiry thus makes reply :—

> Penso (risponde) alla città, del regno
> Di Giudea antichissima regina,
> Che vinta or cade ; e indarno esser sostegno
> Io procurai della fatal ruina ;
> E ch'è poca vendetta al mio disdegno
> Il capo tuo, che il cielo or mi destina.*
>
> G. L. xix, 10.

---

* I think (replies he) of the city, the ancient queen of Juda's realm, that now is conquered and falls. And vainly I tried to be her help against the fateful ruin. I think that thy head is small satisfaction to my disdainful wrath, thy head that heaven now promises me.

These words begin with Tasso and end with Argante. Argante's rashness sometimes appears as bold wisdom,

> Chè spesso avvien che ne'maggior perigli
> Sono i più audaci gli ottimi consigli,*
>
> G. L. vi, 6.

and, usurping the throne of fate, may pass into sublimity :—

> Puote in vece di fato e di fortuna
> Darti la destra mia vittoria intera.†
>
> G. L. vi, 8.

Tancredi and Rinaldo

Tancredi and Rinaldo are the most outstanding heroes of the crusading host. Both are love-bitten, but Tancredi's love is the tender passion in its deepest manifestation, while Rinaldo's, being that of a younger and more forceful man, displays curiosity, youthful abandonment, and impulsive animalism, rather than depth. Besides, the love of the latter is due to enchantment, that of the former to the effluence of the virginal beauty of the chaste *bellatrix*. The passion of Tancredi is dolorous, and sometimes lugubrious, the relations between Rinaldo and Armida resemble those between Hercules and Omphale, with perhaps a more flaccid Hercules and a more amorous Omphale. Tancredi is the soul of chivalry, and of that finer sort in which self-respect does not pass into self-assertion. Rinaldo is a passionate but open youth, with something of Achilles about him, a thunderbolt of war and mover of mountains. In the last and supreme battle, his warlike work beggars description—he slaughters kings, overwhelms infantry; his sword flashes as rapidly and as deadly as three ; he deals blows that kill more than the men hit. These are Ariostean reminiscences, or a Carlovingian survival.

* For in greater perils it often happens that the boldest counsels are the best.

† My right hand, taking the place of fate and fortune both, can give thee complete victory. (These and the above words were said to Aladino.)

Rinaldo is the official hero of the epic, and *deus ex machina*, as distinguished from purely heroic, aspects of him are not wanting. There are bits of autobiography in the drawing of Tancredi, and we feel their presence.

Godfrey

It is sometimes said that Godfrey plays an unimportant part in the action of the poem. In depicting the generalissimo of the Christian army Tasso had to observe fidelity to history, for it is in him that the historical aspects of the epic are in a way focussed. Godfrey's task as controller of mutually jealous princelings and nobles was not an easy one. A hothead like Rinaldo would have ruined the cause, and no amount of personal bravery would have counteracted the destructiveness of his manner. Hence a politic, dignified chief was required for the army, a man of mature years, and one who rather reposed on past deeds than burned to perform new ones. And such a chief was set at its head. The Eternal Father chooses, at Tortosa, Godfrey as leader for his holy zeal and lack of personal ambition. When his natural bravery asserts itself under Argante's stinging taunts, he is not allowed to adventure his person. He is the head and not the arm of the crusading host. Ugone says to him in the dream in which Rinaldo's recall is counselled :—

Tu sei capo, ei mano
Di questo campo : e sostener sua vece
Altri non puote, e farlo a te non lece.*

G. L. xiv, 13.

Yet Godfrey finely insists on scaling the walls of Jerusalem like a common soldier, and in the fight with the Egyptian army combats like the other leaders, slaying Rimedon and Emireno.

Titular leaders do not always show well in poetical

* Thou art the head, and he the hand of the army, another cannot take his part, and thou art not permitted to do it.

accounts of great enterprises. Agamemnon has an *aristeia*, it is true, but it is conventional rather than striking, and he is surely the inferior of Godfrey in the virtues of leadership. Vasco da Gama is a pious admiral. He is an admiral, and he is pious, that is about all Camoens says about him. Being an admiral he can plan a voyage and accomplish it, and being pious he is the favourite of the gods, but I should not say that he is superior in his epic to *il pio Buglione* in our present one. Splendid activity in the Jerusalem Delivered is committed to others, to Rinaldo, to Tancredi, etc., but the poet's Godfrey is not a bad representative of the historic Baron of the Holy Sepulchre.

The quality of Tasso's style

Tasso's style is pronounced and variegated. One does not read far without being arrested by it, and made conscious of a combination of graces. It displays nobility, and colour, and force, and tenderness, and the relation between these qualities is not that between rich abundance and modest presence, for they are all met with in pleasing maturity. Tasso is strong in the last quality, but his reader is no stranger to the others. Of course, in all full styles, colour and force are, strictly speaking, present at any time, though it may be in different degrees. The one may overshadow, but cannot efface the other. The one is the other sometimes, for, while words have usually a birth-mark entitling them to be classed as colouring or force-giving units, force is got not only from groupings and definite postings of the latter units, but from the artistic employment of the former. Tasso's style has the stamp of power and the stamp of colour, but I should say that its power is the power that is colour. Be it always remembered, however, that a foreigner is not able to judge accurately of the relations between power and colour in a foreign vocabulary. In regard to Tasso's style as a whole, it may be said that he is not so tearful and languishing, so weakly soft, and so adjectivally pretty, as he sometimes appears in verse translations.

Specimens

I remember one passage, among others of the same quality, which I think all readers will agree to call sublime. There had been a time of drought in the Christian army, on which had followed open discontent. Godfrey had made a solemn appeal to the Eternal Father, who heard the appeal and nodded his will to the universe :—

> Così dicendo il capo mosse ; e gli ampj
> Cieli tremaro, e i lumi erranti e i fissi :
> E tremò l'aria riverente, e i campi
> Dell'oceano, e i monti, e i ciechi abissi.
> Fiammegiare a sinistra accesi lampi
> Fur visti, e chiaro tuono insieme udissi.
> Accompagnan le genti il lampo e il tuono
> Con allegro di voci ed alto suono.*
>
> G. L. xiii, 74.

There is a fine nobility in this swift travelling of nature's sympathy and obedience, a mixture of Olympian and biblical solemnity.

Within the first thirty stanzas of Canto XX are to be found some fine specimens of Tasso's style. This stretch is quite a mosaic of varied poetic ability—of animation, and beauty, and tenderness, and here, too, if nowhere else, he sounds the heroic trumpet. Take as a proof this bit of rapid narrative :—

> Quindi sovra un corsier di schiera in schiera
> Parea volar tra'cavalier, tra'fanti.
> Tutto il volto scopría per la visiera ;
> Fulminava negli occhi, e ne'sembianti.

---

* Thus speaking, he nodded his head, and the spacious heavens trembled, and the lights wandering and fixed, and the reverential air trembled, and the plains of ocean, and the mountains, and the dark abysses. Bright fires were seen to flash on the left, and loud thunder, as well, was heard. The people accompanied the fire and the thunder with joyous and loud outcries.

Confortò il dubbio, e confermò chi spera ;
Ed all' audace rammentò i suoi vanti,
E le sue prove al forte : a chi maggiori
Gli stipendj promise, a chi gli onori—*

G. L. xx, 12.

and this bit of hortatory heroic (Godfrey speaks) :—

O de'nemici di Gesù flagello,
Campo mio, domator dell'oriente,
Ecco l'ultimo giorno, eccovi quello
Che già tanto bramaste, omai presente—†

G. L. xx, 14.

and this :—

Ma capitano i' son di gente eletta :
Pugnammo un tempo, e trionfammo insieme.
E poscia un tempo a mio voler l'ho retta.
Di chi di voi non so la patria e il seme ?
Quale spada mi è ignota ? o qual saetta,
Benchè per l'aria ancor sospesa treme,
Non saprei dir se è Franca, o se d'Irlanda ,
E quale appunto il braccio è che la manda ? ‡

G. L. xx, 18.

There is a battailous aspect in the following stanza :—

Bello in sì bella vista anco è l'orrore,
E di mezzo la tema esce il diletto.
Nè men le trombe orribili e canore
Sono agli orecchi lieto e fero oggetto.

---

* Then on a steed from band to band, mid horse, mid foot, he seemed to fly. He showed all his countenance through the visor. There shone a light in his eyes and in his visage. He charmed away doubt, and strengthened hope. To the boastful man he recalled his vaunts, and to the brave his prowess. To one he promised greater rewards, to another greater honours.

† O scourge of Jesus' enemies, mine army, conqueror of the east, see, now hath come for you that day, the ending day which you have now so long desired.

‡ But I am captain of a chosen folk : one time we fought, we triumphed together, and then a space, I ruled it at my will. Of which of you do I not know the country and the stock ? What sword is to me unknown, or of which arrow, though it still float quivering in the air, could I not tell if it be from France, or from Ireland, of which could I not soothly tell whose and what arm shoots it.

Pur il campo fedel, benchè minore,
Par di suon più mirabile e d'aspetto ;
E canta in più guerriero e chiaro carme
Ogni sua tromba, e maggior luce han l'arme—*
G. L. xx, 30.

the sheen of spears and the snorting of the charger in this :—

Sembra d'alberi densi alta foresta
L'un campo e l'altro ; di tant'aste abbonda.
Son tesi gli archi, e son le lance in resta :
Vibransi i dardi, e rotasi ogni fionda.
Ogni cavallo in guerra anco si appresta :
Gli odj e il furor del suo signor seconda :
Raspa, batte, nitrisce e si raggira,
Gonfia le nari, e fumo e foco spira—† G. L. xx, 29.

patriotism and pathos in this (Emireno puts the words in the mouth of his country) :—

Guarda tu le mie leggi, e i sacri tempj
Fa che io del sangue mio non bagni e lavi.
Assecura le vergini dagli empj,
E i sepolcri e le ceneri degli avi.
A te, piangendo i lor passati tempi,
Mostran la bianca chioma i vecchi gravi ;
A te la moglie le mammelle e il petto,
Le cune e i figli e il marital suo letto.‡ G. L. xx, 26.

Of quiet and lovely narrative I am to quote some

* Fair too, in so fair a sight, is horror, and from midst of fear cometh delight. Nor less glad and grim an object to the ears are the sonorous and terrible trumpets. But the army of the faithful, though less in number, is more conspicuous for sound and look, and each of their trumpets sounds in more warlike and clearer strain, and their arms have greater lustre.

† Either army seems a deep forest of thick trees ; there is store of so many spears. The bows are bent and the lances in rest, the javelins quiver, and every sling twirls. Each horse, too, gets him ready for the fray, the hate and fury of his rider goad him on. He paws, stamps, neighs, whirls round, outspreads his nostrils, and breathes out smoke and fire.

‡ Guard my laws, and let me not deluge and drench the holy temples with my blood. Shield the maidens from the spoiler, shield the tombs and the ashes of your sires. Aged men, weeping their bygone years, show you their white hair ; the wife shows you her maternal breast, the cradle, her sons, and her bridal bed.

specimens. The first one is the most imaginative and is a commencement to its book :—

Usciva omai dal molle e fresco grembo
Della gran madre sua la notte oscura,
Aure lievi portando, e largo nembo
Di sua rugiada preziosa e pura :
E scuotendo del vel l'umido lembo
Ne spargeva i fioretti e la verdura :
E i venticelli, dibattendo le ali,
Lusingavano il sonno de'mortali.* G. L. xiv, I.

Another is :—

Appena ha tocco la mirabil nave
Della marina allor turbata il lembo,
Che spariscon le nubi, e cessa il grave
Noto, che minacciava oscuro nembo.
Spiana i monti delle onde aura soave,
E solo increspa il bel ceruleo grembo ;
E di un dolce seren diffuso ride
Il ciel, che sè più chiaro unqua non vide.†

G. L. xv, 9.

The above passage is contained in the account of the voyage from Palestine to the Isles of Fortune for the bringing back of Rinaldo. The voyage is interesting and gives good matter. It is guided and commented on by the *fatal donzella* of the angel semblance and the many-tinted gown. I put here a few more lines from this account :—

Giace l'alta Cartago ; appena i segni
Delle alte sue ruine il lido serba.

---

* Sable night now issued from the soft and cool bosom of her great mother, bearing light breezes and a copious shower of her pure and precious dew, and shaking the dank border of her veil, sprinkled therefrom the flowerets and the grass. And the gentle gales, beating their wings, charmed the sleep of mortals.

† Hardly has the wondrous ship touched the marge of the sea, then in storm, than the clouds disappear, and the stormy south wind that threatened a black tempest, ceases to blow. A gentle breeze levels the mountainous waves, and does but ruffle their fair azure bosom, and the sky that never appeared clearer than now, smiles with sweet calm widely spread.

Muojono le città, muojono i regni:
Copre i fasti e le pompe arena ed erba:
E l'uom di esser mortal par che si sdegni.*

G. L. xv, 20.

I may cite now one or two examples of Tasso's tenderness. Tancredi, on recovering consciousness after the swoon that followed the death of Clorinda, says:—

Io vivo? io spiro ancora? e gli odiosi
Rai miro ancor di questo infausto die?
Dì, testimon de'miei misfatti ascosi,
Che rimprovera a me le colpe mie.
Ahi! man timida e lenta, or chè non osi
Tu, che sai tutte del ferir le vie,
Tu, ministra di morte empia ed infame,
Di questa vita rea troncar lo stame.†

G. L. xii, 75.

From the same canto I take the narration of Clorinda's last act:—

Di un bel pallore ha il bianco volto asperso,
Come a'gigli sarían miste viole:
E gli occhi al cielo affisa, e in lei converso
Sembra per la pietate il cielo e il sole:
E la man nuda e fredda alzando verso
Il cavaliero in vece di parole,
Gli dà pegno di pace. In questa forma
Passa la bella donna, e par che dorma.‡

G. L. xii, 69.

---

* Lofty Carthage lies low, hardly does the shore retain traces of her lofty ruins. Cities perish, perish kingdoms; grass and sand cover pomp and pride, and it seems that man disdains to be mortal.

† I live, I still breathe, and still look on the hateful rays of this luckless day, O day, that, witness of my dark misdeeds, rebuketh in me my sins. Ah, fearful and laggard hand, why then dost not thou dare, thou that knowest all the ways of striking, thou, the instrument of cruel and shameful death, why dost not dare to cut the thread of this guilty life.

‡ The whiteness of her face is overspread with a beauteous pallor, as if violets were mixed with lilies. She has raised her eyes to the sky, and sky and sun seemed turned to her in pity, and, in place of speech, raising her bare and cold hand to the knight, she gives it him as a pledge of peace. In this way passes the fair maid and seems to sleep.

There is Virgilian reminiscence in—

Giace il cavallo al suo signore appresso :
Giace il compagno appo il compagno estinto :
Giace il nemico appo il nemico, e spesso
Sul morto il vivo, il vincitor sul vinto.*

G. L. xx, 51.

The tenderness here is rather verbal, and the next four lines drag it along quite forcedly. The following stanza is a fine one, of which I quote these lines :—

L'arme che già sì liete in vista fôro
Faceano or mostra spaventosa e mesta ;
Perduti ha i lampi il ferro, i raggi l'oro :
Nulla vaghezza ai bei color più resta.
Quanto apparia d'adorno e di decoro
Ne'cimieri e ne'fregi, or si calpesta.†

G. L. xx, 52.

Allusiveness

All the poets of the literary epic are allusive, and Tasso shines in this regard. Allusiveness gratifies the taste we have for rich flavour in modern work, and for the incorporation of the past in the present. It is a mark of age in literature, and is resorted to by a poet when in a self-conscious or illustrating mood. When Armida flies from the battle that the Egyptians fight with Godfrey, she is followed by Tisaferno, as was Cleopatra by Antony. When Clorinda stands on a high tower of the battlements of Jerusalem with quiver and bow, ready to shoot, she is compared to the Delian maid shooting arrows from heaven through the lofty clouds. When Tancredi and Argante abandon weapons, and close in the last grip, the bout, for vigour, is rather in-

* The horse lies beside his rider, companion lies nigh companion in death, enemy lies nigh enemy, and often the living on the dead, the victor on the vanquished.

† The arms that erewhile were so gay to view made now an awful and saddening show. The steel has lost its glitter, the gold its lustre, there is no delight more in the fair colours. All of adornment and finery that appeared on crest and badge is now trampled under foot.

appositely said to resemble that between Alcides and Antæus. And so on.

There are many similes in the poem, most of them copies or echoes of the antique. This appropriation is not theft, for similes are common property, nor is the workmanship mechanical, for Tasso was the very man to freshen a simile, or turn it tenderly. We have in the Gerusalemme nearly a hundred of these figures. Indeed, one could pretty well use our poet's collection as a satisfying *corpus* for a study of simile. I shall notice two similes that appear to me new. Both concern Armida. The first refers to her tearful reception of Godfrey's announcement of his inability to serve her :—

Similes

Le guance asperse di que'vivi umori,
Che giù cadean sin della veste al lembo,
Parean vermigli insieme e bianchi fiori,
Se pur gl'irriga un rugiadoso nembo,
Quando su l'apparir de'primi albóri
Spiegano all'aure liete il chiuso grembo ;
E l'alba che li mira se n'appaga,
Di adornarsene il crin diventa vaga—*

G. L. iv, 75.

the second is the sighing prologue of her plaint against abandonment :—

Qual musico gentil, prima che chiara
Altamente la lingua al canto snodi,
All'armonia gli animi altrui prepara
Con dolci ricercate, in bassi modi :
Così costei, che nella doglia amara
Già tutte non oblía le arti e le frodi ;

* Her cheeks, bedewed with those bright drops that fell down even to the border of her robe, appeared flowers of crimson and white set together, should a dewy mist wet them, what time, at the appearance of dawn's first streaks, they display to the glad breezes their shut bosoms. And the dawn, as she looks at them, gets delight therefrom, and becomes eager to adorn with them her hair.

Fa di sospir breve concento in prima,
Per dispor l'alma in cui le voci imprima.*

G. L. xvi, 42.

The story of this epic

It cannot be said that the story of the Jerusalem Delivered is not told on the whole with animation, though, so far as the actual account of the siege is concerned, there is a good deal of wandering narrative. The truth is that the action proper is scant, and Tasso had either to write a shorter epic, or to invent much. The episodes are original, but, in reading the poem, we do feel at times that Calliope is borrowing too much assistance from Erato and Euterpe.

The Ismeno portion

The Ismeno portion of the epic is weak. It takes fibre from the poem. The enchanted wood was not the only means of proving the recovered prowess of Rinaldo and his divine agency. For this enchanter and his enchantments there might profitably have been substituted, say, greater offensive action on the part of the besieged, or some stories connected with the defence or the defenders. Why should not some more capital have been made out of the city Jerusalem? The wizardry is rather foisted in, but it may have been found more reconcilable to the subject by Tasso's readers than by us. It is very strained allegory if that explanation be adventured. The supernatural will always be a great difficulty to a modern epic poet, especially if his poem concern a comparatively modern time. It is true that Ismeno is the agent of Pluto, and represents the malign supernatural. This, however, has large representation, that of Ismeno, Alecto, Armida, etc. Indeed, there is too much supernatural machinery in the poem.

Tasso's story has a burdensome weight of romance, but

* Just as a pleasing singer, ere he set free in song the loudly-sounding notes, prepares other minds for the music with sweet preludings in soft tones, so she, who in her bitter dole did not yet forget all her art, all her guile, utters first a short concord of sighs to win the soul on which she is to imprint her words.

it is a good story and bears it. Tasso's theory of the epic poem permitted the mingling of the classical and romantic, and no such poem could, at his time, or now, be written without the admixture of the romantic. Why, romance is as old as the Odyssey. There is the romance of wonders, wonders that were once believed, and that we can even now believe in imagination. There is romantic handling, which dwells on the lighter humanities of life, such as love, and the joy of living. This may be said to belong to the new epic, though love itself is in the epic as old as Apollonius. Then there is the romantico-supernatural, which, more than romantic wonder, for it is used not merely for embellishment but has a structural value, needs careful and unexaggerated adaptation to time and subject. Much, however, is forgiven to good poetry embellishing with its art and its chosen embroidery a fit story. The age of Godfrey undoubtedly believed in magic, and there is that justification to be pleaded for its use, but Tasso has suffused his whole subject with it, and modernity exclaims against the tint.

The romance

I find the part played by Armida far more excusable and defensible than that played by Ismeno, but it, too, is vulnerable. Why should not Rinaldo, it may be said, have fallen naturally in love with Armida, and taken her, say, to Cyprus? Why should they not have done their dalliance there, on Idalia, in a *quondam* haunt of Venus, lovely by nature (heightened nature if you will) and association? The voyage would have been shorter—and the voyage is good—but not too short for a memory fertile in reminiscence of the past. We should then have had Armida the woman, and her pretty ways, without the improbabilities, and Rinaldo could have been brought back to duty without all those ramifications of the supernatural. But no. It is not merely that the woman in love is attractive in the poem, although

The part of Armida

she is attractive, but that the witch and her surroundings contribute to the maintenance of the high imaginative pitch at which the poet worked, without which much of Tasso's best in the way of heightened sentiment and lyric exaltation could not have found fit and free utterance. And a Rinaldo of this stamp, with his culpable suppression of manliness, would not have suited. The mighty lordship of Love would not have excused him. A voluntary slipping into such sin would have damned an epic hero who is also a soldier of the cross. I should not call such a caviller an incorrigible proser, for there is something in what he says. An admirer of Tasso must, however, feel that a change in the direction indicated would not only impart a soberer tint to the epic, but would conventionalise, if not vulgarise, a most attractive portion of it. And Armida, as she is, the sorceress, is indispensable to the story as told and conceived. As more than woman she is involved in the theory and working out of the plot, and she may be said as more than woman to have a share in the *dénouement*.

The enduring worth of the G. L.

In the Gerusalemme Conquistata Tasso made changes of the sort I have mentioned. I have not read this poem, and so do not know to what extent, if any, the poet altered the romantico-supernatural of his previous poem. But the improved Jerusalem has never displaced, or even brought into neglect, the original one. Were we not dealing with epic, a species of poetry in which gravity, and strict humanity, and intelligible divinity have been and always will be standing characteristics, it might be asked if anything is improbable, from the point of view of literature, that exhibits poetry and poetical truth. And it is the poetry of Tasso that is his fascination, that, and his sympathetic handling of a great theme, and his revealed subjectivity.

Tasso's characters remain abidingly with us, and, if

they do not awe and capture the imagination, and stand for themselves, like Achilles, and Beowulf, and Hagen, and Count Roland, they linger in our memories as long as the sensations associated with them, and the recollection of these, remain, and this is no short time in the case of a poet that sinks himself well nigh inextricably into the softness of the human heart, as does Tasso. It is the fact that a great poet, a poet of vital force, sculptures characters that remain as entities in our minds to the forgetting of the impressions that went to give the finished result, while a less poet, of no sculpturing power, fashions figures of airier consistency that fade, and are remade, according as we are weakly or sympathetically conscious of our original impressions.*

Tasso's characters abide with us

No one on a first perusal of the Orlando Furioso would say that its strong point is unity. The reader is swept from character to character, from country to country, by an errant impetuosity that is at the same time deliberate art, and a teeming redundancy that forces its possessor to give it outlet at many points. Now he is in France, now in Britain, anon in Africa, and anon in the East; now Angelica is on the stage, now Bradamante; at one time we read of the deeds of Rinaldo, at another of those of Ruggiero, or of Orlando, or of Mandricardo; we sail for the nonce over a tract of story of long vista, when suddenly the poet arrests his voyage and tacks obliquely on to another course, to be abandoned for a third, which in turn is left for one we had thought derelict.

Ariosto's Orlando Furioso: its constant changing

* Tasso's heroic verse (that of the South) may be thus described:—The stanza is an octave (*ottava rima*). There are alternate rhymes in the first, third, and fifth lines, and in the second, fourth, and sixth. The seventh and eighth lines rhyme in direct sequence. The normal line is hendecasyllabic with feminine rhyme (*verso piano*). A masculine rhyme makes the line decasyllabic (*verso tronco*). The feet are iambs, but trochees are admitted. Elision and slurring play their part.

There are some master-threads in the ganglion that forms the story of the poem. These are the marriage of Ruggiero and Bradamante, the madness of Orlando, and the Saracen war. Unity is present, and to be seen for the searching, although the search is a little puzzling. It is not exactly an organic unity, that is, a careful suiting of part to part with perfect inter-functional adaptation, nor, on the other hand, is it a mere unity of landscape with associated features and a total aspect differentiating it from others of the sort, but the existent unity is more like the unity of a pattern wrought on a web, which we see after reflection and examination to possess some symmetry of plan and harmony of colour.

The nature of its unity

Some say that Ruggiero is the real protagonist of the poem, that its main end is to celebrate the nuptials from which sprang the house of Este. I daresay Ariosto meant that an exoteric audience should be able to take out of his epic such a seeming purpose. But no discernible historic aim is to be found in the poem, and the poet meets with poor success in any insertions meant to commemorate facts relating to this family. The madness of Orlando, the titular subject, only furnishes material for the thickening of the plot, and is in no way an end that the poet has chosen to follow with a fixed plan and from purpose prepense. Nor is the celebration of the deliverance of Christendom from the yoke of the infidel anything else in the poem than one feature among others. There is properly speaking no end in the poem, no epic unity, save such as results from the play of a well-directed fancy on chivalric details. Chivalry in Ariosto is a life without any definite end, reckless, vagrant, cosmopolitan, and insatiably thirsty of combats and adventures.

Its purpose, ostensible and real

It is only serious poems that have real purposefulness.

If a poem has no serious aim, and has only in contemplation the production of a subjective emotion, say, amusement, there is no need to search for an object of pronounced purview. Laughter arises from inharmonious and unexpected opposition between facts and ideas. None of us can be made to laugh, unless by means of accidents that are either lawless or of a capriciousness defying explanation, or by aid of dissonances that are not to be reduced to concord by any prevailing principle of unity.

Aim and means in serious and non-serious poems

A serious epic poem has an aim to accomplish and a specific line of direction to take. It tries to please the imagination by means of exalted emotions and ideas. Its poet has the sensation of law, and the unity he imparts to his poem reflects this sensation. On the other hand, any æsthetic poetical narrative that aims at pleasing or rejoicing a reader must have no rigorous, intrinsic, or organic unity. Let there be a certain loose enchainment of the facts of the plot; let such order as exists be make-shift, and superficial, not organic, or dynamic.

Ariosto spreads out before us with epic pomp an entertaining story, lit up by the light of fancy, and adorned by marvellous grace of expression, and richness and spontaneity of style, with no lesson to teach and no special impression to make. As is congenial to the nature of his task, he is not tied down by any effort to preserve an informing unity or a moral elevation of tone. He duplicates events, displaces his story, piles up comicalities, but retains the interest of his reader, in fact, almost convinces him of the verisimilitude of his poetic embellishments.

Ariosto's story is more entertaining than epical

The epic of Ariosto is the most outstanding specimen of romantic epos. It gives expression to the sentiment of the noble that was felt to exist in chivalry. Chivalry and the love of the chivalrous were not native products of Italy. They passed into that country along with the Carlovingian legends, and were grafted into an Italian stock to be embellished by the national imagination and manipulated to suit popular audiences. Chivalry, meaning by that the idealised heroic life of the centuries that abutted on the one side on barbarism, and on the other on incipient civilisation, is the one unifying principle of the world pictured to us in Ariosto's poem.

Chivalry in the Italian epic

In the chivalrous life individual liberty existed, untouched by positive or extrinsic law, and realised perfect independence, raising itself above ordinary life by muscular force, mastery of arms, courage and disposition. The hero of chivalry was a divine man, and more poetic than any incarnate deity could be. Chivalry was taking and attractive in so far as it abounded in force and spirit, and was free from the prosaic reality of the life of the day, but ridiculous for its lack of breadth and object.

Virtues and faults of the chivalrous life

Ariosto puts into the light of day the principal faults of chivalry, viz., the disproportion between the pomp and noise of appearances and the smallness and emptiness of the result achieved. We have not merely a depicting of heroic individuals emancipated from rules, but also an outpouring of banter.

The characters of our poet are all living and speaking entities, although they belong more or less to the domain of the supernatural or the fantastic. Although there exists an undeniable affinity between groups of characters, yet these characters are not cast from the same mould, and do not fail to put on individuality.

The characters of the poem

In the Orlando Furioso we have a commingling of the

jocose and the serious. These two elements run the one into the other, harmoniously, imparting to the reader a pleasure of varying quality. The alternation of gravity and gayness gives the reader a sensation of joy, calm and gleeful, and presupposes in the writer an engaging irony, sarcastic, and Socratic, with a pleasant causticity that leaves one in doubt whether he is speaking soberly or jesting pleasantly.

The grave and gay in the poem. The presumptive mockery

One is haunted by the suspicion that Ariosto mocks behind the scenes at the personages introduced and the deeds solemnly set forth, although he nowhere directly professes to move us to laughter. He depicts chivalry, as it were, on the wane, detaches the nullity of its results, and exhibits these as utter folly and ridiculous delirium.

Anyhow, Ariosto wedded and welded together, with remarkable success, the natural and the wonderful, the human and the fantastic. Even on the wonderful and the fantastic he bestowed a quantum of naturalness.*

To write a complete argument to the Orlando Furioso would be to fill needlessly a large number of pages. I shall try to give an outline of the argument that may serve to give a general idea of the matter of the poem :—The Orlando Furioso continues the story of the Orlando Innamorato of Boiardo. It has a plot consisting of many stories with inter-connections. It contains the story of the defence of Paris by Charlemagne and his peers against the Saracen king, Agramante, who is beaten off and has to retreat to Africa, where he is killed, while fighting in the company of two champions against Orlando, Oliviero, and Brandimarte. It records the wanderings and love adventures of Angelica, the daughter of Galafrone, King

Brief outline of the story

* In the above survey I have borrowed from and built on the criticism of Vincenzo Gioberti.

of Cathay, who had sent her and her brother Argalia, Boiardo says, into France, that they might by force or craft bring into his power the Christian peers. This fickle fair, beloved alike by paynim and peers, finally elected Medoro, a comparatively obscure African, whom she had nursed while suffering from a severe wound, into the place of a husband, and fled with him to Cathay. Orlando, on discovering Angelica's choice of Medoro, became mad, and wandered through Spain to Africa, where he was cured by Astolfo of his madness, and, at the same time, of his infatuation for Angelica. He then took part in the successful siege of Biserta, and, after fighting with Agramante as aforesaid, returned to Paris, where he was accorded a magnificent reception by Charlemagne. Our poem tells of the various events that led up to the marriage of Bradamante, the amazon sister of Rinaldo, and Ruggiero, the Saracen hero, who was really of Christian lineage.

Rinaldo, one of the lovers of Angelica, has much to do in the Orlando Furioso. He was sent by Charlemagne on a mission to Britain, and brought back help both from England and Scotland, to which latter country he was driven by a storm. In Scotland he saved Ginevra, the daughter of the king, from disgrace. He returned to Paris with his knights just in time to save the city from a determined assault of the Saracens led by Rodomonte. As the chosen champion of the Christians, he fought a duel with Ruggiero. This duel was treacherously interrupted by Agramante, moved thereto by Melissa, in the guise of Rodomonte, but his treachery did not avail him aught.

Astolfo, son of the king of England, and cousin of Rinaldo, has more varied adventures in the poem than any of the other characters. It was he who ascended to the terrestrial paradise, where he was received by St. John and taken to the moon. There he saw many wonders, and got in a phial the lost wits of Orlando, whom he was thus enabled to restore to reason before Biserta. Atlantes is an enchanter and does much of the villainy of the poem. Alcina is a witch ; Logistilla, her sister and superior, is of better character. Melissa is a beneficent fairy and patroness of Bradamante.

The attraction in Ariosto

What most impresses one in Ariosto is not his measure of heroical verisimilitude, for in the heroico-fanciful part of the poem feigning is too palpable, and only amuses, sometimes, indeed, bores a serious reader, but his general poetic power and expression, the manliness and mellowness of his thought, and the mould-like finish of his work. If we feel no thrills over the Orlando Furioso, we certainly experience much pleasure over the poet's facile, salient, and sympathetic delineation of the multiplex human mood.

Illustrations of his manner

I have under my hand a passage that will serve to illustrate the wise homeliness of Ariosto :—

Alcun non può saper da chi sia amato,
Quando felice in su la ruota siede ;
Pero c'ha i veri e i finti amici a lato,
Che mostran tutti una medesima fede.
Se poi si cangia in tristo il lieto stato,
Volta la turba adulatrice il piede ;
E quel che di cor ama, riman forte,
Ed ama il suo signor dopo la morte. *

O. F. xix, 1.

The wording in the following passages has character and style :—

Il Sole appena avea il dorato crine
Tolto di grembo alla nutrice antica,

* No one can know by whom he is loved when he sits happy upon the Wheel (Fortune's), for here he has true and false friends at his side, who all display one similar faith. If now his joyful estate is changed to a sorrowful one, the flattering crowd turns on its heel, and he who loves from the heart remains firm and loves his lord after death.

E cominciava dalle piagge alpine
A cacciar l'ombre, e far la cima aprica, etc.*
O. F. xvii, 129.

Chè'l Sonno venne, e sparse il corpo stanco
Col ramo intinto nel liquor di Lete :
E posò fin ch'un nembo rosso e bianco
Di fiori sparse le contrade liete
Del lucido oriente d'ogn'intorno,
Et indi uscì dell'aureo albergo il giorno.†
O. F. xxv, 93.

Ariosto is famous for his well-turned similes. I quote this double epic one, of which the first member seems original :—

La fiera pugna un pezzo andò di pare,
Chè vi si discernea poco vantaggio.
Vedeasi or l'uno or l'altro ire e tornare,
Come le biade al ventolin di maggio,
O come sopra'l lito un mobil mare
Or viene or va, nè mai tiene un viaggio.‡
O. F. xvi, 68.

Vigour appears in these lines regarding Rinaldo :—

Di qua e di là col brando s'aggirava,
Mandando or questo or quel giù nell'inferno
A dar notizia del viver moderno.§
O. F. xvi, 83.

Rodomonte with our poet is a strong character,

* The sun had scarcely raised his golden locks from the ancient mother's breast, and commenced to chase the shadows from the Alpine slopes and irradiate the crest, etc.

† For sleep came, and sprinkled his (Ruggiero's) weary frame with the branch dipped in the water of Lethe ; and he slept till a cloud of rose and white strewed all round with flowers the joyous quarter of the radiant east, and day then issued from the hostel of gold.

‡ The fierce battle a while went equally, for small advantage was discerned therein. Now the one side, now the other, was seen to advance and retire, like corn-stalks in the breeze of May, or just as on the shore a swift-moving sea now comes, now goes, and never holds one way.

§ Now here, now there, he turned him with his brand, sending now this one, now that, down to hell to give news of the life we presently live.

impiger, *iracundus*, *inexorabilis*, *acer*, and much else not so honourable :—

> Rodomonte, non già men di Nembrotte
> Indomito, superbo, e furibondo,
> Che d'ire al ciel non tarderebbe a notte,
> Quando la strada si trovasse al mondo, etc.*
>
> O. F. xiv, 119.

He pushed truculence into mercilessness :—

> Religion non giova al sacerdote,
> Nè la innocenzia al pargoletto giova :
> Per sereni occhi o per vermiglie gote
> Mercè nè donna nè donzella trova :
> La vecchiezza si caccia e si percuote ;
> Nè quivi il Saracin fa maggior prova
> Di gran valor, che di gran crudeltade ;
> Chè non discerne sesso, ordine, etade.†
>
> O. F. xvi, 25.

There is spirit and sententiousness here :—

> Fu il vincer sempre mai laudabil cosa,
> Vincasi o per fortuna o per ingegno ;
> Gli è ver che la vittoria sanguinosa
> Spesso far suole il capitan men degno ;
> E quella eternamente è gloriosa,
> E dei divini onori arriva al segno,
> Quando, servando i suoi senza alcun danno,
> Sì fa che gl'inimici in rotta vanno.‡
>
> O. F. xv, 1.

---

* Rodomonte, assuredly not less dauntless, proud, and furious, than Nimrod, such a one as would not cease to mount to heaven till night, if the path thereto were discoverable in the world, etc.

† Religion avails not the priest, nor innocence the little child; for bright eyes or for rosy cheeks, nor dame nor damsel finds mercy. Old age is hunted down and receives blows ; nor does the Saracen here give stronger proof of great valour than of great cruelty, for he discerns not sex, or rank, or age.

‡ Conquering was always a praiseworthy thing, be it conquered by fortune or by skill. It is true that the bloody victory is often wont to make the captain of less worth; and victory is then everlastingly glorious, and nears the mark of divine honours, when, saving her own without any loss, she so acts that the foe disperse in rout.

There is at least in these lines chivalry, ay, and something more :—

> Io dico e dissi, e dirò finch'io viva,
> Che chi si trova in degno laccio preso,
> Sebben di sè vede sua donna schiva,
> Se in tutto avversa al suo desire acceso ;
> Sebbene Amor d'ogni mercede il priva,
> Poscia che'l tempo e la fatica ha speso ;
> Pur ch'altamente abbia locato il core,
> Pianger non dè', sebben languisce e muore.*
>
> O. F. xvi, 2.

Zerbino is more troubled by his uncertainty about Isabella's fate than by death, or what follows :—

> Ma poichè 'l mio destino iniquo e duro
> Vuol ch'io vi lasci, e non so in man di cui ;
> Per questa bocca e per questi occhi giuro,
> Per queste chiome onde allacciato fui,
> Che disperato nel profondo oscuro
> Vo dello'nferno, ove il pensar di vui,
> Ch'abbia così lasciata, assai più ria
> Sarà d'ogni altra pena che vi sia.†
>
> O. F. xxiv, 79.

The following is a favourite comparison in poetry, and is here finely finished :—

> Come purpureo fior languendo muore,
> Che 'l vomere al passar tagliato lassa,
> O come carco di superchio umore
> Il papaver nell'orto il capo abbassa :
> Così, giù della faccia ogni colore
> Cadendo, Dardinel di vita passa ;

---

* I say, and said, and will say while I live, that, whoso is taken in worthy toils, even if he see his lady fleeing from him, and all estranged from his burning desire, even if love deprive him of all reward, after he has spent his time and trouble, he, if only he have highly placed his heart, needs not to weep, even though he wastes and dies.

† But since my harsh and cruel fate decrees that I leave you—in whose hands I know not—I swear by this mouth, by these eyes, and by this hair which so entangled me, that I go despairing into the dark depth of hell, where the thought of you, whom I have thus left, will be much more cruel than any other pain that is there.

Passa di vita, e fa passar con lui
L'ardire e la virtù di tutti i sui.*

O. F. xviii, 153.

The Orlando Furioso is a storehouse of literary treasures, and I have simply made a few quotations at random, unhackneyed, I think, save the last, to illustrate the statement that prefaced them.

The Divine Comedy: its naming

Most epics bear their poetic style on their face, and yet I hardly think that any reader will off-hand pronounce the Divine Comedy an epic. It has, however, been enthusiastically described as such. Competent critics have allowed the description, and in their references to the poem use the name 'epic' with somewhat submissive acceptance.

It is an allegory, and written with a purpose

One of the many categories to which Dante's poem may be referred is that of allegory. The beginning of the poem is allegorical. The wood and the mountain, the leopard, the lion, the wolf, and the delivering hound, contain a double allegory, and have been interpreted both politically and ethically. Virgil and Beatrice represent allegorically human and divine science. Everywhere, in fact, if such be our bent, we shall find allegory. Can we say that the allegorical is hidden, since it is actually and confessedly part of the very fibre of the poem? Allegory and epic are usually opposed terms. Allegorical personages cannot as such be made to put on reality. But are Dante's personages purely allegorical? Most certainly not. They are real, in fact, sometimes realistic; they are not abstractions masquerading as persons, but felt realities of actual or typical significance.

* As a purple flower languishes and dies, a flower that the share in passing cuts down and leaves, or as the poppy in the garden, laden with excess of moisture, droops its head, even so, all colour fading away from his face, Dardinel passes from life; he passes from life, and makes to pass with him the boldness and the valour of all his men.

Dante put his world—his politics, his loves, and his hates into his poem; he put also into it his mediæval religion—his theorisings, his hopes, and his convictions; but the personal and mediæval colouring of the work does not interfere with its universal validity. He meant to write a didactic poem, meant to fashion his readers to perfection in political and spiritual truth, but the didactics may be correctly said to be in solution, and we must consciously employ a disuniting agent before they are precipitated.

Quality of the allegory

The Divine Comedy is an allegory largely in a philosophical sense. I do not mean that it cannot be proved to be literally an allegory, but it concerns me to mention an acceptable mode of regarding the allegorical in it. We can call the poem an allegory, from the standpoint of the idealistic philosopher, who calls the world the realisation of the divine thought, and who would add that in the world is to be found that which figures the divine ideas. So with the Divine Comedy. It is the projection of the poet's mind exhibiting purposeful elaboration, and contains a theory of life that is often allegorically set forth. For long we may, and do, unless prompted, remain unaffected by the allegorical in the poem. It is in the Purgatorio that the untutored reader is first strongly conscious that something besides the story is being conveyed to him. Before that stage he will be content to feel the poem to be, what it on the surface is, an itinerary of Dante's experiences in Hell, Purgatory, and Paradise.

Quasi-epic significance of the poem

It is only when we conceive of the Divine Comedy as an allegory, as well as a story, that we can discern its so-called epical significance. It is the epic of the human soul, they say, which has to struggle to perfection through temptations that have to be overcome, through mortifications that have to be imposed, through contemplation that has to be undertaken. It symbolises the work of emancipation in a man's life, and life is truly an epical action. It is then not in the first intention that our poem displays epic traits, but in the second. In the same sense one may say that specimens of statuary, and tableaux representing the seven ages of man, are epics. Such are, however, only epics by adumbration, it will be said, while the Divine Comedy actually projects to meet our gaze, the purposeful action of a representative of humanity. In the endowments and experience of the principal figure, our proxy and an actual partaker of our lot, we see the semblance of the endowments and experiences that are to determine the pattern, and form the warp and woof threads of the web of our life's story.

It is idle to pretend that this account of the epical in Dante's poem is satisfactory. The poem appeals to our sense of objectivity, and, when our reflection has added meaning to the itinerary, we gain the illusion of an action of fair unity, but it is the action of one agent, for the other personages are not agents in any proper epical sense, but merely a cloud of onlookers, or provocatives of action, or simply scenery. There is no way of getting unity out of the action, save by clinging to the person of Dante. Otherwise, the action is multiplex and nondescript. Certainly the manner of the poem has a fulness and grandeur that suggest epic work, but matter that can be so surcharged with recondite meaning is not the matter of the epic poet, who usually says the things he means. Dante's poem is, I fear, something *sui generis*.* Its action is epical of a sort, and epical in virtue, not of what it is, but of what it signifies.

Is the scenery of the poem such as suits the presence of epical quality in a fable? Is it even adapted to our

* I am pleased to find Mr Bosanquet, in his *History of Æsthetic*, p. 153, describe the Divine Comedy as 'absolutely unique in form.'

notion of the soul as agent? We must, I take it, accept Dante's scenery with his action, and yet, is it not by divorcing, in a measure, the scenery, which is panoramic and superabundant, and does not admit of rationalisation, from the part played by the human actor, that we have been able to regard the content of the poem as quasi-epic action? The scenery, it is true, is often allegorical action. If the Divine Comedy is an epic, the name must in its case mean an epical monodrama with incomprehensible scenery. In describing the form of this poem we ought to keep to the term 'vision,' for this description forces on us no reconciliation between alleged form and known content.

Its scenery

Dante is too intense for an epic poet. He grasps one and says, "Look here, look there, look yonder." The reader of epic is not required to bestow this attention. His matter is often too difficult for epic, which is not hard but readily followed and easily understood. There is little difficulty in his manner considered as a whole. He is definite and precise, to a degree, and his gift for objective realisation is marvellous. But the thing realised is a passionate subjective - objective, and such matter cannot have the substantial, self-asserting, and self-illumining quality of what is objective in its own right.

The poet too intense for an epic poet. The matter too hard to be epical

The Divine Comedy has been called the epic of the conscience. How can an epic be the epic of the conscience? Do we not in thus speaking, if the statement be an *ex cathedra* one, forsake the paths of definiteness. The phrase is simply a metaphor like an Iliad of woes, an Odyssey of wanderings, an Inferno of tortures. It is a compliment couched in figurative language. As are the troubles, hopes, struggles, and dooms of the body

Is the Divine Comedy the epic of the conscience?

in effort, when looked at epically, so are the same accidents of the soul in effort. All such uses of the term epic are figurative, and as such have a certain intelligibility, but we cannot justify their literal application. In this sense every biography is an epic, and life in general is an epic or drama, or lyric, according to the temperament of the describer, and the nature of the lot idealised. I have not yet seen the Pilgrim's Progress called an epic, but it might after the same intention be so described.

Writers who have called the poem an epic

It is Mr Symonds who calls the Divine Comedy the epic of the conscience, but he does so apologetically, and as a means of furnishing a grand estimate of the poem, otherwise I should not care to dispute the judgment of such a notable and inspiring critic. The fight of the conscience, or the soul's pilgrimage, has a right to figurative description and commendation, but no poetic account of such activity can, I think, be made to exhibit the character of epic in the literary sense of the term. Shelley, too, calls Dante's poem an epic, but Shelley's enthusiastic generalisations and ennobling of poetic half-truths are not to be taken too literally. Mr Lowell is another who uses the same term, but seems to do so by way of eulogy, and not definition.

The Divine Comedy an epic because not definitely anything else. Yet it is dramatic

Why is the Divine Comedy an epic? Because it is not dramatic (not formally so), not lyrical. Because it is a narrative poem, and written with high intent. I am not sure that Dante himself would have rejected the appellation 'drama,' for he calls the Æneid *alta tragoedia*, and the name *commedia*, comedy not tragedy owing to the happy ending, argues a consciousness of dramatic quality. If we will insist on referring the poem to one of the genera of literature, and not rather call it a species which in virtue of differentiation would rank as a new genus, if it had or could have fellow-members, 'drama' would be a better term to compound on than 'epic.' Dante knew the Ars Poetica of Horace, and must have sufficiently realised the difference between poetic varieties. We have set before us in our poem a series of pen-pictures dramatically drawn with various interludes. But Dante many times is too realistic for drama. In one way the more realistic, or rather real, a drama is, the better, but there is usually something typical, or representative, or feigned about a drama that prevents us being betrayed into anything but sympathy. We are sympathetic but disinterested spectators, if I may risk a seeming contradiction. Between Dante's presentation and our comprehension there often intervenes no thought of editing, there often hangs no veil suggesting remoteness. There is a note of verity about the narration ; we seem to be listening to a *procès-verbal* with all the actuality of real life. And yet the whole poem is an allegory, and many of the particulars are allegorical.

The spectacular of Dante is not the spectacular of the drama which presents action, and by the manner of its accomplishment and completion seeks to capture our sympathies, but a descriptive spectacular that deals in details, and exhibits a sequence too emotional to be organic, if its manifestations be not too dispersed to be recognisable. There is in the Divine Comedy a preponderance of dialogue, which gives the poem quite a dramatic air, the strong mixture of the spectacular being contributory to the production of this impression. We are asked to reconstruct mentally a series of tableaux, of which the descriptions are given, and that vividly enough, to make the reconstruction an easy matter. The intervals during the progress of this process are filled with didactic, illustrative, and explanatory comment. Dante is not only an actor in his own poem but a sort of cicerone to it.

The Divine Comedy is, of course, no more a drama than it is an epic, but it has got certain external dramatic aspects. The constant obtrusion and finger-pointing of the author, the apparent threadlessness of the action, which needs a strong and deliberately instituted synthesis before any unity can be discerned, effectually prevent us giving it formal classification among literary products.

It is a philosophical poem with a theory of the physical and moral universe. It is a political testament.

Remarks in definition

It is a religious manual. It is also the Revelation of Dante the Florentine. It is neither in intention, nor in execution, nor yet in impression made, an epic. Only vagueness or *schwärmerei* will induce us to speak in favour of such a definition. As a piece of literature its value is not to be enhanced by approximating it to this or that variety. One is not troubled in reading it with doubts about location. We are then in no critical or loitering mood. The poet lays hold of us, and his earnestness, and power, and that omnipotent touch by which feelings, as well as scenes, are painted, impel us onward. There are local and petty events enough in the poem, which to us in those days need comment and explanation, but we are willing to leap over these and defer their elucidation, beckoned on, as we are, by the invitingness of the realising and revealing style. The wonder is that the allegorical and doctrinal purpose of the work does not arrest our progress more frequently.

There is a certain grossness and materialism about the Inferno that of itself largely enchains our attention, but

The Inferno and the Purgatorio

Dante does not need such accessories. We mount with him the terraces of Purgatory, and the compelling power he exercises is still great, all the greater, I think, that the dead air of the woful realms has now lifted. The Purgatory has all the advantage that beauty has over ugliness, that life has over death, and the sapphire-tinted morn of Ante-Purgatory, with its strong contrast to the sigh-laden atmosphere of the cis-Acherusian Hell, radiates expectations that are not overclouded or dimmed. The Inferno is an effortless because a hopeless place. The activity that only emphasises helplessness cannot be called effort, and is sure, from the sameness of impression made, to generate satiety, and it must be said that the grim punitive aspect of the first *cantica*, in spite of the vigour and variety of the depicting, begins after a time to affect us with a certain weariness.

The Purgatorio exhibits effort, and effort quickened by hope. The effort that was somewhat magisterially enjoined by Cato on Casella's listeners was one fed by a hope that had no surcease, but that was itself aye renewed and strengthened by the releasing angel as the climbers passed up higher into joy. Whatever of doctrinal there is in the second *cantica*, whatever that requires the consciousness of the mystic, these, if they arrest, do not interrupt the fine flow of humanity that begins with Casella's song, and that continues all through the healing pathos of the efforts to make oneself fair.* And at the end of the Purgatorio the necessities imposed by the poet's modes of thought and the whole strain of the fable require solemnisation and a mystic initiation.

The Paradiso. Deity in Dante and Milton

It needs some purging of the visual nerve to rise in contemplation with Dante through the circles of the Paradiso, but we can stand afar off and gaze, as a spectator so placed can, at the poet's progress. There are enough circumstantial data given, there is enough radiance shed from

* The souls at the base of Mount Purgatory, when they saw that Dante was, by reason of his breathing, a living man, paused, 'as if forgetting to go to make themselves fair':—

Quasi obbliando d'ire a farsi belle.

Purg. ii, 75.

saints enswathed in light, to enable us to realise his upward course, swift as thought, and as the change in light of Beatrice's eyes.

It is a mystical view that Dante takes of Deity, and he is slowly approached. Dante, though as theologically-minded a man as need be, does not make the Deity a theologian. He is for him a beatific vision, a mystic trinity. Dante leaves theology and speculative detail to Beatrice, to St. Thomas Aquinas, or other saints. Milton, it will be remembered, makes God the author, the redactor, and the exponent of theology. The exigences of Milton's story required an earlier detailed reference to the Divine Being, and though Milton was too much of a poet and artist to drop us plump, as he has been almost accused of doing, into a cabinet council, a meeting of executive with a membership of one, preluding as he does by his magnificent invocation to Holy Light, which is an abstract and not realistic description as are Dante's descriptions, still his first mention of God bears, in a way, this aspect. Milton, although in words he surrounded God's throne with starry sanctities, yet could not have flooded the heavens with Dante's celestial light, and its description would have been too much for even his inner vision.

CHAPTER VI

THE SPANISH AND PORTUGUESE EPICS

The Poema del Cid: its fable

THE fable of The Cid begins with the banishment of Ruy Diaz. It is sometimes said that the loss of lines from the beginning of the poem is considerable, and that much of the Cid's previous life must have been described in these lost lines. This need not have been. An epic is not a biography, and, with the existence of a Cid cycle of poetical legend, the hero's youth cannot have stood in need of commemoration.

The banished chief had to raise money to maintain himself and his family. This he did, by depositing with the Jewish money-lenders, Rachel and Vidas, two chests, supposed to be packed with valuable loot got in the Moorish wars, but really filled with sand. They advanced him money on the contents of the chests and undertook not to open them for a year. The Cid subsequently purged himself of the guilt of this deception by ransoming the chests. During his enforced absence from his country, he left his wife, Doña Ximena, and his daughters, Doña Elvira and Doña Sol, for safety, in the monastery of San Pedro de Cardeña under the care of the abbot, Don Sancho.

Martin Antolinez entertained his master at Burgos in spite of the king's prohibition, and followed him into banishment. Other adherents of the Cid did the same, among them Alvar Fañez, Pero Bermuez, Muño Gustioz, etc., and the amount of his following soon rose to hundreds. Food and lodging were got at the expense of the Moors. The Cid soon possessed himself of the Castle of Alcocer, and, on being hemmed in and besieged by superior numbers, sallied out and inflicted on the enemy a severe defeat, badly mauling in the battle the Moorish king, Fariz. He quitted Alcocer, and carried on a guerilla warfare, utterly defeating Count Ramon Berenger of Barcelona, who attacked him for his maltreatment of tributary Moors. It was at this time, and from Don Ramon, that he got the famous sword Colada. (Tizon, his other sword, was taken by him from King Bucar, whom he defeated at Valencia, whither he had gone to avenge his brother Yucef.)

The Cid now obtained possession of the important city of Valencia, to which he brought his wife and children. Hard on its capture he had to fight by the city walls the king of Seville. This king he defeated, pursuing his routed army as far as Xativa. Thousands of the Moors were drowned in the Xucar, where, as the poet quaintly puts it, they had to drink lots of water. He was not allowed to remain in undisturbed possession of Valencia. Yucef, king of Morocco, landed an army to attack and capture it. This king, too, was routed and driven off the field, bearing with him the marks of the hero's regulation three blows. The Cid, mounted on his charger Babieca displayed great gallantry in the battle. He next despatched an embassy with presents to King Alfonso. He had done this before, to conciliate the king into permitting his wife and children to join him, but he was now a more important personage. He was ruler of Valencia, and kept semi-royal state. The king was dazzled by the success of his subject, and proclaimed his peerlessness. The Infants of Carrion, members of a family that had been hostile to the Cid, attracted by his power and wealth, desired, using the king as spokesman, to marry the great chief's two daughters. The Cid, who personally did not like the match, loyally met the king's wishes in the matter, and the marriage was celebrated with great splendour.

The Cid's sons-in-law proved unworthy men. By cowardice in battle and cowardice before the Cid's lion, they made themselves the butt of the observant and outspoken society at the court of Valencia. Things got so hot for them that they solicited leave to quit Valencia and go to their estates at Carrion. Their wives they took with them, and on arriving at a certain wild place, near Corpes, they laid violent hands on the women, stripped them, and treated them despitefully with spur and saddle-girth. The poor women were found by Felez Muñoz, who had suspected the cowardly counts and followed them. The Cid demanded justice of the king. This was granted him at a session of the Cortes in Toledo, where three champions of the Cid challenged three of the counts of Carrion to a sort of trial by combat. The Cid's men conquered, and extracted from the conquered an acknowledgment of defeat. The epic ends with the announcement of the betrothal of the Cid's daughters to princes of the royal houses of Navarre and Aragon.

The metre

The metre is mazy, and no one seems to be able to set down anything positive about it. The normal line is said to be one of fourteen syllables, but this number may be increased or diminished at the will of the poet, who sometimes pays out an extraordinary number of syllables, sometimes fetches himself up abruptly. The cadence is called trochaic, but iambs certainly appear at the beginning of the line and occur elsewhere, and seem—though in the uncertainty one cannot be sure of anything—to be too common to be due to an occasional substitution of iamb for trochee. A complete account of the metre of this poem will have to say something of definite import about elision, slurring, and accent. There is a pause in the middle of the line and at the end of a word, sometimes following an accented syllable, sometimes not.

If the reader will begin at the end of the line, marking the assonance (vowel rhyme), or consonance (correspondence both of accent-bearing, and other syllable), and work his way backward, simultaneously noting with a glance of his eye the central pause, he will be in a position to recite the lines with something approximating to satisfaction. Practice, the two fulcra I have just mentioned, and a little pious belief, will even enable him to hear a little harmony in his recitation.

The Cid a heroic poem in the narrow sense

The Cid is a heroic poem in that narrower sense of the adjective which implies a distinction between such a poem and an epic poem proper. There is as much difference between a heroic poem and an epic poem, in the large sense of the adjective, as between a biography of personal detail and the biographical narrative of a period of history, a large portion of which has been made by one excellent man whose biography the narrative expands and connects with the world and with God.

Its strong and natural story

The strength of The Cid is in the story, in the narration pure and simple. There are no literary fireworks, there is, one might strictly speaking say, no literary manner. Anyhow, the graces of allusion, of simile, of high-sounding sentiment, of natural description as such, are pretty well absent. Still there is in the poem enough to hold children from play and old men from the chimney corner. It is a record of manliness, of readiness of resource, of kingship of men, of large projects and solid accomplishment.

The poem tells of the disfavour into which the Cid fell with the king, and of his triumphant emergence therefrom. Whatever portions may be lost from the beginning, it is a complete enough whole as it stands, and the plan of the story is as satisfactory as need be desired. It is a tale of a king's ingratitude and a subject's worth. It is an even and natural narrative, with a hero and his following, with adventures, and deeds, and glory won, much thinner in significance than some of the big epics, but possessing an honest action and interesting actors.

The fighting is sane and an every-day accomplishment

The fighting in the poem is intensely sane. The blows are masterly, but not theatrical, and have no such incredible results as, say, those of the Song of Roland, though the strokes and thrusts of the combatants in the fight between the Cid's followers and the Infants of Carrion do seem a bit managed by the poet.

Battling has more than one aspect in this epic. It is a means of living, and not exclusively a means of self-glorification, or a pathway to honour, an aspect which it pre-eminently bears in many epics. For example the Cid, on learning of the approach of King Yucef against Valencia, says regarding his wife and daughters who had but lately come to the city :—

En estas tierras agenas verán las moradas commo se fazen :
Afarto verán por los oios commo se gana el pan.*
P. del C. 1643.

Men took to fighting naturally in those days, as to a vocation ; they lived and throve on it. The following is said of one of the hero's chieftains, when asked for his advice on the proposed sally from Alcocer :—

Primero fablo Minaya, vn cauallero de prestar :
De Castiella la gentil exidos somos acá,

* They will see how our lives are spent in these foreign lands ; they will see clearly enough with their eyes how bread is won.

Si con moros non lidiaremos, no nos darán del pan.
Bien somos nos VI cientos, algunos ay de mas.
En el nombre del Criador que non pase por al:
Vayamos-los ferir en aquel dia de cras.*

P. del C. 671.

Then, men went to battle rejoicing in their strength. They called their swords pet names; they loved them as dearly as a craftsman loves a serviceable tool. Valour in those days was not only a virtue, to be exhibited when occasion required, but a preventive of harm, to be constantly used as a safeguard. The battle belonged to the strong, and this adaptation of means to ends gave to bravery a steadiness and self-confidence that make all old fighting epical and worthy of contemplation, and endowed it with an attractiveness that it is likely to lose when it passes into divestible and calculated fury. I do not mean that war was the trade of the swordsman, the venal mercenary, but that in the more multifarious (not more tumultuous, certainly) individual life of that age, warring was an arm of human activity, and as such was recognised and provided for. What honest and fascinating, as well as daring activity, was that of Pero Bermuez, when he bore the Cid's banner into the thickest part of the Moors, and forced his lord to save his honour, and to make impetuosity the mark of that day's fighting. It reminds one of the still finer act of the Douglas, when, as a provocative to valour and an omen of victory, he cast, alas abortively, his casket into the ranks of the same Moors.

The poem has many strong situations, and is full of manly activity and broad humanity. The actors are

* First spake Minaya, a knight of vigour:—"From fair Castile we have come hither; if we don't fight with Moors they won't give us bread. We are, I say, six hundred, some there are besides; in the name of the Creator let there be no move to anything else. Let us go to attack them on the morrow's day."

transparently natural, and act with all straightforwardness, and not as if they were puppets with parts assigned them by the poet, as, for example, is the case with Lucan's actors. The story is told frankly and unmysteriously, as in all simple heroic. It babbles on like a brook, clear as crystal, now in shadow, now in shade. There is absolutely no padding. The poet disdains all such devices, and refuses to embrace any opportunity for divagation. He says of a journey of Minaya :—

The story is frankly and simply told

> Dexare-uos las posadas, non las quiero contar.*
>
> P. del C. 1310.

Had the matter of The Cid come into the hands of a poet who was not only a master in story-telling, but the possessor of literary art, as was the poet of the Iliad, our poem would have had more echo in the world.

In the absence of express flowerings of literary art there is the more reason to notice the vigorous expression that is to be met with in the poem. When a man is called 'Lying Mouth' (*boca sin verdad*), as was Diego Gonzalez by Martin Antolinez, we simply say, that the language is strong and saltish, but when one man dubs another 'Tongue-without-hands,' (*lengua sin manos*)† as Pero Bermuez did Ferrando Gonzalez, we say that it is both vigorous and fetching, perhaps more so than the piled-up vituperation of 'Wineskin! Dog's-face! and Deer's-heart!' The whole scene of the defiance thrown at the nobles of Carrion in the sight of the Cortes of Toledo is most animated. The reader will remember that, when Achilles quarrels

The vigorous expression

* Look you, I shall pass over the halting-places ; I have no mind to tell of them.

† Compare P. del C. 2174, Que es largo de lengua, mas en lo al non es tan pro (who is large of tongue, but in other things is not so distinguished), said of Assur Gonzalez.

with Agamemnon, the poet, to relieve the tension of the situation has recourse to Athena, who makes her presence felt by Achilles. The poet of The Cid tempers the tragic situation, and allays the apprehensions of the reader by introducing a little comedy, and by giving to some of the challenges a humorous turn, which would have caused any such audience, barring, of course, the parties hit, to smile amusedly.

The duels with the Counts of Carrion

The description of the single combats between the Cid's champions and the Counts of Carrion is as vigorous a bit of narrative of the kind as could well be desired. The bravery is not all on one side, for the fighting is of the give-and-take order, and yet ends auspiciously, that is, for the behoof of the gallant challengers. From the point of view of an account of duelling it is far and away a stronger bit of narrative than Camoens' story of the fight of the Portuguese champions (called the Twelve of England) in defence of the injured ladies. The latter is too cramped—the poet in fact declines to give details—and antithetical.

The Poema del Cid and the Nibelungenlied

It is the fashion to make or suggest a comparison between the Poema del Cid and the Nibelungenlied. I do not see the resemblance between the two poems. That aspect of the Nibelungenlied which may be supposed to recall a sagaesque and presumably original matter, presents a weirdness that is perfectly foreign to the Poema, and the retouched and retoned Nibelungenlied that we know is most dissimilar, embodying, as it does, conceptions, and containing mannerisms the like of which are not to be found in the Spanish poem. The Poema celebrates rational and intelligible exploits in a natural and picturesque manner. We can hardly say this, without reservation, of the other poem. I am not denying the literary reality that is in the German epic ;

far from it, but it has not the living objectivity of the Spanish one.

Ruy Diaz, the Cid, and hero of the poem of the same name, is not haughty or reserved, but open, and with much of broad human sentiment. He understands a joke. He is shrewd, humorous, and brave, a mixture of jolly brigand and patriot. He cheated the Jews, Rachel and Vidas; he outwitted his enemies by craft; he chaffed his followers; he was lavish of his person in danger.

Ruy Diaz

He was a most lovable man, and with strong natural affections. The care and love he evinced for his wife and daughters are most pleasing traits in his character. His wife is his 'dear and honoured wife,' and his daughters and she 'my heart and soul.' The parting from his wife, after the sentence of banishment, was like the rending of nail from flesh :—

> Asis parten vnos dotros commo la vnna de la carne.*
>
> P. del C. 375.

No one ever served the Cid without due acknowledgment, and, in the long run, reward, according to the measure of his generosity and ability. As the poem says :—

> Qui a buen sennor sirue, siempre biue en deliçio. †
>
> P. del C. 850.

It was always a multiplex return that Ruy Diaz made for services rendered.

Our hero was a man of infinite jest. When Don Ramon Berenger, the sovereign of Valencia, interfered to prevent the Cid removing the booty he had won, and was badly defeated for his pains, the Cid treated him generously, but too jovially for the circumstances, and invited him to dine. Don Ramon was too sore over his

* Thus they part, the one from the other, like the nail from the flesh.

† He who serves a good master lives always amid delight.

defeat by ragamuffins, as he deemed them, to consent, and said that under the circumstances, he preferred death to dining:—

> Non combré un bocado por quanto ha en toda Espanna:
> Antes perderé el cuerpo e dexaré el alma,
> Pues que tales mal-calçados me vençieron de batalla.*
>
> P. del C. 1021.

He was a-dying for three days, until the Cid, grasping the situation, promised him and three companions their liberty if they partook of a good square meal. This generous but roguish proffer completely disarmed the count, for he pocketed his pride, and with his three companions acquitted himself as only a valiant trencherman could. The Cid slyly assured the count that this gift of freedom did not involve the restitution of any property, all of which was now permanently alienated through his own default:—

> Mas quanto auedes perdido non uos lo daré:
> Ca huebos me lo he e pora estos myos vassallos,
> Ca commigo andan lazrados, e non uos lo daré. †
>
> P. del C. 1043.

'And,' said he at parting, 'if your countship deems that he has been treated too cavalierly by me, it is open to him to correct the mistake fortune has made.' The Cid was a man easily found by his friends, and still more easily by his enemies.

It is at this stage of the story that the poet lauds the honour of Rodrigo:—

> Vna desleatança ca non la fizo alguandre.‡
>
> P. del C. 1081.

---

* I will not eat a mouthful for all that is in broad Spain. Sooner will I lose my body and surrender my soul, seeing that such poorly-shod devils have conquered me in battle.

† But that which you have lost I will not give it you. For I have need of it for myself and for these my vassals, since, to their own sorrow, they go with me, yea, I will not give it you.

‡ A disloyalty, why, he never committed any.

Count Ramon, it seems, had his suspicions of the Cid's honour, over which the poet is hotly indignant, and says so. He has not forgotten the Rachel and Vidas episode, but he apologised for the act at the time, and others than Jesuits will be found willing to excuse the temporary, and perhaps venial lapse of such a pattern of chivalry as the Champion of Bivar.

The Cid at the Cortes of Toledo

The Cid makes a notable appearance at the Cortes called to adjudicate on the quarrel between himself and the Counts of Carrion. He first rises and demands the surrender of the swords Colada and Tizon from approved cowards. His demand is granted. He rises a second time and demands that they give back the presents they had received on departing. The Counts profess their inability to do so. Their personal effects are then poinded and taken at a valuation. For the third time the Cid rises and demands vengeance for the outrage on his daughters. Then follow mutual recriminations and some very salt speech ending in the three challenges.

The religion of the Cid

Our hero was a good Catholic. He sanctified his conquest of Valencia by making the city a bishopric with Don Jeronimo as bishop. He was pious after the fashion of the times, and perhaps more so, for we read that, after a census had been taken of his subjects in Valencia, he said to Alvar Fañez :—

> Grado a Dios, Mynaya, e a Sancta Maria Madre!
> Con mas pocos yxiemos de la casa de Bivar.*
>
> P. del C. 1267.

It is plain, then, that the Cid of the poet had some religion in his soul, for this little aside is a better revealer of character than a big overt act.

The Cid was courteous, and spoke courteously, but, on

* Thanks be to God and to Holy Mother Mary, Minaya, we came out of the Castle of Bivar with a poorer following.

occasion he had a most biting tongue. Count Garcia of Carrion twitted him before the Cortes with his overgrown beard. The Cid replied that his beard had remained intact from all affront and injury, which was more than could be said for the count's, for at the taking of the Castle of Cabra it had been plucked by boys, and had suffered so much from his own violent tug that it had grown in awry. These words must have stung like a whip.

His courtesy

The Cid's beard is often referred to in the narrative. He had not trimmed or touched it in any way since his banishment, *por amor del rey Alffonsso*, says the poem. A victory of his is thus described :—

His beard

> E vençió esta batalla poro ondró su barba.*
>
> P. del C. 1011.

He is even complimented in terms of his beard. For example, he is called 'Fine Beard' (*barba tan conplida*). Again :—

> Dios commo es alegre la barba velida !
> Que Albar Fanez pagó las mill missas.†
>
> P. del C. 930.

The initial wording of this citation is of common occurrence. For example, just a line or two above, we have :—

> Dios commo fue alegre todo aquel fonssado !
> Que Minaya Albar Fanez assi era legado.‡
>
> P. del C. 926.

The Cid has many epithets and descriptions. He is 'My Cid,' 'My Cid of Bivar,' 'My Cid the Warrior,' 'My Cid of the long beard,' 'the perfect one,' 'he who was born in a lucky hour,'

His titles

* And he gained this battle and thereby honoured his beard.

† God, how joyful is Bushy Beard that Alvar Fañez paid for the thousand masses.

‡ God, how joyful was all that host that Minaya Alvar Fañez was thus returned.

'he who in a lucky hour girded on sword' (*Myo Çid, Myo Çid el de Bivar, Myo Çid el Campeador, Myo Çid el de la lengua barba, el caboso, el que en buen hora nasco, Myo Çid Ruy Diaz que en buen ora cinxo espada*).

The other characters in the poem are clearly drawn. We are conscious of an individuality in each one. The principal one is Minaya Alvar Fañez, the Cid's 'right arm,' his 'better arm' (*el myo diestro braço, el myo braço mejor*), his organiser of victory and principal contributor thereto, of whom his lord says:—

The characters

> Mientra uos visquieredes, bien me yrá a mi Minaya.*
>
> P. del C. 925.

Others are Pero Bermuez, nicknamed Peter the Dumb (*Pero Mudo*), a man of deeds and not of words; Martin Antolinez, 'the Burgalese of prowess,' 'the noble Burgalese' (*el burgales de pro, el burgales cunplido*), the type of a faithful vassal, ready to peril his property and person for his lord's sake; and the fighting pilgrim-prelate, Don Jeronimo, 'loyal priest,' 'priest of vigour' (*coronado leal, coronado de prestar*), who could pass one into immortality:—

> El obispo don Ieronimo la missa les cantaua,
> La missa dicha grant sultura les daua.
> El que aqui muriere lidiando de cara,
> Prendol yo los pecados, e Dios le abra el alma.†
>
> P. del C. 1703.

The jealous king is always in the background, well wooed by the Cid, proud in spite of himself to have such a vassal, and almost persuaded to be permanently just and generous, but, though this is rather a shadow thrown by the Chronicle, still fickle and fitful.

* While you live, Minaya, it will go well with me.

† The bishop Don Jeronimo sang them the mass. The said mass gave them complete absolution. "He who will die here, fighting face to face (with the foe), I absolve him of his sins, and God will take his soul."

The story of the Lusiads

The story proper of Os Lusiadas begins with the showing to us of the Portuguese ships under sail to India. A council of the gods is held on Olympus to decide on the future of the expedition. At this council Jupiter displays an inclination to befriend the Portuguese, and announces his determination to procure them a friendly reception on the African coast. Bacchus, who was afraid lest the glory the Portuguese might win in India would eclipse the glory he had won in the same land, opposes this decision ; Venus and Mars support it. We return to the fleet, and find it sailing between the Isle of St. Lawrence (Madagascar) and the mainland. It touches successively at Mozambique, Mombasah, and Melinde. At the first place Bacchus plots against the voyagers by instigating an attack, which failed, and by causing them to be supplied with a treacherous pilot. The better to affect his purposes he had assumed the form of a well-known and respected Moor of Mozambique. Venus saves the Portuguese off Quiloa, and, by her own personal efforts and those of the Nereids, prevents them sailing into the harbour of Mombasah to their own destruction. She and her assistants oppose their persons to the passage of Gama's ship across the bar, and push it back constantly, in spite of the efforts of the crew to sail on. The plotting Moors and the treacherous pilot take fright at the delay, and jump, some into the boats around the ship, others into the sea. The treachery and the delivering miracle are both at the same time revealed to the admiral, who thanks Divine Providence for preservation. The ruler of Mombasah, purposing treachery, had invited Da Gama to land, and the latter had consented on hearing of the presence of many Christians in the land. He had despatched two messengers to verify this report, who found a priest, Bacchus in disguise, worshipping God according to the Christian rite. Thyoneus worshipping Jehovah, a false god adoring the true—such things are to be met with in the hybrid supernatural of Camoens. Venus, after rescuing the Portuguese at Mombasah, ascends to heaven to solicit the active interference of Jupiter on behalf of her favoured nation. Jupiter accedes to her request, prophesies the future glory of the Lusitanians, and sends Mercury to Melinde to prepare them a hospitable reception. Da Gama, warned by Mercury in a dream, leaves dangerous Mombasah, and sails to Melinde. The king of this place, an impressionable person, who had heard the story of Lusitanian renown, welcomes the strangers and promises to visit the fleet. He keeps the promise, and craves from the admiral a description of his country and its history.

Da Gama's narrative to the king occupies three cantos. It tells of the history of Portugal from the foundation of the monarchy by Count Henrique down to the despatch of the fleet to India by Dom Manoel. It mentions the battle of Ourique, in which the Portuguese overcame the Moors, and that of Aljubarrota, in which they defeated the Castilians. It contains the episodes of Ignez de Castro and of Adamastor, Dom Manoel's dream of the Ganges and Indus, and the farewell of the Old Man of Belem. The part of the voyage that preceded the arrival at East Africa is then described.

After the entertainment by the king of Melinde the Lusitanians set sail for India with pilots and provisions. Bacchus now attempts to rouse the sea-gods against the hated nation, and for this purpose descends to the palace of Neptune, in the depths of the sea, which palace is described by the poet. He succeeds in arranging a storm for the torment of the voyagers. The poet makes Velloso tell the story of the Twelve of England, twelve Portuguese nobles who championed the honour of twelve English dames. Venus and the sea-nymphs calm the storm that has now broken loose, and after a little the ships approach Calicut. The admiral sends a messenger to the shore, where he meets Monsaidé, a Mahometan, and a native of Barbary, who could speak Spanish. This person proves most useful to the Portuguese. Da Gama is invited to land by the king, and is placed under the guidance of a catual, or ruler of the kingdom. He visits the king, or samorim, as he is called, and makes on him a favourable impression. The catual, in quest of information, boards the admiral's ship, and while there, asks Paulo da Gama to describe the pictures and figures to be seen on silken banners. Then are introduced the names of leading Portuguese with little bits of recital. Some of these names have had mention and celebration already. Bacchus stirs up the Mahometans, and these poison the minds of the natives and their king. Da Gama and his companions run some risk, but finally are able to set sail on the return voyage, taking with them Monsaidé, who becomes a Christian. Venus prepares for their reception and refreshment the Isle of Loves. In the tenth and last canto, at the banquet given by Tethys to Da Gama, a nymph sings of the future exploits of the Portuguese in the East. After the banquet Tethys takes the admiral up a mountain, and shows him, suspended in the air, a wondrous globe of several orbs. Some astronomy and much geography are then given, and an account is also furnished of the martyrdom of St. Thomas. The Portuguese leave the Isle of Loves, and renewing the return voyage, arrive at Lisbon.

Camoens has many asides. He has an address to Dom Sebastiam at the beginning of the poem, and an exhortation at the close. He has personal notes—elegiac song, indignation in verse, philosophical reflection, and hortatory ethic. These personal notes contain some of the most fascinating work of the poem.

Virgil's Venus is in heaven already. The description

of her flight thither adds much to the attractiveness of Camoens' digression. Her upward passage impassions all space. The heaven, the stars, and the air—the great things of space—do homage to her beauty. With a bold but fine exaggeration in the manner of the romantic poets, her eyes are said to have fired the poles, and to have instilled desire into the frigid zone. Virgil's Venus merges the woman in the goddess, and it is a goddess, though a tearful one, that reasons with the thunderer; Camoens' is more of a woman than a goddess, and in addition possesses the allurements and potency of the mother of reproduction, *hominum divomque voluptas*, who entangled Mars and dazzled the eyes of the Phrygian shepherd. Camoens paints with the warm sensuousness of Spenser and Milton, painting, too, not the meretriciousness of mere repose, but an animated and aggressive beauty.

The plaint and intercession of Venus

Virgil's Venus is less astute than the Venus of Camoens, and more reproachful, being indeed a trifle censorious. The Roman is stiffer than the Portuguese, and does not see so many possibilities in the theme. The latter fills in the picture, and colours all its parts. The strength of the portraiture of the former is in its reserve, a reserve of great expressiveness, suggesting tenfold more than mere words convey. The tender grace of *tristior et lacrimis oculos suffusa nitentes* and the severe chastity of *oscula libavit natæ* are, if not so sensuously pleasing, far more eloquent than honied descriptions of the amorous coquetry and corporal charms of the Camoensian Venus. The Jupiter of the Venus episode has with Virgil the Olympian manner; the Jupiter of the same portion of the Lusiads has the air of a celestial *roué*. The dignity he has is the dignity of Virgilian reminiscence.

What in Virgil is suggestion, and with him properly so, is in Camoens expanded and elaborated. The one manner is as legitimate as the other, and Camoens, the child of romance, was perforce—to say nothing of the constraints of natural propulsion—compelled to write romantically. It is thus that Camoens' treatment of this incident exhibits far more developed art than Virgil's. To exercise this art, he gives us, in addition to his filling-up of the Virgilian outline, the passage of Venus to heaven, and her offer of vicarious sacrifice with its fine weeping *aposiopesis*.

Jupiter's consolatory forecast in the Æneid is better than that in the Lusiads. It is more compact and continuous and has more scenic suggestiveness. It is graver, and better dressed, and has decidedly better phraseology, and a better feeling for national ideas and aspirations. Virgil is a better national mouthpiece than Camoens, and has a more penetrating vision of historic verity. He has better, because more ideal, historic portraits, and more historic distinctness. The Virgilian forecast covers a longer time, and consequently has more perspective.

As a whole it is much finer, because possessing more unity, and the details are more impressive, because more poetical, and pictorial too. 'Romulus in the wolfskin,' 'Augustus laden with the spoils of the east,' 'conquered Phthia, Mycenæ, and Argos,' 'hoary Faith,' and 'the Race of the Gown' are of more literary value than Camoens' heraldic announcements, and all too vainglorious boasts about the Lusians. These announcements are too circumstantial and of too miraculous matter. Virgil's presentation reposes on features of great national and human import—a dynastic survival, a triumph of poetic justice, a divine reconciliation, and an empire in perpetuity. And at the close we have the fine vision of the Pax Romana.

Perhaps a Portuguese is the best judge of the quality of his poet's enumeration of national achievements, but I confess there is to me a flavour of pettiness and mendacity about the ever-victorious Portuguese, the stormless storm,* twice-subjugated Ormuz, the deadly backward flight of arrows,† the two sieges of Dio, dominant Goa, and generally the chart-like delineation of events. Virgil has in his episode the art to deal in generals, and what there is of the particular has a strong symbolic value. Camoens, in his, deals too much in particulars, his tone is ultra-patriotic, and his manner somewhat ruffling.

Ignez de Castro

The episode of Ignez de Castro is one of the gems of the Lusiads, and certainly one of the noblest bits of elegiac writing in all literature. Its subject is a fine one, as youth and beauty done to death must always be. And Camoens was not a poet likely to miss an opportunity of making capital out of the attractiveness of youth and the glamour of beauty.

The old king, Alfonso, had deserved well of his country. He had established her position in the Peninsula. He was a neighbourly and politic prince. He had assisted his son-in-law, the king of Castile, to rout the Moor. But his statecraft drove him into crime.

The immediate settling of the episode is a strong one. Hard on the victory over the Moor comes the assassination of a woman. The national hero becomes the domestic murderer. A noble past is sullied by a cowardly deed. In the narration the poet constantly, by suggestion or by direct allusion, brings home to us the counterpoise of glory with cruelty. The mighty falling-off of the king is not the only extraneous bit of colouring in the episode. At its very beginning, and repeatedly throughout, reference is made to future punishment. The wings of the Erinyes brood over the narrative. We have an intuition

* It is said that once in a dead calm the waters of the sea boiled furiously before Da Gama.

† In a fight with the Persians, off Ormuz, the arrows these shot against the Portuguese were driven back against themselves by a great wind, with fatal results.

of the sureness of a dogged though slow retribution. Every now and then we hear the distant but still perfectly audible tolling of the tocsin of coming vengeance. The victim is not to be deprived, even by death, of the regal pomp that the alliance with the king's son makes her right. All this comes in well as a sort of background of poetical justice. Our pity and indignation crave this solace and gratification.

Ignez de Castro was butchered in the king's presence, as the poet has it, by those assassins—*algozes* (hangmen), they are called—who did not wish to be governed by the offspring of a *mésalliance.* The deed was done in spite of impassioned appeals on the part of the victim, appeals which softened even the sternness of the worldly-wise old king. Poor Ignez, pleading that her only crime had been to love him who had known how to gain her love, entreated to have her life spared, if only for her children's sake :—

> Ó tu, que tens de humano o gesto e o peito,
> (Se de humano he matar huma donzella
> Fraca e sem força, só por ter sujeito
> O coraçâo a quem soube vencel-a)
> A estas criancinhas tem respeito,
> Pois o nâo tens á morte escura della :
> Mova-te a piedade, sua e minha,
> Pois te nâo move a culpa que nâo tinha.*
>
> Os Lusiadas iii, 127.

The pathos of the last line of her entreaty reminds one of the simple pathos of the entreaty of Sejanus' daughter, who asked to be told her crime, and said that she would not commit it again. The entreaty moved the king, but not the Hyrcanian tigers of courtiers. She had wept and

* O thou that hast a man's face and breast (if 'tis manlike to kill a feeble and frail girl, and all because she ruled the heart of him who knew how to conquer her), have regard to these little ones, though thou hast it not for the shameful death of the mother; and may pity for them, and for myself, move thee, though my crime that is no crime moves thee naught.

pleaded in vain, and in vain had uplifted her eyes, for she could not uplift her bound hands, to heaven. What a really moving picture! It is not the pretty pathetic that we find in the episode, for in it we hear, as it were, the voice of Nature weeping for her children.

The poet has known how, by allusiveness, to lend association and scope to his verses. Ignez was done to death, as was done Polyxena at the tomb of Achilles, for the benefit of others, and not for her own crime. The sun well-nigh veiled his face, as he once did, at sight of the awful meal purveyed by Thyestes. Nature is enlisted as judge, as chorus. The sun threatened to withdraw his light, the hollow valleys retained and re-echoed the victim's last cry, the waters of the Mondego are feigned to have been swollen by her tears, and to have murmured the name of her lover to the mountains and the tiny flowers. The precise localisation of the poet gives local colour and additional reality to the story. Mondego suggests Ignez, and Ignez, Mondego. And the Fountain of Loves, whose waters are the tears wept over Ignez by the daughters of Mondego, gives a local habitation to the story.

It is not so much the beauty of the daisy stanza in itself that commends it, as its prominent place in a lengthy piece of fine poetry, whose merit consists in the long-sustained pitch of literary excellence. The wording of the stanza is not superior to the wording of the verses that tell of the deaths of Euryalus and Pallas, the former falling like a flower uprooted by the plough, or drooping like a drenched poppy with neck aweary of its head, the latter laid on his bier like a delicate violet or a drooping hyacinth plucked by a maiden's hand, still lovely and bright, but dissevered from nurturing and strength-giving earth. The words of the stanza are these :—

Assi como a bonina, que cortada
Antes do tempo foi, candida e bella,

Sendo das mâos lascivas maltratada
Da menina que a trouxe na capella,
O cheiro traz perdido e a côr murchada ;
Tal está morta a pallida donzella,
Seccas do rosto as rosas, e perdida
A branca e viva côr co'a doce vida.*

Os Lusiadas iii, 134.

The fate of Ignez was due, says the poet, to imperious and ruthless Love. His reproachful address to Love has not the pseudo-scolding tone of lighter compositions couched in the orthodox erotic vein. These half-serious, half-conventional apostrophes to tyrant Love and cruel Cypris, do sometimes, however, suggest things of tragic and deadly earnestness, and the fictitiousness of the manner enhances by contrast the terror of the facts. This is the case with Camoens' address.

The Dream of Dom Manoel

Just before dawn there appeared to Dom Manoel, as he reclined on his golden bed, the river-gods Ganges and Indus. In his dream the king had been rapt in spirit to the first sphere, whence he looked eastwards, over various worlds and thronging peoples, on a vista of mountains, down the sides of two of which there flowed two mighty streams. Hard on this sight followed the apparition of the river-gods. These twain, of reverend and yet rugged aspect, crowned by a coronal of branches and herbs, their hair-tips emblematically exuding the watery element, and their colour tawny, as is the colour of a river, addressed themselves to the king, and, the Ganges being spokesman, invited him, as the head and representative of his nation to enter into possession of all he had in view.

* Just as the daisy that is plucked before its time, the daisy bright and beauteous, on being maltreated by the wanton hands of the little maid who put it in her chaplet, has lost its fragrance and wears a faded colour, even so lies dead the pallid dame, all withered the roses of her cheeks, all gone with sweet life the lilies and the brightness of her hue.

The portent of the river-gods exalts the imagination of the reader, sublimates the narrative, and publishes at fitting time the sanction of Fate that is written over the projects of the Portuguese. An experiment in this sort of writing is not more highly poetical than it is venturesome, and its successful accomplishment argues the possession of lofty inspiration. Camoens' Dream of Dom Manoel is no unworthy adaptation of the dream of Æneas at the beginning of the eighth book of the Æneid. It is more swelling, and more brightly painted no doubt, but equally effective, and how finely dismissed. The dream disappeared with the morning light, when Phœbus spread abroad his bright mantle, and morning painted the sky with colours of purple and rose :—

> Estendeo nisto Phebo o claro manto
> Pelo escuro Hemispherio somnolento ;
> Veio a manhâa no ceo pintando as cores
> De pudibunda rosa e roxas flores.*
>
> Os Lusiadas iv, 75.

The Old Man of Belem

The Old Man of Belem voices the feelings of the practical and unemotional citizen, who may support his grumblings and buttress his reasonings by considerations that possess validity and sometimes repose on high sanctions. Rash enterprise has indeed cast down crowds of men, and reckless adventure has ruined many states. Consolidation and conservation, however, are not always best attained by the respective acts of consolidating and conserving, but, on occasion, by extension and dash. It doubtless requires a high intelligence, or, it may be, dæmonic instinct, to recognise or intuitively discern that the acts of consolidating and extending do not, in a special instance, neutralise or nullify one another, but, by distribution, insure

* Meantime Phœbus spread his bright mantle over the dark hemisphere sunk in sleep, and the morning came painting in the sky purple flowers and the blushing rose's hue.

an increase of activity that will give a resultant force of surpassing power and sweep.

The old men of Belem have not this intelligence or instinct. They invariably hark back, expressly or unconsciously, to a bygone time of betterness, and reinforce their retrospective reasonings with the wise saws of a lifetime, which have general but not particular infallibility. Such men do not always restrict themselves to exclamatory indignation and damping prophecy. The original old man of Belem pointed to the Moors. "Gain," said he, "the glory of daring and the reward of piety by exploits accomplished at your very gates. There is a false brilliancy and a grain of cowardice in your present action. You seek too far afield, the Ishmaelite is an approved antagonist, and his conquest will bring you not only fame but lands and wealth." The presentation of this alternative on the part of such grumblers is a dishonest proceeding. They would have equally objected to the alternative as an adopted course of action. Contemplative inaction is their dearest employment, and humdrum activity, which least interferes with this bestowal of time, is therefore to be properly and piously recommended to others. Their exhortation to exhibit the prime wisdom of attention to the daily duties of life has not much virtue about it, and is not due to an etherealised conception of what are usually called the minor concerns of life.

Camoens' Old Man of Belem is not, however, the mere exponent of senile hesitancy and mistrust of novelty tempered by Philistinism. It is matter of history that Da Gama's voyage was regarded with disfavour by a considerable section of the populace. The poet meant to record and dress up for us this view of the voyage. It is incumbent on the staid portion of society to give expression to its legitimate dislike of foolhardy adventure, and Camoens' own experience of the dust and ashes of human hopes, and the grains of bitterness that come with all fruition, had been of such a nature as to make him take kindly to a little pessimistic sermonising :—

> Oh gloria de mandar ! Oh vâa cobiça
> Desta vaidade a quem chamamos fama ! *
>
> Os Lusiadas iv, 95.

In the poem the recording of the forebodings of the fearful serves a purpose. It throws into strong relief the sturdy daring of the members of the expedition. The poet has known, by this and kindred means of lending colour and heightening contrasts, how to glorify his heroes. Da Gama's resolution was not unmixed with apprehension. He prepared his men, as he told the king of Melinde, for the death that always stalks before a sailor's eyes. Friends, relatives, and clergy came to speed the parting sailors. A wife says to her husband :—

> Ó doce e amado esposo,
> Sem quem nâo quiz amor que viver possa ;
> Porque is aventurar as mar iroso
> Essa vida que he minha e nâo he vossa ? †
>
> Os Lusiadas iv, 91.

Sadness, and not joyful anticipation, was the dominant feeling.

Camoens has historical and poetical justification for his Old Man of Belem. He is at once the mouthpiece of the formal opposition to the voyage, and a sort of spectators' chorus. The poet himself, in person, often performs the duties of this chorus. But the creation is utilised in another way. It is made a vehicle for reminiscence, the means for a serving up of old Horatian fare (Od. i, 3, 10):—

> Oh maldito o primeiro que no mundo
> Nas ondas vela poz em secco lenho ! ‡
>
> Os Lusiadas iv, 102.

---

* Oh glory of commanding ! Oh empty craving of the vanity that we call fame !

† Oh dear and loved spouse, without whom Love hath not willed that I can live, why dost thou go adventuring on the angry sea the life that is mine and is not thine ?

‡ Cursed be thou that first in the world placed sail over a floating tree-trunk !

The following lines from the same stanza sound familiar to our northern ears :—

Nunca juizo algum alto e profundo,
Nem cithara sonora ou vivo engenho,
Te dê por isso fama nem memoria ;
Mas comtigo se acabe o nome e a gloria ! *

Adamastor

The conception of Adamastor is a fine one, and his appearance in the poem is novel and impressive.

For five suns the Portuguese had sailed the seas with fair winds, when, one night, Da Gama, as he stood on the prow watching the progress of his vessel, was conscious of the presence right overhead of an obscuring cloud that conveyed the sense of a shock, and filled the heart with a vague terror. The admiral had only time to ejaculate a prayer to God when the cloud took shape, the shape of a robustious and tall giant, of sour and somewhat ungainly aspect, with unkempt beard and sunken eyes. His mien was menacing and evil, and, it is added, his mouth was black and his teeth yellow. The colossal shape proceeded to deliver himself of multifarious prophetic threatenings directed against the Portuguese nation and individual Portuguese. Da Gama interrupted, and asked his lineage, whereupon the giant's threats melted into narrative that ended with pathos.

Adamastor is not only an awe-inspiring spectre, but a spectre with a pedigree and a romance. He was of the race of the giants that warred on Jove. Just before the conflict of his brethren with Omnipotence he had become enamoured of Thetis :—

Todas as deosas desprezei do ceo,
Só por amar das aguas a princeza ;

* May no lofty and profound appraising, may no sounding lyre or living art give thee for this or fame or remembrance, but may thy name and glory end with thee !

Hum dia a vi co'as filhas de Nereo
Sahir nua na praia ; e logo preza
A vontade senti de tal maneira
Que inda não sinto cousa que mais queira.*

Os Lusiadas v, 52.

The wooer was aggressive, and threatened war on the domain of ocean. Doris was intimidated by his threats, but Thetis bantered the wooer and promised conditional acquiescence, meaning to serve her forceful, though infatuated lover a trick that would damp and demean him. On the night in which Doris had promised to consummate for him his happiness, the poor love-sick giant thought he saw far in front of him the form of the silver-footed goddess. He gave chase, reached the enticing semblance, and rained down on it, promiscuously, fond and fatuous kisses, only to find that his promised delight had evanished, and that the substance behind the shadow was a rough mountain of savage girth and with thorny brakes :—

Como doudo corri de longe, abrindo
Os braços para aquella que era vida
Deste corpo, e começo os olhos bellos
A lhe beijar, as faces e os cabellos.†

Os Lusiadas v, 55.

One feels a strong sympathy with the heavy lover and his intensely human lament over his disillusionment. Altogether, he is an interesting creation, Adamastor. Full of sorrow, and with a past, he cannot hear a question of personal import addressed to him, without remembering, and unburdening his memory of, his bygone sorrows. His story is neither too long nor too short, having just

* All the goddesses of the heaven I disprized, and this for naught but love of the princess of the waves. One day I saw her advance, with her sister Nereids, without tire, to the shore, and straightway I felt my desire smitten in such wise that even now I am conscious of nothing that I more desire.

† Like one demented I ran from afar, opening my arms for her that was this body's life, and began to kiss her beauteous eyes, her cheeks, and her hair.

enough narrative to surround sublimity with interest. The poet first impresses, then interests, and lastly, moves us to pity.

Adamastor fled from the scene of his rude disenchantment, but had meted out to him a portion of the punishment that had overtaken his brethren. He was changed into, and became corporeally identical with, the Cape of Storms :—

> Em fim, minha grandissima estatura
> Neste remoto cabo converteram
> Os deoses : e por mais dobradas magoas
> Me anda Thetis cercando destas agoas.*
>
> Os Lusiadas v, 59.

The 'black mouth' and the 'yellow teeth' abstract somewhat from the sublimity of the conception. Perhaps they are meant to be a sign of age hastened and made ugly by unrequited love and cruel deception. Camoens sometimes imports considerable circumstantiality into his descriptions. He describes Triton as having seaweed for hair, a lobster-shell for a cap, and a body covered with marine creatures. Perhaps they are meant to represent some aspect of nature, some black and yellow effect of the towering promontory.

Adamastor became guardian of the cape, and a sort of nature-power. He represents, in this respect, one of the creations of the imagination of the venturesome but superstitious, and consequently timorous, sailor.

Bacchus, to further his plans, seeks the home of Neptune and the Nereids. Before the assembled divinities of the sea, he speaks of the impertinent daring of the Portuguese, of his own discomfiture in Olympus, and of the depreciation of his exploits to be produced by the success of the sons of Lusus. He con-

The Palace of Neptune

* Finally, the gods converted my huge form into this distant cape, and to redouble my grief Thetis goes circling round me in these waters.

descends to tears, and obtains thereby the aid he desires. A buffeting storm of wind is sent against the Portuguese.

The abode of Neptune is well described. By a wave of the enchanter's wand there rises before us on the silver sands of the ocean plain the turreted and transparent crystal palace of the god of the sea :—

> Descobre o fundo nunca descoberto
> As arêas alli de prata fina ;
> Torres altas se vêm no campo aberto
> Da transparente massa crystallina.*
>
> Os Lusiadas vi, 9.

With its golden doors of pearled marquetry it stands before our imaginations in realistic similitude.

The sculpture on the door represents chaos and the elements. Self-sustaining fire, Prometheus' gift, the source of life to all living things, is represented ; the omnipresent air and the teeming waters are represented. The sculpturing that represented the earth is takingly described by Camoens—earth mountainous, clad with her green mantle, and with trees in bloom, dædal earth, and also earth the mother of all living.

The subject is doubtless a reminiscence of Ovid's chaos and evolution of the elements. It is appropriate enough to serve as an embellishing sculpture for the palace of an elemental god. It is broadly conceived and satisfies the imagination of the reader. There are other sculptures on the palace front, among them the *gigantomachia*.

The assembling of the gods to the council by blast of Triton's conch is finely told. There are a noble circumstance and spaced-out reality about the narration that recommend it to the reader.

The whole matter of this fine digression and its arrangement satisfy our imagination ; there is a satisfactory garnering in of allusion, and the phrasing is apt.

* He explores the bottom never yet explored, and the sands there of fine silver ; lofty towers appear on the open plain, of substance crystalline and transparent.

Virgil, when he describes (Æneid vi, 20) the carvings on the temple of Phœbus, built by Dædalus on the Cumæan shore, has the advantage of the modern poet in the subject imagined. His subject is more human, more amenable to the art of description. It is pictorial, and becomes, in Virgil's hands, stately. It has life and story, and variety and pathos, and that virgilian touch whose rare exquisiteness is to be felt, not defined. Camoens was a great poet, but he had not the magistral art of Virgil.

When Silius Italicus describes the ornamentation on the temple of Hercules at Gades, he jots down mixedly the details of his description of Hercules' labours, and sticks Mount Œta in the middle. Silius was an artist in jumbled juxtaposition.

Venus, in pursuance of her intention to provide a period of rest and enjoyment for the Portuguese mariners, determined to enlist as aid her son Cupid. Her chariot, drawn by billing doves, passed over the Idalian mountains in quest of the boy-god. Him she found preparing an expedition to punish and reform mankind, who had overstepped the limits of liberty in their abuse of certain things that were given not for indulgence but for use. He was to punish the Actæons of humanity who preferred field sports to domestic duties, the devotees of Philautia, dangling and flattering courtiers, false and greedy churchmen, and all varieties of evil-disposed transgressors. The poet thus created an occasion for animadverting on the faults of his day and generation.

The Isle of Loves. Venus seeks the help of Cupid

Round about the god his brother Cupids were preparing the avenging artillery—darts, pointed by flames of desire over fuel of human hearts, and tempered by the waters of the tears of wretched lovers. This pretty anacreontic conceit is very pleasing and of positive propriety. Its legitimate effect reminds me of a big effect

Statius tries to produce by his outrageous conceit in the matter of Harmonia's necklace. This ornament (*Harmonies dotale decus*, Theb. ii, 272), had for constituents bright emeralds, diamonds carved with sinister figures, gorgons' eyes, ashes of thunderbolts, gleaming hairs torn from the brow of green dragons, tears of the Hesperides, fateful gold from the golden fleece, one of Tisiphone's serpents, and witchery from the cestus of Venus.*

Cupid the reformer

Cupid the reformer is more than the son of the Cyprian. He symbolises some punitive and guardian aspect of the divine love. His function as reformer seems to be marred by the commingled exercise of some of his tricksy attributes. The god's wounds are healed by nymphs, some plain and some pretty, and both, the wounds and the nymphs, are called antidotes (*triaga*—θηριακά). Nymphs, in ordinary thought, inflict the wound, but, I daresay, may be looked on as Cupid's balm for Cupid's wounds. Spenser says of a similar wound :—

> Which to recure no skill of leaches art
> Mote him avail, but to returne againe
> To his wounds worker, that with lovely dart
> Dinting his brest had bred his restlesse paine.
>
> F. Q. vi, 10, 31.

Cupid helps his mother

Cupid is addressed by his mother, almost in Virgil's words, as her bulwark, her arm of offence, and the despiser of the Typhoean bolts, instructed of her intent, and taken into her chariot. He advises his mother to take Fame as an ally. Fame is to run on before the chariot, sound the praises of the voyagers, and thus prepare the hearts of the impressionable fair ones for their approaching lovers. Statius, of whom I have just made mention, has a similar use of Fame in the second Thebaid, feigning her to fly before

* Compare what is said of Armida's girdle, G. L. xvi, 25.

the chariot of Mars, uttering *facta* and *infecta*, just as Camoens' Fame utters truths and glozings that have the sound of truths.

Tethys and her nymphs are wounded and quite fordone by the darts of Cupid. They are then led by Venus in dancing clusters to the floating Isle, and instructed in amorous usage. The Isle is then driven athwart the path of the approaching vessels and fixed Delos-wise to the bottom of the sea. The nymphs discern the advent of the healing Venus in the shape of the white bellying sails of the fleet. The crew sighted the island just at the time that Memnon's fair mother rose into the sky.

The island itself was a veritable paradise of the senses. All the natural delights of eye, ear, and tongue were to be found in it, with the addition of facile nymphs not all sisters of Phœbus. Trees of noblest kind, flowers of all hue, choirs of singing birds, fruits of delicious taste, all were there. The colours of the sky were to be seen on earth, and the colours of the earth in the sky, so much so that it was hard for an imagination, so disposed, to determine which was borrower, and which lender:—

The aspect of the Isle

> Para julgar difficil cousa fôra,
> No ceo vendo e na terra as mesmas cores,
> Se dava ás flores côr a bella Aurora,
> Ou se lha dâo a ella as bellas flores.*
>
> Os Lusiadas ix, 61.

This is a pretty conceit, and Camoens' use of it is not the first.

Such was the Isle of Venus, with its beach of ruby shells, and its tapestried sward, and its three mountain peaks with down-running streams uniting in the valley into a

* Seeing in sky and earth the same colours, it had been a difficult thing to judge whether fair Aurora was giving colour to the flowers, or whether the fair flowers give it to her.

water that reflected the circumjacent loveliness. The Portuguese mariners, on seeing the island, landed to obtain water. Some of them took guns and cross-bows, meaning to shoot down the wild game of the island. They found quarry they little dreamt of. Velloso and his mates caught sight of bright colours moving among the trees, and gave chase. And then animate nature followed the example of inanimate, and went a-playing.

The faring in the Isle of two types of Portuguese youth

Velloso is a forward, rattle-brained sort of youth, with no undue modesty or pensiveness about him. Leonardo has not Velloso's sparkling effervescence; he has been unfortunate, has perhaps required from life a more thorough, a more complex happiness than his fellow, and been correspondingly disappointed and disheartened. Such natures are not buoyant enough to be boisterous, and too manly to sink into blank despair. They anticipate, and prepare themselves for, misfortune, but reason themselves into hopefulness, and this hopefulness, thank God, does not always cheat them. Velloso found his affinity among the nymphs without overmuch trouble. Leonardo's chase had like to have proved a baffling quest. Ephyre, who practised the sweet reluctant amorous delay recommended by Venus, was taken too seriously by her philosophical moody lover, who with self-conscious gloom murmured, as he ran, mild aspersions of fate and melancholy forebodings of failure. A final outburst of fatalistic tenderness and resignation that reached the ears of the fleeting fair determined her to abandon her attitude of feigned reluctance, and gratify her panting and enamoured lover :—

> Pôes-te da parte da desdita minha ?
> Fraqueza he dar ajuda ao mais potente.
> Levas-me hum coraçâo que livre tinha ?
> Solta-mo, e correrás mais levemente.

Nâo te carrega essa alma tâo mesquinha,
Que nesses fios de ouro reluzente
Atada levas ? * Os Lusiadas ix, 80.

When a righteous power dispenses rewards it is not merely happy-go-lucky individuals like Velloso that ought to partake of such, but thoughtful and disappointed seekers after an ideal, like Leonardo and Camoens.

The meaning of the Isle of Loves

Venus meant the navigators to receive refreshment and reward in the Isle of Loves. In this land they were to look back with self-satisfaction and self-gratulation on their past toiling and moiling, and their pleasure was to have all the sweetness of pleasure after pain. Here they were to be regaled with all the happiness in the gift of boon Nature and kindly Venus. Such is the goddess' own account of her proposed feast of delights. The poet says that the whole of the island episode is in allegory. Its delights and diversions symbolise and prefigure the rewards that our fellows, and posterity, and providence, will confer on virtue. On virtue there waits an exceeding great recompense—the applause of the good, the self-consciousness of high desert, some outward regalia of lordly office or noble aspect, and an embalmed memory. Nay, more, its fame is immortality, and its goodness is godhead. For the nymphs of ocean, so fair as they are, Tethys, and the painted Isle angelical are nothing but the honours that exalt our lives and confer undying repute. Noble high eminence, triumphs, a brow crowned with palm and laurel, glory and wonder-rousing state are the delights of this Isle, and ought to be the reward of merit. The heroes of old got them immortality by merit, and the gods climbed to heaven by the pathway of virtue. The

* Dost place thyself on the side of my ill-fortune? It is cowardice to give help to the stronger. Dost take from me a heart that was free? Pray loose it, and thou wilt run more lightly. Doth it not o'er-weight thee, this so trifling soul that thou takest away entangled in these tresses of bright gold.

Island of Venus is the paradise of a euhemerist, and the entry to it is obtained by self-repression, by general virtuous activity, and by philanthropy.

So far as the events of the Isle of Venus form a part of the story of the poem, they represent not a fixed state, but one temporary and recreative, after lofty and vigorous effort. So far as they symbolise a sort of worldly Elysium, they imply that men who have dared and done something deserve to have dispensed to them some big favour. Camoens in his Isle foreshadows and antedates this dispensation, meaning, too, in his royal way to anticipate any perversity of fortune. Virgil's Elysium is in the other world, but even in this life he would never have given heroes such rewards as Camoens gives. He held out to his heroes a settled habitation, a home for their penates, but he never, even in allegory, uplifted from off their heads impending doom. There is in their way as much difference between a Mahometan paradise and the paradise around the throne of God as between the Isle of Venus and Virgil's Elysium. Camoens' bliss is earthly, largely of the 'youth on the prow and pleasure at the helm' order, and yet all is meant to be within the bounds of decorum. He expresses in language of sensuous exuberance the human right to fruition.

The alleged indelicacy of Camoens

The alleged indelicacy of Camoens' language in the episode of the Isle of Loves, and elsewhere, is not a question for hasty determination. It is a matter of race and temperament on the part of the poet, and of pure-heartedness on the part of the reader. It is incontestable that the peoples of the South have warmer feelings than we Northerners. The quantity and quality of the erotic poetry of the South will go far to prove this. To this warmth of feeling must answer a corresponding exuberance in its expression. And a poet who is supposed to think more passionately than his fellows must express himself in language that is correspondingly more glowing than theirs. As a matter of fact all the great poets have exercised a large liberty with the language of passion. Tasso, Shakespeare, Spenser, and Milton have all done this. Who shall gainsay the purity of the Muse of John Milton? And yet he uses language that breeds hot summer in our veins. Shall Camoens, who, in virtue of his temperament, uses language more nearly approaching that of the Book of Canticles than perhaps any of his brother-poets, shall he therefore be called indelicate, and his Isle of Venus the Garden of Cotytto? His descriptions of the wild joys of the sensuous life do not overpass the limits of voluptuous chastity. The glory of the natural life is imperishable, and it shines quite unobscured in the imaginations of a Camoens, and we really ought not to judge of such things by the sometimes narrowing maxims of a negative morality of blank virtue and excremental whiteness.

Flaws in the story. Its lack of a unifying personality

One who is a stickler for epic technicalities will find much to object to in Camoens' poem. If a nation be the heroic agent in a poem it must be represented by different persons at the different periods of a long time, otherwise the one agent of a limited period would be the hero. The transference of one's interest to the various national representatives is tedious to the mere seeker after epic qualities. One's interest is inevitably diluted by the process. The poem is deficient in forward movement. Its movement is oscillatory. A putative epic poem, it will be said, ought to stand the test of the application of epic rules. Because a poem is read with great pleasure it is not therefore an epic. One such rule is that there should be an outstanding personality, and will any one deny, says the stickler, that the lack of such a being, on whom to concentrate one's interest, is a prominent defect of the Lusiads. The various incarnations of the people-hero are a trifle distracting, and we miss run in the story owing to the existence of this lack. The sensations that one has on reading the descriptions of the 'pictures' are really the sensations that are impressed on the reader of the poem. No reader consciously accepts as protagonist the people-hero.

Its episodic character

The episodic character of the narrative undoubtedly gives to the poem a limping movement. Of the absence in it of epic unity proper there can be no doubt. Tasso has far more unity in his poem. The Portuguese nation is the hero, and just as Æneas or Ulysses by narration supplies the events of the poem that are first in order of time, so Vasco da Gama, the proxy of Portugal, tells the story of the people-hero with historic sequence and heroic pomp. The manner of the telling is the poet's own, and the subject loses nothing thereby.

The narrative at Melinde only the response to a request

As a prelude to Da Gama's recital of Portuguese history to the king of Melinde, Camoens ought to have introduced some circumstances such as are present in the Demodocus incident in the Odyssey, which would have made us believe the king of Melinde a sympathetic listener, as sympathetic a listener as Alcinous or Dido. This only needed poetic art, for, as a matter of fact, the king of Melinde probably knew as much of the Portuguese as the king of Scheria or the queen of Carthage did of the warring round Troy.

The piecing of the voyage and the history into a whole

It may be said that the repeated harking back of the Lusiads prevents us perfecting the suture between the past of the history and the present of the voyage. Apart from the avowed intention of the poet, a certain measure of harking back would have been imposed on him by the comparative scantiness of the details of the voyage proper, a scantiness which Camoens has known how to remedy by other expedients than that of historical retrogression, by the introduction, for example, of such episodes as that of the Old Man of Belem, and that of Adamastor. It is even said that, after the piecing of the two sundered parts has been effected after a fashion, there still remains the fault of too abrupt an ending. But the prophecies of the tenth book are meant to project, and do project a shadow in front of the voyage.

The strict matter of the voyage

The strict matter of the voyage is rather meagre in actual incident, as a means of introduction and a medium of presentation for the story. Such means, such media, such antedated middle or final parts of a total story should themselves furnish an ample sequel of interesting and cognate incident. The ampleness of this sequel is, in Camoens' case, also detracted from, to the thought, at least, by the short space covered by the events of the voyage when compared with the centuries of historic incident. I say, to the thought, because to the consciousness of the reader the discrepancy is not so apparent, the episodic form being quite fit to convey to his mind, without unpleasing sensations of the lapse of long periods, the transactions of ages. And in the history conveyed by such devices as the description of the banners, etc., time from the manner of the conveyance forms no element. The poet in this way lightened his big episode.

Certain cantos

For my part I should say that Canto V, containing the real beginning of the story of the voyage, is dexterously fitted into the previous narrative, and that by means of high poetic ornament the part of the poem devoted to Da Gama and his comrades assumes most respectable proportions. Cantos V and VI are very fine. Cantos VII and VIII are a bit prosy, but contain some fine Camoensian characteristics. Canto IX is the Isle of Venus canto. Canto X lags, and has a good deal of padding.

A certain looseness of the parts is discernible in the

The looseness and the strong element of unity in the Lusiads

Lusiads, due to the absence of a central bond of connection, such as a common undertaking would supply. There is no bond save that of nationality, and this hardly furnishes enough coherence. A sympathetic reader of the Æneid says :—" I have followed the wanderings of Æneas with interest, I have commiserated him when buffeted by fate and suppliant of others, I have been alternately puzzled and pleased by the Dido delusion, I have been solemnised by the Descent, I have rejoiced over his welcome by Evander, I have been harassed by his varying fortunes, and I have been consoled by his crowning victory." Can a reader of the Lusiads give any such connected account of his impressions? No. His sensations have been in detached groups. His attention has been lifted and concentrated anew, over and over again. And yet there is a strong element of unity about the Lusiads. It is not got from one main action or one main actor, although the story of the voyage to India is always made to suggest to the mind of the reader that the action is the replica, if I may so speak, of the big action of generations, and that the actors are the representatives and peers of a long line of heroes. It is nationality expressed in continuous heroic activity that is the thread of unity in the theme of the Lusiads. I think, too, that the frequent obtrusion of the poet's own person contributes powerfully to the impression of unity. It is an external unity, no doubt, and makes, I suppose, the poem into a new species of the genus epic. All the same, it is a sort of tire binding together the various segments of the circular unity.

The mythology of the poem

Camoens was a patriotic poet, who chose the epic form as the most dignified, in which to set forth his panegyric. He chose, also, mythology as a part of this form. Surely his adaptation of the epic manner is better than the servile and stupid literalism of Silius Italicus and Voltaire.

His employment of mythological machinery is a concession to use and wont, and is pure play of the fancy.

A homage to use and wont, and not inappropriate

Inasmuch as mythology introduces divine agents, and therefore confuses and weakens our conception of the action of the Supreme Agent of a Christian Epic, it is in these respects a less satisfactory vehicle for supernaturalism than the angels and sorcerers of Tasso. The action of angels and sorcerers is more reconcilable with, and suggestive of, delegated power than the action of the Olympians with its associations of masterful and supreme authority. I am not sure, however, that the employment of subsidiary agents of Christian pattern would have suited Camoens' subject as it suited Tasso's. In the first place, the main scene of Tasso's epic is in the East, the land of mystery and magic, and that ought to go for something; in the second place, a historical episode with religious bearings, as was Tasso's, round which romantic accretions had grown, is better fitted for the action of spirits and sorcerers than national history. No one finds fault with a Christian poet for addressing an invocation to Calliope or Urania, and why should we not allow ourselves to be borne by poetic illusion still further, and accept Camoens' deities in the spirit in which he employs them. Their employment has given us much fine poetic embellishment, many, in fact, of the finest parts of the poem, witness, The Ascent of Venus to Jove's presence, The Palace of Neptune, The Isle of Loves. Even Adamastor himself has attachments to the ancient mythology.

Let us adopt the following device, and I maintain that Camoens will be justified of his mythology. Let us in

A device to justify its employment

thought banish from the poem all Christian machinery and allusions—for in spite of the strong-flavoured Christian propagandism about the expedition, this may, so far as form goes, be quite well done—substituting pagan equivalents in their place, and we shall be so struck with the comparatively flawless use of the antique mythology as to cease to be unreasonably censorious.

The gods lent grace to poetry and they lend something to this poem

Camoens' deities are puppets used out of homage to antique form for purposes of poetic art. And yet they are more than puppets. We must never forget that Camoens was the first modern to write an epic on a scale, and with a purpose, at all corresponding to the scale and purpose of the grand epics of the old world. The gods of Olympus in the hands of the proper artists are far more effective in poetry than angelic underlings of the Almighty. They bring with them the associations and the power of the old mythology, of that time when nature, in virtue of its vitalisation, borrowed some of the charms of personality; when the world was not so lonely; when the beautiful features of nature had not only their own compelling attractiveness, but were clustering-points for the imagination; when life could be lived as a whole without the annihilation or dwarfing of any of its activities; when divinity itself had a variety corresponding to the recognisable and intelligible varieties of nature and humanity, and was not swathed in attributes of pompous mystery and arid tautology. We live in the cold shades of monotheism, and if, as regards the heart, and in a measure the intellect, we can reasonably satisfy our religious instincts, there can be no doubt that with the old mythology there have passed from the world many fair humanities of great import. The gods have been driven forth, and the dispeopled earth is poetically the poorer. The life of the senses, of which mythology was in many cases the expression, has been too much depreciated, we have banned the wild joy of living, and made life more leaden.

It is Camoens' mythology that gives sky, and atmosphere, and colour, and sensuousness to his poem. Without it the epic would be a poetised log with historical interludes.

Camoens is a master-poet. There should be no question of that. He has a charmed power and style that surmount all difficulties, answering nobly to all the demands that pure imagination or descriptive ardour make on them. He can set before us old beauties, he can interpret for us hidden ones, he can originate groupings of loveliness, he can flash before us effects produced by the sunshine or storm of the feelings. Camoens has the poet's eye for the beauties of nature, and the poet's tongue for the description thereof. He sees nature in poetical fulness, and also under its traditional poetical aspects.

Camoens' descriptive power

The flavour of our poet's allusions confers on the poem a definite rank and status. These allusions in their quality, are an evidence and proof of its homogeneity with the great epics. Camoens' allusiveness is as frequent as that of Milton, but not, I should say, of such copious expression. It is usually apposite, or, which comes to the same thing, the poet wins us into an opinion of its appositeness. It is difficult to adjudicate on the merits of two such vendors of classical allusion as Milton and Camoens, but, speaking generally, one may say that Milton's allusions have more grandeur than those of Camoens, and exhibit a more living incorporation into the narrative. Camoens' allusions are ornamentation, and their extraneousness is perhaps perceptible.

Allusiveness

There are in the poet of the Lusiads an arrogation and an easy entering into possession of the grand manner. He assumes it at the outset and maintains it throughout. He had the self-consciousness of genius. He had also the *furor poeticus*. His language is often largely magnificent in virtue not merely of external glitter, but of an inner content of real grandeur.

Grandeur

He is a master of the sterling sublime. I daresay his thought sometimes overleaps itself and falls into the quasi-sublime. But that is only the defect of a rare and precious virtue. I should not say that Jupiter, when he harangues the gods in favour of the Lusians, and fortifies his eulogy of their merits by a reference to Viriathus and Sertorius, is guilty of bathos, for, since every hero occupies his pedestal by reason of the laudation of some sacred poet, a great creative master of song, like Camoens, has a right to name his heroes, and, in so naming, to instal them in the national pantheon. Mars' championship of Venus, outspoken, and enforced by grounding his spearshaft on heaven's pavement, is quite a striking feature of the god's council. That thud on the floor made Apollo pale his light. It would be dangerous for a lesser poet than Camoens to express himself thus.

INDEX

(*To supplement Table of Contents*)